From The Writings Of
Richard A. Harris

simple/truths
volume I
sharing the simple truths of Christ love

Xulon
PRESS

Printed in the United States of America

ISBN 9781612151212

www.xulonpress.com

Jeff,

To a fine young man who has been a great help in the ministry. We appreciate your efforts and great attitude.

We look forward to seeing how God will use you in the years to come.

Blessings,
Richard A. Harris

Acknowledgments

⚜

Simple/truths revolve around many of the people in my life, to some of the most influential of those lives I must pause and give thanks:

Many blessings to John and Margaret Williamson who have believed in my ministry and loved my family for more years than any of us care to acknowledge. They supported this project from the beginning and without them it just does not happen.

A great thanks to Kyle Vaughn who gave up hours in editing this volume, making sense of my simple truths is simply a hard job to do. Kyle thanks for your patience and perseverance.

To the loving family of God at Lawson Road Baptist Church who have provided a great many prayers and served as a sounding board for my writings; thanks for your love and support for these many years. Thanks to all who have been there from the beginning of Loaves and Fishes right through to simple/truths. God has seen us through much, I am glad I traveled it with you.

To my father Eli Harris who created in me first a love to care for all people and then a love of writing. From the two newspapers on the front porch every day to an encouragement to follow my dreams your influence lives deep in my heart and seeps into each page. This book is a combination of your two greatest influences; loving people and writing. Thanks dad!

For my children who endure much for the sake of ministry including being subjects of many of my writings. Your patience and endurance mean the world to me. You are God's greatest blessing, each one of you making my life special in your own way. The simple truth is that I love each of you very much.

Most importantly I dedicate this book to my wife Kim. You encouraged me to start writing six years ago and without you there is no book to share. Your ability to edit without criticizing and to be honest without bruising my ego is a special touch. When it comes to special touches you are gifted with many; a loving wife, caring mom, forgiving soul, sacrificing spirit, partner in ministry and friend to those who need one. You are underappreciated by many and taken for granted by others. You put up with much and ask so little. There is an extra special corner of heaven reserved for someone as special and deserving as you. I am blessed to be your husband, and your children are blessed to call you mom.

Table of Contents

Looking at the year in Rear-view

This time of year, everyone seems to be looking at the past year. Most call it the year in review. I have seen a host of things reviewed everything from celebrity deaths to the top scandals, from the top 50 songs to the most important news stories of the year. Of course, all of these lists are subjective, so you get a different view from each source.

Each of these "year-in-review" programs takes you back to the past year and gives you a visual, written, or audio reminder of what happened. Some you are glad to remember, and others, you would just as soon forget.

Here we can all relate; there are some things in each year I love to remember while there are others I would just as soon forget.

Each year comes and goes, and each has a mixed bag of emotions to go in it. There are words we wished we had said, while others we wish we had kept to ourselves. There are moments we are proud of, ones that defined us as the type of person we want to be. Then there were the moments of tears in loss and happiness in victory. For the most part life comes at us in a balance of emotions.

Sure, some years have important milestones, and you hate to see them go. Others seem to be filled with heartache, and you can't wait for a new year to begin. Overall, our lives live out in a balance of experiences: good, bad, and somewhere in the middle.

Though looking at the past year can make for interesting viewing, I believe it is best in our world to look at the past year in the "rear view mirror" instead of looking at it in review. Some people can never get past the past and become stuck in their current circumstance. Know this: God does not waste any experience on us, but He never expects us to stay in one experience forever.

Here are some thoughts on looking at life with a rear-view mirror perspective:

In the rear view mirror you can see where you have been, but you are moving away from it, and you are moving forward. There is nothing wrong with looking back on our lives as long as we are learning from it and are moving in the right direction, forward. The wrong response is to be sitting still.

In rear view mirror living, you only take a glance. If you spend too much time looking at the past, you will have a wreck moving forward. Same with life—just take a glance. Don't get too hung up on your victories or too beaten up by your defeats. Get from the experience what God has intended for you and move on.

The best part of rear view mirror living is that it is behind you! Your mistakes, they are done; seek God's forgiveness, soak in His grace, and let it go. All of life is in front of you.

The start of a new year is a great chance for a fresh start. Remember we cannot change the past only learn from it. Let's do the right thing; put the past year in the rear view and then move full speed ahead!

Scripture: Philippians 3:12-14: "Not that I have already obtained all this, or have already been made perfect, but I press on to take hold of that for which Christ Jesus took hold of me. Brothers, I do not consider myself yet to have taken hold of it. But one thing I do; forgetting what is behind and straining toward what is ahead, I press on toward the goal to win the prize for which God has called me heavenward in Christ Jesus."

Prayer: Dear Lord, we thank you for seeing us through another year. Please guide us and lead us toward a more Christ-centered life in the New Year, one that pleases and brings honor to you. We ask these things in the name of Christ, Amen.

Holding Things Loosely

My family and I just returned from our annual trip to San Antonio for New Year's Eve. It has become a family tradition that we all love to do. We love getting away, we love the fireworks on New Year's Eve, we love the market, we love the river walk, and we love the Mexican food on the river.

The river walk is a beautiful place this time of year with Christmas lights giving romance and color to the surrounding area. As much as I like the river, it does hold a challenge for my youngest children. Once again, I must use Caleb as my illustration for this devotional; he seems to be getting a lot of devotional space lately.

Caleb is an excitable kind of guy. He loves to chase birds and dart out of nowhere into places he really does not need to go. A river is a very inviting place for him, especially one with ducks and boats going by. Even worse is the fact that around most of the river walk in San Antonio, there is little or no railing separating you from the river. It is an accident waiting to happen for young and old alike.

All of this makes it very important that Caleb's hand be held at all times while on the river. As he walked, we would trade out holding his hand, and once, while it was my turn, I received a lesson in holding things loosely.

If I held his hand too tight, it would bother him, as it should have, and he would pull back and try to get out of my death grip. If I held his hand too loose, he would be able to dart wherever he wanted without my having any control at all. In that case, I might as well not have been holding it at all.

I had to find a happy medium, one that was tight enough for control, but loose enough to allow him some freedom of movement. I found that special touch by holding his hand just firmly enough to be able to connect quickly without squeezing the life out of him.

I find that like Caleb's hand, I tend to go to the extremes in life, especially in regard to my children. A part of me wants to tighten the grip, hold on tight, and micro-manage every aspect of their lives. Of course we do this out of love. We want them to be safe, we want them to have the right friends, and we want them to suffer no pain. So we hold on tight and pull them in whenever we see danger.

The danger in this is that they, like Caleb, will pull back many times and rebel against such authority and lack of freedom, thus, leading them into the very danger we hoped to avoid by holding on tight to them.

Some go the other extreme of handling them too loosely, with little control. They figure that children can learn by making mistakes. They claim that the freedom is good for them no matter what the danger. I have seen this in action many times as young teenagers are allowed to run free and make adult decisions that lead to serious consequences.

Everyone needs someone to be accountable to. All of us need some control in our lives, and it is far better to learn from others' mistakes as opposed to our own, no matter what our age. Experience is a great teacher, but we all need a little hand-holding, no matter if we like to admit it or not.

So we walk the balance between too tight and too loose. Here are two things to keep in mind as we walk the tight rope that is parenthood:

1) God created each child to be different; some need a tight grip, while others respond better with a loose grip. You have to know your child. Make sure you do.
2) Most grips need to be loosened slowly. If you let loose too fast, they jerk back and fall in the river. Allow for responsibility to be earned by trustworthy and mature behavior.

Over the next 12 months, my grip will be greatly tested. I will have one child getting married, one going off to college in a city several hours away, and one graduating from high school who wants to go on mission trips in places I did not know existed. I will have to hold them loosely while eventually letting go.

If you have been blessed with children, you have either already walked the road I am walking or are walking it with me. Children are a God-sized task requiring a great deal of love, time, and mostly prayer.

Word of caution: Watch your grip.

Scripture: Ephesians 6:1-4: "Children, do what your parents tell you. This is only right. 'Honor your father and mother' is the first commandment that has a promise attached to it, namely, 'so you will live well and have a long life.' Fathers, don't exasperate your children by coming down hard on them. **Take them by the hand and lead them in the way of the Master.**" *The Message*

Prayer: Dear Father, it is hard to be a parent. We seek your help in doing a job that honors you. We know you give us the strength and wisdom, so we thank you for it. Remind us to lean on that strength daily. We thank you for the gift that children are, and we ask all these things in Jesus' name. Amen.

Resolving to Have Resolve

Some people think making New Years Resolutions is silly. I respectfully disagree. The very best thing about the New Year is not the parties or staying up until midnight to watch the ball fall in Time Square. No, the best thing is being able to start fresh and new. That is a true gift from God. It is the best time of year for a second chance. The slate is clean for this coming year; that is the very best thing about the New Year.

By the time you read this, you will have had the opportunity to set some goals for the New Year. I hope you have taken a good look at your life, especially your spiritual life, and set some attainable goals.

Let us consider Jonathan Edwards, who is considered one of the greatest preachers of all time. He was a fiery man of God who preached with a great love for God and His word. He preached during the 1700s and was a big part of the first Great Awakening in this country. His theology has a great influence on America to this day. When he made a resolution, it was worth taking note of.

Here are Jonathan Edwards' resolutions. **"Resolution #1: I will live for God. Resolution #2: If no one else does, I still will."** That quote tells you why his theology has a great influence on America to this day. He was determined to live for God, and he was not going to let anyone else stand in his way.

We may not be one of the greatest preachers of all time, but we can still have an influence on the world in which we live if we resolve to live for God. If we determine in our hearts to stand for God, we will study His word, we will be active in worship, we will be devoted to prayer, and the Holy Spirit will lead us in our actions.

Edwards' second resolution is where many of us fall short today. We resolve to live for God, but when we find that the world around us is living in conflict with God's way, we give in and fall short. **It takes good old-fashion gumption to say "no matter what I do or where I go, I will stand for the Lord" and stick to it.**

Edwards' quote says quite simply my living for God will not in any way be affected by how you decide to live your life. In a world of trends and followers, to stand for God this way is the only way and is sorely needed.

Remember, no matter what your resolutions are, they are yours and yours alone. When you stand before God, you will stand alone. When you complete this year and look back on what has happened in your spiritual life, the results will be of your own doing. There will be no one else to blame or to give credit.

Exercise:

**Take a moment and write down where you are right now in your spiritual life. For example, how is your study life, your faithfulness to worship, or your prayer life? Perhaps you might evaluate whether the way you live matches the way you believe.

**Take a moment and write down where you would like to be in a year. For example, be more faithful to worship, read through the entire Bible or even the New Testament over the next twelve months. You might need to commit to change some of your actions to better match what you believe.

**Take what you have written down and evaluate it through the year. Determine that you will live for God and that no one else will affect that resolve. Remember that with God, all things are possible, and you can do all things through Christ who gives you strength. You're not in this alone. As you live for God, His Spirit will enable you.

May God give you a blessed and fruitful year as you seek to live for Him. May you allow no one to stand in your way during the journey.

Scripture: Joshua 24:15: "But if serving the Lord seems undesirable to you, then choose for yourselves this day whom you will serve, whether the gods your forefathers served beyond the River, or the gods of the Amorites, in whose land you are living. But as for me and my household, we will serve the Lord."

Prayer: Dear Lord, help us to be strong and have courage in our daily walk. Give us the wisdom to set goals that please you. Give us the strength to stand firm in the wake of a world that will attempt to lead us to oppose You. We thank You for Your Spirit and how You give us many chances. We ask these things in the Name of Christ, Amen.

Outliving the Predictors

On June 25, 1904, Ruth Bookhout was born in El Paso, Texas. She was born with a heart defect that doctors told her parents would prevent her from living past childhood.

Her own father died when she was six, leaving her to be cared for by an uncle. The uncle hired a nurse to care for Ruth as she struggled with illness and many bouts of high fever. Her illness was so serious that it kept her from attending school.

A heart defect in 1904 was far more serious than it is in 2006, let me assure you. The loss of a father and constant bouts with fever are very serious, too. You might think the next part of this devotional will tell you of Ruth's untimely death, and so it will.

Ruth Bookhout passed onto the other side on 10/28/06. Oops, I might need to tell you that the '06 stands for 2006, not 1906. The young baby that the doctors predicted would never make it out of childhood lived to be 102 years old. At 100 years old, she joked that she had outlived all of the physicians who had predicted her death.

She lived 102 fascinating years. She was a businesswoman when women were not as active in business. Her obituary in the *Dallas Morning News* told of a business career that spanned 65 years in real estate and insurance. She had a passion for her city that led her to run for political office in the 70s. Ruth was quoted in the *Morning News* over 130 times and had a great desire to help the elderly and neglected teenage girls. The list of her accomplishments took a full column in the paper.

To say the doctors missed their prediction is a gross understatement. It is in this prediction business I want to pause and give thought today. What predictions have people made about you? Let me lay a few out and see if I can hit any:

1) You're not smart enough to amount to anything.
2) You're just like the rest of your family; you're no good.
3) With looks like that, you will never get a husband/wife.
4) Being disabled, you will never have a job or do anything of value in this world.

5) You've messed up your life so much, you can never serve God.

Here is the deal: people make predictions out of the negatives they see. They see a little girl with a heart defect: "sorry, you will never make it." They see a person not achieve in school and declare doom for their future. They see a wheelchair or a speech impediment and declare the world will never accept you, etc, etc.

Here is the other side of the deal: God sees the positive side of your life and has a plan. Is it that God does not see your negative traits? No, not at all. He sees the entirety of your life. He sees the youngster not challenged by conventional school but gifted with great desire. He sees a heart with a desire to beat, and He keeps it beating. He sees a sharp mind and great will hidden behind a wheelchair, etc. etc.

Many negative predictions made by people, especially people close to us like parents, grandparents, siblings, teachers, and supervisors, can scar us and set us back for a lifetime if we let them. No matter what your tag, don't buy it. Buy into what God says. You are His creation. He knew you before you were born. He has a plan for your life. Why, you know what? God can even use your negatives as positives in His grand plan for your life.

Here is my prediction; God has a plan for you. He will see it to the finish, and it is far greater than you could ever imagine.

Scripture: Ephesians 3:20: "Now to him who is able to do immeasurably more than all we ask or imagine, according to his power that is at work within us." *NIV*

Prayer: Dear Lord, help us to drown out the world around us and hear the good that you have to tell us. Have us to lean on you for our help and for power. We thank you that you love us and we ask all of these things in Christ's name, Amen.

A God Moment

Just so you know, I program phones for a living. There are many different styles of phones, but there is one style of phone that I have been working on for the last couple of years that, friends, let me tell you—it never breaks. Well, it almost never breaks.

I have worked on the same account for over ten years and have built a solid working relationship with most of the other technicians that work with me. We talk on the phone daily, I know their family situations, and if something is going on in each other's lives, we normally know at least a little something about it.

One particular coworker's father recently became ill and had been in the hospital for about two weeks in intensive care. Each day, I would talk to him. I would check on how his dad was doing. He would share with me the details, and then we would carry on with our work.

Last week, we started to go through the routine. He told me his dad was doing worse and shared with me that he was more than likely taking the next day off to go and see him. Nothing unusual about the conversation or the morning up to that point, but things were about to change.

He happened to be doing his checking on the phone that never breaks. But this morning he plugged one in and it made a horrible noise. Now, I had heard noises before, but not on this phone, and not like this. We worked on it together for a minute, him at the desk and me on the computer that controls the phone. After both of us acknowledged that this rarely happens, we had no choice but to get another phone. So, I sent him off to get another phone. He said he would call me in a couple of minutes. Indeed, he called in less than two minutes.

He opened the conversation stating that he was giving the phone to another tech that happened to be with him. I thought that was strange but no big deal. Then the next sentence brought things into focus. He said he had just received a call that his dad had passed away. Before he could finish, he began to sob, and my heart began to break with him. We took a minute, I shared my sympathy, and then

23

we prayed together. He hung up the phone, handed it to his good friend standing next to him, and headed home.

I have had some time to think about that moment and the one thing I cannot get out of my mind is that this was most certainly a God-ordained moment.

Let's line it up. An unbreakable phone breaks. Coincidence? I think not. Had he not had to go and get another phone, he would have never had need to call me. I would never have had the chance to pray with him, and though it is not about me, I would have never had the chance to pray a blessing on a friend of ten years. I believe God can break a phone or do whatever is necessary to line people up in the proper place.

How many people, you might ask, does it take to install a phone? One. But for some reason my friend had someone with him. Why, I have no idea. The person with him normally never works on phones; he pulls cable. The person with him also was a good friend of his, an older gentleman with a sweet heart and a love for family. He was the right guy at the right time. I believe God can arrange work schedules for people to be in the right place at the right time.

Deny God if you like. I care to believe. Say He no longer works in people's lives if you care to, but do so at your own risk. I care to believe He is right in the middle of the action just like He always has been.

I am thankful God woke me up last week, and He allowed me to be at my desk at just the right time, just as He had planned. I am thankful He had a cable puller working on phones, and I am thankful that God had a relative make the call at just the right moment.

What a great God that He allows us to be a part of His work, that cares for us enough to set people up in the right place when He knows we will need them the most. Last week I was caught in the middle of an undeniable "God moment." I can't wait to see what He has planned for this week.

God is still on the throne, creating God moments. Open your eyes, be available, and jump right in.

Scripture: Psalm 29:3-5, 7, 8, and 10: "The voice of the Lord is over the waters, the God of glory thunders, the Lord thunders over the mighty waters. The voice of the Lord is powerful; the voice of the Lord is majestic. The voice of the Lord breaks the cedars; the Lord breaks in pieces the cedars of Lebanon...The voice of the Lord strikes with flashes of lightning. The Lord shakes the desert; the Lord shakes the Desert of Kadesh...The Lord sits enthroned over the flood; the Lord is enthroned as King forever."

Prayer: Dear Lord, keep our eyes open to see your hand at work, help us to be open and available. We thank you for your love and care for us. We praise you that you set things in order and bless us with your presence. We ask these things in Christ's name, Amen.

Complete Surrender

September 3rd, 1939 was the beginning of WWII. It was the day Britain and France declared war on Hitler's Germany. Hitler had only hours earlier invaded Poland and left the British government little choice but to declare war. By the end of this conflict, over 50 million men, women, and children around the world would die. That is an amazing and sad number.

But what were they fighting for? This is what Neville Chamberlain said in his speech to his nation on that day in early September: "Now may God bless you all. May He defend the right. For it is evil things that we shall be fighting against—brute force, bad faith, injustice, oppression and persecution—and against them I am certain that right will prevail."

Reading those words makes me think that indeed those were good things to fight against: brute force, bad faith, injustice, oppression and persecution. Those are indeed evil things. Fortunately for the world in general, though the battle did not always go their way, the British people and the people around the world never gave up the fight and eventually did prevail.

Prevailing against evil is not a battle that knows only the borders of nations, but also takes place in the souls of all mankind. It is this battle that we must concern ourselves with this day and each day that follows. It is a battle that must be fought on two fronts—in our own hearts and within the hearts of others.

We look at people like Hitler and think we could never be a person like that, and for most of us, that is correct. But within our hearts lie the evils of this world: hate, lust, unforgiveness, covetousness, disrespect, and selfishness. If we ignore these things in our hearts, then we too can do unspeakable evil. To pretend as though these elements of evil do not exist will spell certain personal defeat.

The only way that we can win this battle is total surrender. Yes, surrender. Not to the enemy, but to the victor, our Lord. If we attempt to fight the battle against the evil in our hearts on our own, we are doomed to failure, and the evil one will occupy our hearts and control our lives. We must surrender each part of our life to Christ and allow Him to guide and direct us by paying close attention to His word and by devoting ourselves daily to prayer.

The war can be won, but it is a battle, and like all battles it is best to have the most powerful weapons. When we have the Holy Spirit living in our lives, the ultimate power of an all-powerful and knowing God, we can have victory. Remember we gain this power by surrender not personal control.

As we win the battle from within, it allows us to stand strong in the world in which we live. With God as our strength, we should stand up against the things that are evil in this world. I am not calling you to politics as much as I am calling you to love your neighbor, care for the sick, feed the poor, remember the forgotten and love the unlovely. As we strive to fight the battles of evil in this world with a loving Christ-like spirit, we will have a great effect on the battle in other people's lives. They will see a different love that they, too, will want to surrender to.

The war is real, the battle is tough, but like all battles that have a good and righteous cause, it is worth the fight. Remember, victory comes only after complete surrender.

Scripture: 1 John 5:4: "For whatever is born of God overcomes the world. And this is the victory that has overcome the world—our faith."

Hymn: "Faith is the Victory"—Words by John Yates; Music by Ira D. Sankey
Encamped along the hills of light,
Ye Christian soldiers, rise.
And press the battle ere the night
Shall veil the glowing skies.
Against the foe in vales below
Let all our strength be hurled.
Faith is the victory, we know,
That overcomes the world.
Faith is the victory! Faith is the victory!
O glorious victory, that overcomes the world.

Prayer: Dear Lord, help us to surrender to your will, to do all we can for the world you have placed us in, and to draw upon your strength to keep our lives free from sin. We ask these things in the name of Christ, Amen.

Problems

As I was sitting in a meeting the other day, a co-worker made what I think is a profound, yet simple statement that I know I needed to hear. We were in discussion about a problem another co-worker had found themselves in, and after a long pause, as we thought about it, she said, "Where there are people, there are problems."

How very true that is, and we would all agree that this is a very simple statement. But in reality, our actions and expectations say otherwise. For some reason, we seem to think that we should all be immune to problems. We get very upset and even act surprised and shocked when problems come our way from the people around us.

We go even further. We set up organizations and set them up for sure failure by declaring that these places should experience no problems. Cases in point: the family and the church.

Here is the bad news: the church and the family are packed full of people, and, thus, are destined for some kind of problem. Let's take the family first. Here is a group of people that you live with each and every day. They know each and every one of your qualities, good and bad, and you the same with them. Somewhere, somehow, someway, these differences are going to cause problems. It is even very possible that at least one person in this group is going to shock you with their actions and make some extremely bad personal decisions in their life. What is worse is that the person making the really bad choice might be you.

Then, there is the church. People expect everyone here to live in blessed, peaceful harmony. There is a picture we have of everyone agreeing on all things: being good friends and working together for the common good. Though this would be nice, let me warn you about something at the church. There are people there, and we have already established that where there are people, there are problems.

The church is to be unified but that does not mean one of us won't make a really bad choice somewhere down the road. We are to work for the common good, but that does not mean that someone is not going to get on your very last nerve.

I am reading your mind and hearing your next question. If the church is so full of problems, then why bother? If the family is going to give me issues to deal with, why be committed to one? Good questions, easy answer. Because God created you to be a relational being; you were created to need people.

A part of you desires to have lasting, loving relationships with other people. You cannot help it. Yes, you can worship in silence alone, but God created the church for you to worship corporately with other problem people just like you. Yes, you could live a solitary life, but God created us to support, love, and nurture one another, especially with all the problem people who are a lot like you.

Now that answers your questions, but I have another one. What do we do with all of these problems and problem people? Is it good enough to say "where there are people, there are problems?" NO. I do not think God just expects us to live through our issues with relationships. He expects us to grow from them.

I could not live without my family. They are figuratively, spiritually, and physically a part of who I am. Are they perfect? Am I? No, on both accounts. But without them, I would not have learned things like patience, unconditional love, forgiveness, sacrifice, support, faith and giving. Within the family we see real love learned and nurtured, and there within those walls, we see the design of a loving God, that we one day will fellowship with.

I love my church family, not because they are perfect or because I get along with everyone perfectly and they never create any problems by bad choices. No. Not at all. I love them because God has placed me in that family and I have learned a lot about God, about them, and especially about myself as I have spent time with them. I know for a fact that I am further down the road with Christ because I have been around them, especially during the problem times.

The world has high expectations for the family and for the church. That does not bother me. As a matter of fact, I want to do my best to live up to those expectations placed upon me. Taking it one step further, we should not merely be concerned about expectations from a worldly perspective, but more importantly from a Godly perspective. We should always seek to be as much like Christ as we can possibly be.

Here are some short thoughts on problems with people and their choices:

1) Don't freak out when they happen. Know this: they will happen.
2) Do not put higher expectations on others than you are willing to put on yourself.
3) Learn to resolve issues lovingly and respectfully, not like you're in a battle.
4) When someone makes a bad choice, cover them with the prayer and support you would want to be covered with, and then some.
5) Always keep in mind your shortcomings. Believe it or not, you just might get on someone's very last nerve.
6) Keep in mind the old saying that if a church was perfect before you joined, it no longer was after you became a member.
7) Do not withdraw simply because you have a problem with a person. This only makes things worse, and you learn nothing that God had intended for you to learn.

Where there are people, there will be problems, so until we run out of them, let's seek out God and see what He has in store for us in the midst of the problems.

Scriptures: Genesis 2:18: "The Lord God said, 'It is not good for the man to be alone. I will make a helper suitable for him.'"

Hebrews 10:24 & 25: "And let us consider how we may spur one another on toward love and good deeds. Let us not give up meeting together, as some are in the habit of doing, but let us encourage one another—and all the more as you see the Day approaching."

Prayer: Dear Lord, help us in our desire to love the people you have placed in our lives. Fill us with the fruits of your Spirit. Help us to learn from each situation you place us in. We ask these things in Christ's name, Amen.

2 and ½ Hours

I read a report yesterday that stated that Americans get 2 and ½ less hours of sleep a night then they did 100 years ago. Being the mathematical genius that I am, that equals out to 17 and ½ hours a week. That is a lot of missed sleep.

Keep in mind 100 years ago much of America was working on farms and were going to bed early and getting up very early. They were working from sun up to sun down, if not more. So let's don't fool ourselves into thinking we are working any harder or longer than they were. With that in mind, I started asking myself, "are we making good use of those hours?"

So let's be honest here for the next few minutes. Consider this:

- In 2003, the average American spent 1,745 hours in front of the television. Here is a side note: most American homes now have more televisions in them than people.
- The average American works 47.1 hours a week, and I am thinking with the onset of the home computer, that number is low.
- A Ball State University study says the average person spends 2 hours a day on the computer; not work related.
- The average American spends 3 minutes a day in religious activity on a normal weekday. For the sake of my mental well being, let's not visit weekend church attendance.

Those are just stats, and who can argue, but even as you consider some of those things, we all know we fill our time with endless meetings, sports, and entertainment. Then we drop into bed exhausted and wonder where the day went, only to get up and do it again the next day.

My thought is that we are missing out on the important at the expense of the mundane. Instead of taking a beating from the numbers, let's turn them and make something positive of them. For example, what if we remove some of the needless items in our life? For example, how about a 30-minute sitcom? We can add some positives. Below are some thoughts, and then you have an assignment today.

- What if you took your 30 minutes and read and meditated on scripture?
- What if you spent those 30 minutes with the TV off playing with your kids? Not teaching them, not doing homework with them, but having fun with them.
- What if you slept those extra 30 minutes so you would be refreshed and feel better for your family, work, and Lord? Sleep is not a sin, by the way.
- What if we lay in bed and held our spouse in a non-sexual way for 30 minutes. Just love on them, and let them sleep or enjoy the unexpected moment for 30 minutes. If your marriage is like most, this would be a most unusual and useful event.
- What if you or your family took a 30-minute walk? Good exercise, good time to talk, and a good time to explore. We all could use the exercise!

Your assignment:

1) Write down the things you know you could do without. Pick out just one and release it.

2) Write down one positive thing you could do in your 30 minutes. For example: time with God or family, etc.

Finding the answers should not be a problem. Following through will be. Commit your time to God and ask Him to help you follow through.

Scripture: Ephesians 5:15: "Be very careful, then how you live—not as unwise but as wise, making the most of every opportunity, because the days are evil."

Prayer: Dear Lord, help us to be wise how we use our time in the light of eternity. Help us to keep the important truly important and to be brave enough to toss aside those things that are not the best for our lives. We ask these things in the name of Christ, Amen.

The Great Thief

I often speak to people about their deepest of concerns. They share with me what is on their heart, and I listen. Many times during our conversations, they will say a sentence like this: "I know it is not good to worry, but..." They say this as if they are confessing a sin when it comes to worry. Many will tell me, "Brother So-and-So said you shouldn't worry," or they will give me the verses about worry in the Bible. They know they should not worry, but it is not keeping them from doing it.

Well, I have news for everyone: this Brother So-and-So worries too. I, too, have lain in bed at night and worried about things that might happen or things that have happened. I have lost sleep and spent time on worry. It is not something I do often, or something that consumes me, but indeed I am normal just like you, and to say I never worry would be foolish, not to mention a lie. I believe Jesus knew it would be a concern of ours; otherwise, He would not have addressed it in the Sermon on the Mount. Jesus knows what keeps you up at night, and he knew we would be prone to worry.

Having established that most all of us humans worry let me establish something else that might help us fight against this problem. Worry is a great thief. Leo Buscaglia put it best when he said: "**Worry never robs tomorrow of its sorrow, it only saps today of its joy.**"

Let's think clearly for a few seconds and address this modern day epidemic.

1) Worrying about something has never made it not happen.
2) Worrying about the past will not make the past go away. What is done is done. We need to give it to the Lord and move on.
3) Worrying takes up needed energy we might use to solve an issue or just to take care of our daily business. It is an unnecessary distraction.
4) Worry can make you sick, especially if it is prolonged.
5) As the above quote says, worry steals your daily joy.

Worry is all about control. The less control we have, the more we are likely to worry about it. Control is about faith. When we come to Christ in faith, we give Him all of our life including, or especially, the things we are prone to worry about. As we give our life to Christ more and more each day, we learn to let Him be in control. Maybe we should practice some short prayers to help us with our worries:

- Dear Lord, these are your children. Help me to raise them right and leave them in your hands. Thanks for loaning them to me.
- Dear Lord, this is your marriage. Help me to do my part **but** let you lead it. With your help, I can manage anything that comes my way.
- Dear Lord, you have gifted me with this job. Help me to rely on you to handle the daily pressures with grace and courage.
- Dear Lord, you have gifted me with this body. Help me to take care of it, and give me the strength to live out the days of my life no matter what might happen to it.
- Dear Lord, forgive me for my sin. Thanks for forgiving me and now please give me your Holy strength to walk away from it, never to repeat it again.

This Brother So-and-So does not want you or him to worry because he knows that it all comes down to faith. Christ is in control. When we live our lives with that knowledge at the front of our minds, the thief can no longer steal the great joy that each day has to offer.

Let us live out this day with the great knowledge that we do not know what will happen tomorrow, but we know Who does! He loves us and He is in control!

Scriptures: Matthew 6:25: "Therefore I tell you, do not worry about your life, what you will eat or drink; or about your body, what you will wear. Is not life more important than food, and the body more important than clothes?"

Matthew 6:27: "Who of you by worrying can add a single hour to his life?"

Matthew 6:34: "Therefore do not worry about tomorrow, for tomorrow will worry about itself. Each day has enough trouble of its own."

Prayer: Dear Lord, you know our flesh, that we are prone to sin. Give us your strength to make it through each day. Lay in us a desire to please you and to know you more closely. We ask these things in Christ's name, Amen.

A Man of Many Pardons

President Gerald Ford was known for many things. He was known rightfully so as the only president who was never elected to the office of Vice President or President. Because of that, he was called the "accidental president." He was known, in joking ways, as a man who was clumsy, with Chevy Chase making fun of him each Saturday night on *Saturday Night Live*.

As I have read about him over the last couple of days, I have found that most believe him to be a man of integrity no matter what party they voted for. He was known as a dedicated public servant that never wanted to be President, but really strived to be Speaker of the House. He was the last living member of the Warren Commission, which investigated the death of John F. Kennedy. He was also known as the Most Valuable Player on Michigan's National Championship team in 1934.

He was known for many things, but what brings me to this devotional is that he was known as a healer. He came into the Presidency in a very difficult time in our nation's history. A historian called it the most divisive time in our history since the Civil War. On his plate were two very divisive issues. One was an unpopular war, and he had to make the decision to grant amnesty or pardon for thousands of young men who had fled the country to avoid the draft. The other was the decision to grant a pardon to former President Nixon or to allow the judicial system to carry on in due process.

For many of you, these are very emotional topics even today. A person my age who was just a young teenager at this time cannot put a finger on how passionate people felt on both sides of these issues. Needless to say, I am not here today to say which was wrong or right. I will leave that up to the historians and your conscience.

On both issues, Ford chose pardons. The polls of that date had him as a very popular President until the day he pardoned Nixon. From that moment on, he was not as popular to say the least. He also gave the draft dodgers forgiving terms on returning to the country.

I have to ask myself, if one of my boys had died or been wounded in Vietnam, how would I have felt about this pardon? I have to ask myself, if I had voted for Nixon, or if he had ordered some criminal activity on a family member of mine, how would I have felt about a full pardon for him? I do not have the answer for that.

But I do know that pardons, for some reason, are never popular decisions. We seem to demand justice when it comes to people who have done us wrong. We demand that people get what is coming to them. The closer it is to home, the more justice we demand. The more personal it is, the more pious we are.

Please, for a minute, read an excerpt from a speech that Ford gave to the Veterans of Foreign Wars referring to draft evaders, "As I rejected amnesty, so I reject revenge. I ask all Americans who ever asked for goodness and mercy in their lives, who ever sought forgiveness for their trespasses, to join in rehabilitating all the casualties of the tragic conflict of the past."

You, as President Ford did, have a choice with those who have wronged you. You can choose pardon or you can choose justice. You can choose to forget the times you sought forgiveness and pardon and remember only the times you were wronged. But I warn you; this attitude comes at a price. If you choose to seek justice at all cost, you will find yourself focusing on the past, on the negative, on the wrongs in life and never moving ahead.

Without question, I have found that those who demand justice are the most bitter people I have ever encountered, while, on the other hand, those who have given pardons are the most free.

Is there a place for justice? Most certainly. We will all find justice one day when we stand before the Lord. My suggestion is to leave those people who have wronged you in His hands. His justice is never too light and never too harsh. It is perfect justice, just as His peace will be perfect peace. Why waste your time doing the Lord's job?

In a world of imperfect people who are constantly hurting and causing pain to one another, there are two paths: the path of pardon and the path of judgment.

Ford chose pardon and became unpopular in the process. Come to think of it, so did Jesus and He become unpopular as well.

My friends, free yourself up; become a person known as one of many pardons.

Scripture: Isaiah 55:7: "Let the wicked forsake his way, and the unrighteous man his thoughts; let him return to the Lord, and He will have mercy on him; and to our God, for He will abundantly pardon."

Prayer: Dear Lord, help us to look within, to see our sin and ourselves. Then help us to find your grace and embrace it, enjoy it, and spread it. We ask all these things in the name of Him who paid the price for our sins, Jesus Christ. Amen

The batteries are out on the scale; aw shucks!

Batteries are one of the must-have nuisances of life. In any household, batteries are a necessary evil that helps make the world go around. You never know how much you need them until they go out, and you never know how expensive they are until you go to buy them!

Battery replacement at my house works on a priority basis. For example, when the batteries go out in the flashlights, I am slow to respond but eventually get the job done. When the batteries go out on some of the kids' toys, my response is in direct proportion to how upset the child might be. When the battery goes out in the remote control, well, that is a top priority normally dealt with in an expeditious fashion.

On another note, over the last several months I have been trying to get my weight where it should be. I have been doing pretty well with my efforts. One of my daily routines has been to check my weight as I got up and at times even when I went to bed, looking for any positive news.

As I exercised and ate better, my weight would go down, and I would gladly jump on the scales. But lately, I have begun to slip a little; my schedule has changed, and eating right has been more of a challenge, not to mention that time for exercise has not been there. At least those are my excuses today.

The change in weight loss pattern has caused me to lose my eagerness to jump on the scales. But the other night I reluctantly hopped on, wanting to see where I stood. To my surprise, the battery was out in the scales. Shoot, I did not even think about it having batteries. If I had thought about that, I would have sabotaged that a long time ago! That battery lasted forever.

So now, each day I walk by the scales, knowing the battery needs to be replaced. Needless to say, replacing the battery on the scales ranks pretty low on the "battery replacement" priority list. I will get to it someday, just not real soon.

So why so slow about replacing the battery on the scales? Let's face it, for most of us, the scales tell us things we really don't want to know. By avoiding them, we avoid having to face the tough facts about us and the guilt that comes with not making needed changes.

That same thought process is what leads a lot of people to avoid dealing with God. Without reading the Word, going to church, or praying, we figure we can avoid the guilt that comes from needing to make changes in our life and not doing it. Instead of looking into the mirror of our life with the help of God, we choose to pretend that everything is okay.

Unfortunately, this way of thinking does not work, and eventually there are breakdowns that force us to take a long look at how we have lived or are living our lives. Trust me, it is better to face the truth and avoid breakdowns than to wait too long and face the consequences of avoidance.

Ignore the scales of life, and it will lead to a health breakdown; avoid the truth about life in regards to the living God, and you are headed for a far more serious breakdown: a spiritual one.

My advice: replace the batteries today, the longer you wait, the harder it gets, both physically and spiritually.

Scripture: James 1:22-24: "Do not merely listen to the word, and so deceive yourselves. Do what is says. Anyone who listens to the word but does not do what it says is like a man who looks at his face in a mirror and after looking at himself, goes away and immediately forgets what he looks like."

Prayer: Dear Lord, help us to face your word daily, to take a good look at ourselves and how we are living out our faith. Help us not to just look at our lives, but also to make the proper changes your Spirit directs us to. We thank you that you care for us enough to guide us, to correct us, and to discipline us. We thank you for your love and ask all these things in the name of Christ, Amen.

Taking the Hurdles

Those who run the hurdles in track have always impressed me. The object of the event is to run around the track as fast as you can while jumping over hurdles placed in your way. It takes not only speed, but also great coordination and agility. To see it done really well is very impressive.

To be the very best at this event, you need to be able to get over the hurdles while not getting tangled up in them. Such is life, as well.

Each life has its own set of hurdles that we must overcome. Maybe you were abused as a child, had absentee parents, are poor, or were born with a physical or mental disability. Maybe your hurdles have come in the form of an unplanned pregnancy, or unwanted divorce, or unexpected serious illness. Life is full of hurdles in all shapes and forms. No matter what your hurdle might be, to be the very best in life, you must avoid getting tangled up with them.

When I say tangled up in them, I think of how I have watched runners hit a hurdle and fall face-first into the track. Not only do they suffer injury, at times serious, but also most every time, they are out of the race. We want to avoid these things at all cost in life: injury (spiritual & physical) or getting out of the race. Here are some thoughts on how to avoid taking tumbles over the hurdles in life.

1) **Know hurdles are coming.** If you know hurdles are coming, you can prepare yourself for when they come. Never let your guard down, hurdles *are* coming.
2) **Be flexible.** Runners stretch for hours getting themselves limber enough to go over the hurdles. Flexibility is crucial. Same with life. Be willing to make a change if you need to in order to get over the hurdle. As a matter of fact, many times God sends hurdles so that we will loosen our grip and make a change in life. Be willing to listen and watch what direction God is leading you.
3) **Stay in motion, even if you tip a hurdle.** In every race that involves a hurdle, some of the runners, if not all of them, will tip at least one hurdle but do not fall down. In life, we will tip

hurdles all the time. When this happens, keep your eyes on the prize and keep moving. We will not always be ready or handle hurdles perfectly, but when you tip them, don't look down, look up.

4) **Timing is everything**. A good runner knows exactly how many steps it will take in between hurdles. If that timing is off even a little bit, it can cause disaster. Same with life. Timing is everything. God may use a hurdle to slow you down. If that is the case, slow down. When you hit a hurdle, don't panic, wait for God, move when he directs you to, and stop while waiting for His direction. God has a time for everything, even hurdles. Be in contact with Him; be in tune with His timing. Being off even a little bit can cause disaster.

Exercise:

A) Write down the hurdles you have encountered in life. Give God praise for how He helped you through them.

B) If you are in the midst of a hurdle, write it down and stop for prayer, asking God to help you clear the hurdle as He would have you.

C) Take a moment and seek the Lord. Ask Him to reveal to you what you were to learn from your last hurdle or the one you are in now. Seek His face, and ask Him if there is some change you need to make in your life. Let no hurdle be wasted by failing to learn something from or about God through it.

Scripture: 1 Corinthians 9:26-27: "I don't know about you, but I'm running hard for the finish line. I'm giving it everything I've got. No sloppy living for me! I'm staying alert and in top condition. I'm not going to get caught napping, telling everyone else all about it and then missing out myself." The Message

Prayer: Dear Lord, help us to lean heavily upon you when trials come. Have us to trust you for direction and to stay in good contact with you by prayer and reading of your word. We love you and ask all these things in Christ's name. Amen.

Following the Wrong Leader

Many years ago, I ran in a 13-mile race around the shoreline of a local lake. It was a lot of fun. Many runners jog around the lake, so we all know in what direction to travel.

When you run in these races, if you're the lead runner (not me), you follow a lead car or bike. These lead cars have all the directions and know exactly where to go in order to make the race the exact distance. They have to be trusted, and they have to know the course perfectly. Runners trust them without question.

On this particularly day, there were thousands of people running in this race. We all started off, and just like always, we faithfully followed the lead car and we all followed the lead runners. We finished the race and felt with certainty that we had just run 13 miles. One problem—we had not.

You see, the lead car took a wrong turn and no one caught it until the end of the race. Thus, we all followed and went in the wrong direction. Everyone's time was wrong because we had unknowingly followed a leader that did not know where he was going. We finished the race, but we had gotten lost along the way.

In the world in which we live, there are lots of people following the wrong leaders. They belong to cults. They trust in leaders that appear to know the way to peace, love, and eternity in heaven. Unfortunately, these leaders are following the wrong map, and thousands of people are blindly following them into destruction.

During the race, I just followed the guy in front of me; I trusted that everyone in front of me knew where they were going. In reality, they too had no clue they were heading in the wrong direction. We were all duped.

People in this world are searching for what is missing in their lives. They will follow whatever looks good at the moment. They are eager to find the love and hope they find missing in their day-to-day existence. They put their trust in people; they are just following the crowd. Big mistake.

We need to be careful and make sure we are following the right leader, and that is Christ. The crowd, even the so-called spiritual crowd, will head off in the wrong direction on many occasions. People will guide you in the wrong direction, even with good intentions. We must be very careful that we follow the only One who has the way to the Father, Jesus Christ (John 14:6).

How horrible it would be if we spent our lives following everyone else, then found at the end of the day that we had taken the wrong path. For us, there is only one lead driver, and that should be Christ. Avoid the temptation to follow the crowd.

We are all heading for one destination or the other. One leads to heaven and the other to hell. Make sure you're following the right leader—Christ.

Scriptures: Matthew 7:13-14: "Enter through the narrow gate. For wide is the gate and broad is the road that leads to destruction and many enter through it. But small is the gate and narrow the road that leads to life, and only a few find it."

John 14:6: "Jesus answered, 'I am the way and the truth and the life. No one comes to the Father except through me.'" (read John 14:1-5 as well)

Prayer: Dear Lord, we thank you that you have given your Son as our Savior. Help us to follow Him completely. We pray for those who are following people, religion and possessions in life, we pray they will find you and follow you only. In Christ's name, Amen.

Stunting Your Growth

When I was a kid, I used to hear this saying, "Don't smoke—it will stunt your growth." Since I came from a family of people who were not all that tall, there was no way I was going to be smoking—that was for sure!

I got to thinking about this simple question, "What does stunt your growth?" So I decided to take a look on the internet. What fun that was! I always keep in mind, and you should as well, that what you read on the internet is not always true. With that in mind, below are some things listed that might stunt your growth.

Smoking, caffeine, alcohol, steroids, weight lifting, drugs, a strict dietary regimen, diet pills, and extreme exercising (key word extreme) make the short list on the internet of things that could stunt your growth. Please keep in mind I have no idea if any of these actually do stunt your growth, but it was fun looking the question up.

Now, I have no idea about what will stunt the growth of the human body but I am absolutely certain of the things that will stunt the growth of the believer. The five L's, here they are:

- Low Bible Reading
- Little or no worship
- Lazy prayer life
- Lack of Christ-centered service
- Living a life of sin

Grace is free; growth requires a little work. One thing I noticed about my list of things that might stunt the growth of the body was that most of it required stopping or slowing down something. For instance, less coffee or stopping smoking, but it works opposite in our spiritual life. To avoid stunting our spiritual life, it requires increasing some spiritual discipline.

In both cases, it takes a personal decision. You decide if you are going to read the Bible on a daily basis or put it on the shelf. You decide if you will attend worship or not. You decide if you will spend time in prayer. You decide if you will be a part of service for the Lord. God cannot make you do these things anymore than a doctor can make you stop drinking coffee. God can convict you to do the right thing, but we ultimately will choose if our spiritual life will grow or stop right where it is.

We live in a world that is very concerned about what is going on with their body, and there certainly is nothing wrong with that. What we need more of is a world that is concerned about what is affecting their spiritual life.

The answer is simple: pay close attention to the five L's and decide to correct the ones that are lacking.

Scripture: Colossians 1:9-11: "for this reason, since the day we heard about you, we have not stopped praying for you and asking God to fill you with the knowledge of his will through all spiritual wisdom and understanding. And we pray this in order that you may live a life worthy of the Lord and may please him in every way: bearing fruit in every good work, growing in the knowledge of God, being strengthened with all power according to his glorious might so that you may have great endurance and patience, and joyfully giving thanks to the Father..."

Prayer: Dear Lord, convict us where we need to be convicted concerning our spiritual life. Help us to care about and give time to what is really important, our relationship with you. Help us with the hard things like discipline, time and priorities; convince our hearts to move into action. We ask these things in the name of Christ, Amen.

What is going on here?

It is cold here in Texas, and though that normally means 32 degrees and makes the rest of the country laugh at us, this time, old man winter got real serious. With lows in the teens, we simply do not know what to do. After a while we get a little stir crazy, and my house seems to be in that state of mind.

My kids and my wife know I like things simple, simple look, simple clothes, simple food. My motto is "let's stick to the basics." That might seem boring, but it works for me.

Not only do I like for my life to be simple, I like for the things around me to be that way as well. For example, we have our dog Dudley; he is a cocker spaniel, and he fits the house we live in perfectly. He doesn't like cats, and well, he shouldn't, he is a dog. When anyone takes a seat, he will sit right at your feet just as any good and faithful dog would. He has to get a haircut from time to time, but nothing fancy, just the basic trim you give a cocker spaniel.

Dudley and I have a little disagreement concerning his amount of house time, and he is a little bit of a sissy when it comes to wet grass, but otherwise, he is a good basic dog. I like that. Apparently, not all people like my simple view of dogs.

With the cold weather arriving, we started to take all the necessary precautions to keep all things safe and warm. Dudley, I figured, would be safe because he would just spend most of his time in the house. He likes that anyway. I thought when he did have to go outside, he would be okay. After all, he is a dog, and God gave him all that hair for a reason.

As I walked around the house, I witnessed something I never thought I would see in my home: Dudley wearing a sweater! Some smart person within the house decided he needed a sweater, so they took one of my daughter's old sweaters and put it on him. What is going on here? Has the cold weather frozen our brains?

Everyone got a big laugh out of it as I muttered words under my breath. Of course being the man in charge of the household, I did what all good self-respecting men would do. I shook my head and walked away. As I look around this morning, there Dudley is, brown sweater wrapped nicely around him.

Most people are like me. They like things basic no big surprises. We like our jobs secure, our families nearby, our church to sing familiar songs, our dogs without sweaters, and the people around us to have the same common belief as we do.

God, the creator of all things, is not so hung up on the basics. He delights in bringing on the unexpected. Think you're going to have two kids and a two car garage? He might have five kids and small house in mind. Going to work for IBM all of your life and retire with a nice pension and a gold watch? He might have a lay off in mind that drives you to teach kids in the inner city about business. Thinking small business with few worries? God might have in mind a big company with many concerns but a great influence for Him.

Need some more examples? Try these from the Bible:

Peter: He was headed for great things in the fishing industry. Jesus had being a leader of the first church in mind. Result: Peter becomes a great preacher and is the only person besides Jesus to walk on water.

Moses: Had retirement from public service in mind after some difficulties in that field. Had a nice shepherding business going, but God had plans for him to lead millions out of bondage. Results: Moses watches the people run free, witnesses God write the Ten Commandments, and sees the Red Sea split in two.

David: Had a good future watching sheep and was also the youngest male in the family, so his prospects for leadership were not good. God, on the other hand, had him pegged to be a great king. Results: he sees giants fall and leads Israel during its glory days.

If it were left up to us, most of us would live nice, quiet, boring lives. Thank God it is not left to us.

Scripture: Ephesians 3:20: "Now to Him who is able to do exceedingly abundantly above all that we ask or think, according to the power that works in us." NKJV

Prayer: Dear Lord, we thank you that you know best, and we praise you that you desire to do more for us than we can even imagine. We ask these things in the name of Christ, Amen.

Relieving the Pressure

For those of you who do not live in Texas, let me get you in on something in case you were wondering. It rarely snows in North Texas. When we get something cold and wet, it is usually ice. Those of you from the north, don't laugh at this, but an inch of snow can paralyze Dallas.

Last week was a record-breaking one for us in the snow department. We actually received from 8 to 10 inches and broke the one-day record. Dallas was transformed into a winter wonderland, and five days later as I look out the window, I still see a snowman in my front yard.

Since I am a rookie at more than an inch of snow, there are some things I was not completely ready for. One of those was the weight of snow. As I looked out after the great storm of 2010, all the trees in my yard were beginning to show the pressure of having so much weight on them.

The more I looked at my trees, the more I became concerned. Not so much for the big oak tree in the front, but the little crape myrtles in my flowerbed.

A tree, like a person, can only take so much pressure before it snaps. Pressure must be relieved.

For the small tree, I simply picked up a stick, walked out to the yard, and tapped on the base of the tree. Almost magically, the snow fell off, and the tree limbs bounced back to their original position, relieved of the pressure, ready to move on.

What I did for the tree in peril, God wishes to do for us.

We, for some reason, have this idea that we can carry the weight of the world on our shoulders. When things go bad, we think we can fix them, when the troubles of life begin to pile up on us, we simply work harder to fix the problems. We are most foolish at these times.

After a period of time of trying to take care of business on our own, the weight becomes evident. The pressure makes us grumpy, and that leads to hurt relationships. The added weight of the world often leads us to do things we never thought we would do. On top of that, if we keep at it long enough, the pressure makes us sick.

Don't believe me? Look around you today; check out the overworked, overstressed, over-worried people around you. How's that working for everyone? Maybe even take a look in the mirror; how's that person doing? I know the answer because I see the results often in broken families, crushed relationships, and sick bodies.

God never meant for life to be like this. Come to the Father; let him tap you on the base of your life. Relax in His loving care, give Him the worries, pause for a moment, and let Him help you put things in perspective.

You have probably tried everything else. Remember, even some very healthy trees fall in a mighty storm. You're not the oak tree that can handle all the weight. Come to Him like a frail crape myrtle that needs help. He will be good to provide the needed help, and before you know it, you will have bounced back, pressure relieved and in your original position.

Last word of warning: don't wait too long. Remember, when the limb snaps, the damage to the tree is severe. Recovery takes much longer, if it happens at all.

Scripture: Psalm 55:22: "Cast your burden on the LORD, and he shall sustain you; He shall never permit the righteous to be moved." NKJV

1 Peter 5:7: "casting all of your care upon Him, for He cares for you." NKJV

Prayer: Dear Lord, Help us to lay our burdens at your feet instead of carrying them on our own back. Guide us to trust you with our lives, all of our lives, each aspect. We thank you that you love us and care for us, and that we can indeed throw our burdens to you. We ask these things in the name of Christ, Amen.

Learning to Walk

About a year ago this week, I became sick. No big deal. I did not end up in the hospital, just the basic upper respiratory stuff, it seemed. It only got worse and lasted until the New Year, and this was after several trips to the doctor.

I did get well and have recovered in every area except one: I can't run. I used to run several miles at a time, but no more. I loved to run. It made me feel better, kept my weight down, and freed my mind from all the stuff normally going on in there.

Now if I run about half a mile, I start to wheeze and just can't get it done. I stop for a while, try again, and to my dismay, the same things happens. I thought over time it would go away. No such luck. This lead me to a choice, find something new to do or do nothing. I chose to walk.

I have always enjoyed the speed of running and shied away from walking. Walking, I thought, was for old people who cannot run, or walking is for those out-of-shape people who can't run yet. Walking was just not for me, "was" being the key word.

My exercise dilemma is much the same as my spiritual one. I want to run; God normally thinks otherwise. Let's look at the advantages of walking spiritually:

1) **Know this — if you run too much, too fast, or too long, you will eventually break down.** Most especially this is true for our life. Go 90 mph long enough and you could easily find yourself in the hospital, or without any real friends or meaningful relationships (you ran right past them). You will not really know even those closest to you, not to mention having a washed out relationship with God. People who run in life are normally a mile wide and an inch deep spiritually. I know I have been there.

2) **Walking allows you to see things you would not normally see.** You miss the landscape of life if you are going too fast. You don't appreciate the little things that make us truly happy because we are worried about what is around the next corner.

How many times do we miss listening to the kids because we were preoccupied with some important task we have given ourselves? Trust me, it probably is not all that important.

3) **Walking allows you to take others with you who can't run.** Running for me is an alone sport even if someone goes with me. I don't talk, I just run. Walking allows me to talk with important people about important things like: the kids, bugs, the moon coming up, who made tress and about what the big truck is doing. You know, the critical stuff. Why, at times, you even get to talk to a neighbor.

Here are signs you are running instead of walking in life: You're frustrated with your schedule; others dictate what you do; little spiritual life; no prayer time; lack of communication with those closest to you; anger; continually exhausted and little patience with others, to name just a few. I know them all, well.

Friends, when you see these things in yourself, take off the running shoes and walk for a while. You will be surprised the difference it makes.

Scripture: Proverbs 4:10-12: "Listen, my son, accept what I say, and the years of your life will be many. I guide you in the way of wisdom and lead you along straight paths. When you walk, your steps will not be hampered; when you run, you will not stumble."

Prayer: Dear Lord, help us to find the right pace in life, one that includes you at every turn. Help us to keep a proper perceptive on life and the many gifts you give us. We ask these things in the name of Christ, Amen.

Some Good Bets

The Super Bowl is big. There is no doubt about it. It has become almost a national holiday. Game day stands second only to Thanksgiving as the biggest eating day of the year. As far as television goes, almost nothing stands in its way of being the highest rated show of not only the year, but of all time.

The amount of people who watch tells me one thing for certain. A lot of non-football fans watch the game; it has become a social event. I, on the other hand, love sports; I love to play them, I love to watch them, and I love to participate in them. When it comes to a big game, I do not need a reason to watch a game. Others do. Welcome to the world of betting.

Many people need a reason to watch, especially if their favorite team is not in the game. They feel that if they are going to watch the game, they need something to keep their interest. Make no mistake about it, the NFL is a gambler's paradise, and the NFL knows it; never think otherwise.

According to one source, over 90 million dollars were bet on last Sunday's game in the United States. Over 200 million people were estimated to bet on the game worldwide. Some estimates have the amount bet on the game in the billions of dollars worldwide. Let me assure you, there are not 200 million football fans in the world, soccer maybe, football no way. People love to gamble, and the Super Bowl is the place to do it.

If you wanted to bet on the Super Bowl, here are some things you could bet on:

1) You could bet on if the coin toss would be heads or tails.
2) You could bet on who was going to commit the first penalty.
3) You could bet on how long it would take Carrie Underwood to sing the national anthem. (Yes, that is right.)
4) You could have even bet on how many times the announcers would mention Hurricane Katrina this year since the Saints were in the game.

Here is what we know about gambling: it is risky. Bookies know what they are doing, and they know how to lead us to take a risk — you can take that to the bank. There are also people who, for a small service, will help you make the right pick. If they are absolutely sure they have the right bet for you to make, they will guarantee it by calling it a "lock." As far as the Super Bowl, if you would have asked me who to bet for, you would have lost money, but as for God, here are some "locks" you can be sure to bet on:

1) God loves you, even when we don't deserve it. (Romans 5:8)
2) God loves you; when the world turns its back on you He will not. (Deuteronomy 31:8)
3) God keeps his promises. (Psalm 145:13)
4) God wants you to have an abundant life. (John 10:10)
5) God did not come into the world to condemn it but save it. (John 3:17)
6) God cares for the broken hearted. (Matthew 11:28-30)

In gambling, even the most sure bet comes with some risk, and most people lose as much as they win. With gambling comes uncertainty; with God comes the certainty that He is always true to His word and He never changes. You can bet on that!

Scripture: Psalm 19:9: "The fear of the LORD is pure, enduring forever. The ordinances of the LORD are sure and altogether righteous."

Prayer: Dear Lord, we thank you today that in a world of uncertainties, we can be certain of your love for us. Help us to hold onto that truth each and every day, no matter the circumstance. We ask these things in the name of Christ, Amen.

A Hard Heart is Hard on You

This time of year is not good for me. Around each and every turn, at every store, I am tempted beyond measure, and one of my greatest addictions gets the best of me. I must admit that I am indeed addicted to Necco Conversation Hearts.

These little pieces of candy come out every year just after the first of the year, and I cannot get enough of them. These little hearts of sugar taste great and besides that, they have those neat little sayings that, when used in the proper context can add some spice to life. Sayings like "bear hug," "true love," "love bird," "kiss me," "lover boy," "my baby" to name just a few.

I can eat those things at a ridiculous pace, and without any trouble at all, I can knock a bag down before lunch on a regular workday. This year I went a little crazy, even for me. I was eating my conversation hearts at such a pace that my teeth began to hurt from all the sugar.

I need to note one more thing about my addiction. I love the hard ones. They come in a few different ways, and all the others ways are okay, but I must have the hard ones. My habit is not to put them in my mouth and wait for them to soften. No, I go to crunching on these little hearts right off the bat. I cannot wait!

This brings us to another problem I had this year. After my teeth started hurting, I took a little break. But finally, I gave in and picked me up some more hearts. I started popping them in and crunching away when all of a sudden, I felt something in my mouth that was not candy. It was a portion of one of my teeth. I had crunched on a hard heart and it broke a tooth.

I learned a lesson that day; a hard heart is nothing to chew on. The world we live in is filled with hard hearts. There are people who have, over the course of their lives, allowed their hearts to no longer be tender. They have allowed the world and its many moments of pain and disappointment to toughen their hearts.

No longer can they forgive; they must receive justice. No longer do they have patience. Things must be done their way, and pronto. They no longer see the beauty of life as anything special—the touch of a baby, a beautiful mountain scene, a good joke, a special friend. Their hearts have hardened and stolen their joy.

Hard-hearted people are no fun to be around. They have little joy, few smiles, and are cynical beyond measure. They see the negative before the positive. They have lost their friends as well as their way. Their heart, well, it just cannot be cracked,

How is your heart? Is it hardened? It can happen to anyone. Life gets so busy and can be so difficult. Who can blame you? That being true, do yourself a favor.

Take a moment; allow your heart to be soaked by the presence of the loving God. Slow the pace, seek out a friend, let a wrong go, laugh a while, smile with some friends, hold a hand, worship in silence, read the Word.

Do it now, before your heart cracks.

Scriptures: Hebrews 3:7-9: "So, as the Holy Spirit says; "today, if you hear his voice, do not harden your hearts as you did in the rebellion, during the time of testing in the desert, where your fathers tested and tried me and for forty years saw what I did."

Hebrews 12-13: "See to it, brothers, that none of you has a sinful, unbelieving heart that turns away from the living God, but encourage one another daily, as long as it is called Today, so that none of you may be hardened by sin's deceitfulness."

Prayer: Dear Lord, help us to keep a tender heart, one sensitive to your word and your ways. Lead us in the direction of love and forgiveness, remembering the great things you have done for us, for the grace you have showed us, your undeserving children. We praise you for what a wonderful God you are. We ask these things in the name of Jesus Christ, Amen.

Where is the Fruit?

"But the fruit of the Spirit is love, joy, peace, patience, kindness, goodness, faithfulness, gentleness, and self control..." Galatians 5:22-23.

In Galatians 5, Paul sets before us things that will bud in our lives if we have the Holy Spirit working in our lives. Yes, everyone can have joy and love, etc., but Christians are to have it in such a way that it is supernatural, empowered by God Himself.

I spend much of my life around people who call on the name of Christ. Not only at church, but also in my neighborhood and at work, these people claim to know and love Christ. That claim would indicate to me that the Holy Spirit is dwelling in their hearts and lives. This may very well be true, but I wonder—where is the fruit?

More specifically, let me deal with one fruit on the list: joy. Some of the most joyful people I am around are Christians. They just radiate an inner joy that you know could only come from knowing Christ. You love to be around these folks. They pick you up when you are down, and their joy is contagious.

Then there are folks, many folks, who I have to wonder what happened to the Spirit of joy in their life. Lest you think I am preaching at you, let me tell you that there are times that I can put myself in this category. Yes, real joy comes from the Spirit of God, but we make a choice each day as to how we are going to live our lives and whether or not we are going to allow the Spirit to work in the area of joy in our lives. Joy is a choice.

I read a quote from a 5-year-old girl with cancer who was associated with St. Jude's hospital. It goes like this, **"I can choose to be sick and unhappy, or I can choose to be sick and happy. I choose to be happy. It's a personal choice."** What wisdom from a five year old! I am humbled.

Things are going to happen in life. Circumstances are not always going to go our way. We will not always be on the winning side of the score. Life is just that way; we cannot control many of life's events. Some of you have faced circumstances I could never dream of.

Though all of that is true, it is also true that each day we can make a choice—be happy or be unhappy; let joy reign in our life or spend our life miserable. The harder life gets, the more we have to lean on God and the power of His Holy Spirit to help us. The more we lean on Him, the more He empowers us. Let's face it. The way life falls without God, I can't imagine anyone finding too much joy.

My suggestion is, choose joy. As we do, people will have no trouble finding the fruit of God's presence in our life.

We have a choice whether to be miserable and quench the Spirit of God or find joy and share with the world a ripe fruit, sweet to look at and delightful to be around.

Scripture: Philippians 4:11-13: "I am not saying this because I am in need, for I have learned to be content whatever the circumstances. I know what it is to be in need, and I know what it is to have plenty. I have learned the secret of being content in any and every situation whether well fed or hungry, whether living in plenty or in want. I can do everything through him who gives me strength."

Prayer: Dear Heavenly Father, help us to find joy. Help us to seek your help in being people who bear the fruit of joy in our lives. Be with us as we seek to be content in all that life brings though we may not understand it all. You are a good God, and we ask these things in the name of your son, Jesus Christ. Amen.

The Top 100?

This is probably old news for some of you, but since I strive to keep you informed, I must carry on. Some of you are way ahead of me here, but for the sake of those uninformed, here is the big news. Angelina Jolie was named the top most beautiful woman in the world by *People* magazine.

Let me assure you that one look at Angelina, and she is indeed a beautiful person. For the sake of good journalism, I took a look at some of the top beautiful people and, indeed, without question, as far as beauty goes, these people are beautiful. As a matter of fact, I am not sure how you could tell one from the other in the area of looks.

The question must be asked: how can you come up with such a list, and what are the criteria to make it? Does their hair have to look a certain way? Does their smile have to be picture perfect? Are there any intangibles that can separate one beauty from another?

Then, I would like to know what makes someone an expert at who is the greatest beauty. Do they use former winners as judges? Do they simply use staff at *People* magazine? I mean who is qualified enough to make such an important and subjective decision?

Okay, enough of the questions. Let me tell you what I think. I rarely read *People* magazine, and I have a strong feeling that their definition of beauty and mine are completely different. Since neither my wife nor any of my children made the cut, I think the system is somewhat flawed.

The way I see it, the only person qualified to determine beauty is the one who did the creating. That would narrow it down to God. So let's take a look at his qualifications:

1 Peter 3:3 & 4: "Your beauty should not come from outward adornment, such as braided hair and the wearing of gold jewelry and fine clothes. Instead, it should be that of your inner self, the unfading beauty of a gentle and quiet spirit, which is of great worth in God's sight."

As I read it, according to God, it is not the outside that makes you beautiful but the inside. Let's face it. Some of us have no chance of ever getting on anyone's top 100 list if we use the world's standards of judging beauty. But if we use God's standard, then the playing field becomes level for all of us.

We can all be beautiful on the inside and probably would be if we took as much time and effort on the inside as we put into the outside. How much time is spent on grooming? For example, haircuts, make up, clothes, and manicures to name just a few. I am not saying we should not seek to look our best, no, not at all. I am just suggesting we spend some time, as much time, probably more, on the inside as we do on the outside.

What kind of beauty are you cultivating in your life? One that is based on the outside appearance the world appreciates and in some cases worships, or the kind God desires and blesses?

Remember a few things:

1) God created you. For Him, you are in the top 100. As a matter of fact, you're No. 1.
2) What eventually shows up on the outside is a reflection of the inner beauty. For example, your attitude, your humbleness, your purity, and your speech reveal the heart.
3) Be careful how you judge beauty yourself. Outer beauty fades with age, but inner beauty only grows more beautiful. Remember that when you choose a companion, especially a life-long companion like a mate.

Scripture: Psalm 139:14, 15: "I praise you because I am fearfully and wonderfully made; your works are wonderful, I know that full well. My frame was not hidden from you when I was made in the secret place. When I was woven together in the depths of the earth."

Prayer: Dear Father, help us to be beautiful from the inside out. Help us to see beauty as you do and cultivate our inner beauty by spending time with you in quiet places. We ask these things in the name of Christ, Amen.

Who can you really trust?

I have grown accustomed to our dog over the last year. At first, I must admit I was not a huge fan. But over the year, he has won my heart over with his good nature and the fact he does not destroy my house. I want to put a large emphasis on the second half of that sentence.

Let me assure you that no one, but no one, keeps a better look out for our home than Dudley. For hours on end, he will keep a look out for any unwanted visitors, mostly for those dreaded neighborhood cats. I can see no way that any cat can get within 100 feet of my house without Dudley sounding the alarm. Dudley is always on the job.

For a moment, let me describe to you how Dudley stands guard. First, he positions himself by the front door, where on each side there are windows that he can easily look out. He moves from one side to another unless he sees a cat on the move, then he takes his lookout to a front bedroom window he can also easily see out. For the most part, though, he stands guard at the front door.

Recently, we walked by, and Dudley was at his usual post but was being exceptionally still. Upon further investigation, we saw that Dudley's head was resting on the small ledge of the window. Upon even further review and much to our surprise, we saw that Dudley's eyes were closed. He had fallen asleep on the job!

My faith is now shattered. How can I know for certain that no pesky cat is going to make its way into the yard? How will I know for sure that an uninvited solicitor will not make it safely into Harris territory? How do I know for sure that he is really watching and not just catching a little shut eye? If I can't trust Dudley, who can I trust?

A great many of us think the same way about God. We wonder if we can really trust him. We live our lives out in fear, worried about what might lurk around the next corner. Perhaps our past is going to show back up, leading us into misery of days gone by. Who has any idea if they are going to have a job during the next year? Health, family, the questions can all be just too much. We live our lives as if no one has our back.

In an effort to protect ourselves, we hide behind things like bottles, pills, careers, accomplishments, knowledge, religion, and people to name just a few. All of these, and a thousand just like them, will work for a period of time, and some may even be positive in some way. But like Dudley, eventually you will catch them sleeping on the job. They will let you down.

I have good news for all who have lost hope: there is a God; He loves you, and He is more powerful than your circumstances. When the world seems against you, He is for you. He created you in his image and has a stake in our success. Though others may let us down, He never will. Things may not happen on our time table, but don't let that fool you. He is still standing guard.

Bottom line: God has your back, and He is not going to be caught napping!

Scripture: Psalm 118:6-7: "The LORD is with me; I will not be afraid. What can man do to me? The LORD is with me; he is my helper. I will look in triumph on my enemies."

Psalm 56:3-4: "When I am afraid, I will trust in you. In God, whose word I praise, in God I trust; I will not be afraid. What can mortal man do to me?"

Prayer: Dear Lord, help us to reach for you when fear comes our way. Have us to trust in you and to step boldly in front of our enemies and challenging circumstances with the knowledge that you love us, have a plan for us, and that plan is good. We ask these things in the name of Christ, Amen.

Living with Urgency

If terrorists ever wanted to send the Dallas area into panic, I have their secret weapon. Just say the dreaded four-letter word: you know the one if you are from around here. If you say this word, you send hundreds of thousands of people into an utter frenzy. The word you ask? Snow.

Last week it happened here again. The weatherman comes on the television and tells us there is a chance of snow in the region. This sets off a chain reaction that affects every segment of society. People fill up their cars with gas; folks run to the store and stock up, preparing to be snowed in for days, if not weeks; kids begin immediately praying for school to be closed; parents begin praying for schools to be opened. There are long lines and panic-stricken people everywhere.

People act as if they believe the next day is the last. They prepare for it with a sense of urgency. *In reality, we should live each day that way.*

I wish I could tell you that we will all live forever, but I must tell you the direct opposite. I would love to guarantee you tomorrow, but I cannot in good conscience do that. Will we get tomorrow? Probably, but nothing is for sure.

I am certainly not telling you anything you don't already know. Even though we know of life's uncertainties, we tend to treat life like a snow day in Texas. Instead of being prepared all the time, we wait until the end, then we attempt to get things in order. Sometimes people wait too late. This is a serious mistake; let's stay away from it.

Let us instead live our lives with a sense of urgency when it comes to the things that are really important. Below are some thoughts that will help us prepare:

—Keep your relationship with God in the right condition. Seek his forgiveness when you sin, stay close to His word, and pray often. God calls us to love Him with all of our heart, soul, and mind. Don't wait until the last minute for this one. It is too critical.

65

—Keep a good relationship with your family. Don't wait for a funeral or tragedy to say you're sorry or to say, "I love you." Don't wish you would have made a relationship right, make it right. You will never regret this one.

—Keep your priorities straight. Our family is number one after God, not our club, ball team, the internet, television, or work. Do a log of your time for one week, and you will find your top priorities. If a change needs to take place, do it. Don't put it off. You may have to tell some folks no. Do it. On the other hand, you may have to tell some people yes. Do it.

Needless to say, life is short; don't waste it. Don't wait until the doctor says you have cancer or until someone you love has moved away. Don't risk living a life of regrets; live life with a sense of urgency, and when the day arrives, whenever that day is, you will not have to rush around making preparations for things you should have done years before.

If you need some form of reminder, think, "Snow is coming to Dallas tomorrow," and you will be fine!

Scripture: Ephesians 5:11-17: "Don't waste your time on useless work, mere busywork, the barren pursuits of darkness. Expose these things for the sham they are. It's a scandal when people waste their lives on things they must do in the darkness where no one will see. Rip the cover off those frauds and see how attractive they look in the light of Christ. Wake up from your sleep, climb out of your coffins; Christ will show you the light! So watch your step. Use your head. Make the most of every chance you get. These are desperate times! Don't live carelessly, unthinkingly. Make sure you understand what the Master wants." *The Message* by Eugene Peterson

Prayer: Dear Lord, drive deep within us the desire to live our lives in the pursuit of you. Lead us not to waste our lives on meaningless pursuits, but live your perfect will for us. We ask these things in the name of Christ, Amen.

Swallowing Your Pride at the Thrift Store

First you need to know this—I do not enjoy the thrift store scene. Neither am I a big fan of the garage sale, but that is a whole other subject. People always tell me what great deals they find, and even my own family enjoys going, but it is just not for me. My family knows this; thus, they do not bother me with requests to go.

So it was with some surprise that my wife, Kim, came home from the store the other day and told me about what was going on at the local thrift store. The store was closing down, and they had all their clothes thrown out on the sidewalk with a sign that said they were free. She wanted to go, but she was insisting that I go with her.

We did not need the clothes. We are fine in that area. But our church is having a clothes give-away this weekend, and it would be great to gather some more clothes. With that thought in mind, we jumped in the car and headed that way. When we arrived, sure enough there was a big pile of clothes just waiting to be rummaged through, so we got to work.

At first, I must admit, I felt really uncomfortable. There I was in my own neighborhood where I had lived for years and was digging through a bunch of clothes on the sidewalk of the local shopping center. I was thinking, what if someone drove by and watched me digging through these clothes? What would they think?

Then there were those who were walking by and looking over at us. I was down on my knees just picking through the clothes and handing the good ones back to Kim, who would do a double-check to make sure they were in good enough shape to give away. After a while we had a big stack of clothes. Who knows what people were thinking?

For some reason, Kim and I felt the need to go in and tell the owner who was cleaning out his store that we were collecting all these clothes for a church event, as if telling him what we were doing would justify us taking a big stack of clothes from the side-walk. Why were we worried? The clothes were free in the first place! He just looked at us and acknowledged we spoke to him, but you could tell he could care less what we were saying, or that he didn't believe us.

As I got to thinking of my attitude about this whole affair, I came to one conclusion: I have a lot of work to do with some of my spiritual attitudes.

It is obvious that my biggest area of work is in the needed area of pride. My pride was on the line while I was on my knees. I was worried so much about what others would think, that it made me slow to jump in. My reputation was on the line. Eventually I got over it, but it took some time. When we are worried about what others think of us or what we are doing, it slows us down from doing good, and it sometimes keeps us from doing it at all. At first, my pride almost got the best of me and kept me from going even though, without question, it was what needed to be done. Let me assure you this, you cannot do what God wants you to do if you are worried about what others think of you or of what you are doing.

If it is for God, we are to just do it and not worry about our pride and reputation. After all, in that situation it is not God's reputation we are worried about—it is our own.

The good news is this: after about 10 minutes or so, I was right in the middle of those clothes. People were walking by, and I could really care less. I knew that those clothes being here on that sidewalk was a God thing, something that He had provided. Once I got my head on straight and remembered who and why I was doing it, then what others thought or how it looked did not matter.

God is all about putting you in places you don't want to be, doing things you don't really want to do, to teach you things you really need to know.

Scriptures: Proverbs 29:23: "A man's pride brings him low, but a man of lowly spirit gains honor."

Isaiah 2:11: "The eyes of the arrogant man will be humbled and the pride of men brought low; the Lord alone will be exalted in that day."

Prayer: Dear Lord, where we have pride, humble us. Help us to see things in your light, as you see them. Have us not to think too highly of ourselves but to always be available to bow low and serve others in your name. We ask these things in the name of Christ, Amen.

Same Medicine, Different Color

One time, when I was a child, my mother came home with a bottle of Listerine. I want to make sure you know what Listerine is. It is a mouthwash used to clean all the germs out of your mouth after brushing your teeth. Or at least that is how I think of it. Back in those days, it came in a real bottle and had a nice copper color to it.

I decided that I would try good dental hygiene for a change and check this stuff out. I put a little in my mouth, swished it around, and then started to wonder if this stuff was gasoline or mouth wash! I thought: of course this stuff kills germs in your mouth; it kills everything else as well. Nothing could burn and taste like that and not kill everything it touches. That stuff burned!

I must admit for any of you Listerine fans that indeed, it must have worked, because once I got over the bad taste, my mouth did seem to feel just a bit cleaner than it did before. I also must admit that I rarely touched the stuff after that original experience.

Lo and behold! I looked in my bathroom the other day, and in a nice plastic bottle with a green color to it, I saw the name Listerine. This looked nothing like the original copper-colored bottle, and it had a slogan on it that caught my attention. It said, "Less Intense, Equally Effective."

I thought: the makers finally get it. They are giving me that good working mouthwash that will clean out my mouth and not taste like gasoline. I was eager to give it a try and see the difference after all these years. My mouth was prepared for a nice, minty flavor. My mouth, and the rest of me, was greatly disappointed. It still tasted like gasoline. As far as I could tell, nothing had changed. The stuff still tasted bad, but it still left my mouth feeling cleaner after I recovered. It was the same stuff, just with a prettier color and a plastic bottle.

I guess some things you just can't change. While thinking of Listerine, I got to thinking how some of us present the message of the Good News of Christ. For some, we come across like gargling gasoline. It is a tense, confrontational message, sometimes filled with anger, and rarely does it sound loving. We point fingers; we talk of sin and hell and rarely mention the love of God as represented in Jesus

Christ. Some of us do not intend on making it sound so harsh, but we just come off so negative it is hard to imagine anyone would want to know more about Christ. I must admit guilt in this area in the past.

Perhaps we need to look at our presentation of the Gospel and see what kind of package we are putting it in. Are we presenting it in a Listerine type of way that burns, or a minty-green type of way that attracts? Remember the slogan, "Less Intense, Equally Effective." Sometimes we are so eager to share Christ, and so intense in our feelings, that we present the message in a very harsh way.

I am convinced that we can be less intense and just as effective in our Christian walk. The message of Christ will never change. Christ came to this earth, lived a perfect live, paid the price for our sins on a cruel wooden cross, and victoriously rose from the dead on the third day. Because He died and rose again, we, too, can look forward to victory over death and eternal life with God should we choose to accept that loving sacrifice. Really, it is a simple message and a simple choice. No matter how we package it, it is each individual's responsibility to either accept it or reject it.

Though the message is the same, the way we present it can change. People tend to listen better when someone is not in their face pointing fingers. People tend to want to respond better when the message is shared in love rather than in anger. It is only natural. Think of how you would like the message shared with you.

How blessed we are! We have the greatest message to deliver of all time—the message of a cleansing of our sin by a loving God. That message will never burn going down! Perhaps we are less intense, but the message is just as effective.

Scripture: Romans 5:8: "But God demonstrates his own love for us in this; while we were still sinners, Christ died for us." (Easy Message, Good Taste)

Prayer: Dear Lord, help us to present your loving message of salvation in a loving manner—one that is effective to those that we share it with. Help us to share the words of life with a lost world that needs it so desperately. Most of all, we thank you for your love. In Christ's name, Amen.

Forgiveness—it's A Little Fuzzy

Of all the theological issues of the Bible, I must say that forgiveness is the one I find most difficult. That seems odd even to me. I have read books on the subject, I have scoured the Bible on the subject, and even heard good sermons, but still there is a piece of me that has some struggles here. I read a story the other day that reminded me of my struggles.

Before we go too far, let me tell you that if it were just about God and His forgiveness, that would be no problem. But it is where *people* come into play that it gets difficult. Fuzzy Zoeller was a terrific golfer in his prime. He was popular among many golf fans and was known for his sense of humor and quick wit. It was his quick wit that got him into trouble.

Nine years ago he made an off-color joke about Tiger Woods that offended many people of color. It caused a great uproar in the public arena. To this day, when people think of Fuzzy Zoeller, they think of that statement. I must admit, it crosses my mind as well.

I found this statement in a recent interview with him about the incident: "Well, it's been the worst thing I've gone through in my entire life. What happened to me as a result? I got death threats against me, Diane, my kids, even threats against the house. I received hundreds of terrible letters, almost all of them anonymous, and they're still coming—I got one this morning. It's been more than nine years now, and it still hasn't blown over. If people wanted me to feel the same hurt I projected on others, I'm here to tell you they got their way. I've cried many times. I've apologized countless times for words said in jest that just aren't a reflection of who I am. I have hundreds of friends, including people of color, who will attest to that. Still, I've come to terms with the fact that this incident will never, ever go away." *Golf Digest,* August 2006

Where to start and keep this short? First let me inform you that I am not here to defend what he said but to learn some lessons from the event. Here is one lesson that has little to do with forgiveness. Be very careful what you say. What may be innocent to you may hurt others, and Christ would always want us to keep others' best interests at heart. Words can be very harmful, and I bet if you asked Fuzzy, he would tell you once they are said, that is it. You can't get them back no matter how badly you would love to.

Now on to forgiveness, and let's assume for the sake of this devotional that Fuzzy has asked God for forgiveness. If he has, then God has forgiven him. It is hard to believe that God forgives so easily, but He does. And why is it hard to believe God can forgive so easily? Because we are so crummy at it.

Let's look for a moment at the offended here. It is nine years later and someone is still taking the time to write out a hate letter to someone they probably don't even know. I will not for one second try to put myself in the position of the hurt. I will not make light of that pain or any other for that matter. But I will say if nine years later they are writing letters, they have not begun to heal from it, and they have more than likely become bitter. That is where a lack of forgiveness leads. It leads the offended into a permanent captivity that God would never want.

You spend your time worrying about revenge instead of getting on with the next steps of your life. You spend your time writing letters, or being harsh toward others, and who does it hurt? Does it hurt those who inflicted the pain? No, lack of forgiveness hurts those who become bitter and angry. You want revenge? Look to God who says, "Vengeance is mine, says the Lord." Leave it in His hands.

Speaking of revenge that is where forgiveness gets us doesn't it? We want justice for those who hurt us or those we love. This always gets my attention. I wonder for one second who out there has not hurt someone? Who out there has not said hurting words, hated, or committed some grievous sin in the eyes of others? Yet when we deal with our sin, we want mercy, but when we deal with others who have sinned against us, we want justice. I wonder if those who have written hate letters and made threats against the Zoeller family have looked within their own hearts and lives. When you do that, it gives you a whole different perspective on forgiveness. I am very glad God does not give me what I deserve.

What about Fuzzy who says he knows this event in his life will never go away. I think he is right. If you have offended others, keep in mind that first and foremost, our sin is against God. Know this—

people do not have to forgive you; you cannot make that happen. Though you might love for that to happen, many times, if not most the time, in people's eyes, you are still the offender, and you always will be. Remember what I said about people: they are not too good at forgiveness.

There is only one way to survive. Look upward. Do the right things; ask for forgiveness. Start with God, move to those you have hurt, and then keep looking up. In the end, when this life is over for us, we will stand before a God that is far better at forgiveness than we are.

For us, forgiveness is kind of fuzzy. We want it but have trouble giving it. But it becomes much clearer when seen through the loving sacrifice of our Savior Jesus Christ.

Things to think about:

1) God's forgiveness is complete. People and what they think or do, cannot change that.
2) Harboring a grudge is harmful to your spiritual and physical life.
3) Looking inward instead of outward helps us to better forgive others.
4) People who know the grace of God should be the best at forgiveness.
5) Real forgiveness is unattainable without the help and power of the Holy Spirit. We cannot do it on our own.

Scriptures: Colossians 3:13: "Bear with each other and forgive whatever grievances you may have against one another. *Forgive as the Lord forgave you.*"

Matthew 6:14 & 15: "For if you forgive men when they sin against you, your heavenly Father will also forgive you. But if you do not forgive men their sins, your Father will not forgive your sins."

Prayer: Dear Lord, we come to you humble and grateful for your forgiveness. We thank you for the blood of Christ that washes away our sin. Help us to work through our emotions and to forgive others where they have sinned against us or those we love. We know we cannot do this without your help, so we seek it. We ask all these things in the precious name of Jesus Christ, Amen.

My Adventure Book

I have not been a big fan of the latest Disney movies, but last weekend I caught one that I had hardly even heard of: *Up*. This movie was void of any sexual innuendo or behind-the-scene messages. Let me warn you before you watch it that this movie has several gut-wrenching moments that really make you think. Today we will only deal with one.

When Carl and Ellie first meet each other, they are small kids who desire to be explorers. Ellie lets Carl in her exclusive explorer's club, and a relationship is begun that will last a lifetime. The next few moments of the movie show them as they grow up and eventually get married.

Ellie and Carl, like so many of us, have shared dreams of doing exciting things together. Ellie has a scrapbook called "My Adventure Book" that has all the exciting things her explorer hero had done, as well as a picture of Paradise Falls, a place she and Carl dream of going someday. Throughout the movie, you see the progression of the love and the excitement they had for and with one another.

In the middle of her adventure book was a page that said, "Stuff I am going to do." From time to time during the movie, you would see Carl looking at that page and in his mind you could tell what he was thinking. He was disappointed in himself for not giving his love Ellie all the exciting times she had desired. For most of the movie, he never turns the page to see what, if anything, is behind them.

Before I go any further, let me ask you several questions. What would be behind your "Stuff I am going to do" page? Is there anything on your list or have you let the difficulties of life stop you from dreaming? Are you disappointed in your life as it stands at this moment? Old or young, do you feel like a failure in the "Stuff I am going to do" area?

Know this: it is never too late. Dream a big dream, go for it, take the trip, change your career, write the book, sing the song, go on that mission overseas, learn to dance—whatever it is, just do it. Take advantage of the gifts God has given you, and then go for it. What do you have to lose? Afraid to fail? So what! The Bible is chocked full of failures who did great things for God.

When Carl did finally look behind the "Stuff I am going to do" page, what he thought were empty pages were filled with pictures of him and Ellie. Were they swimming the Amazon or traveling to South America? No. They were doing normal, everyday stuff. Sitting together, sharing a smile, growing old with one another, and enjoying every minute. Carl thought their life was not meaningful because they had never done the adventures they had dreamed of earlier. *What he missed was this: life is an adventure, and it is not about what you do but who you do it with, and, might I add, who you do it for.*

Lesson learned? It is not the size of the dream; it is about the desire of the heart. Adventure is in the eye of the beholder. For some, life is meant for exotic places and fascinating situations. For most of us, our adventure comes in the everyday dreams and blessings. *No matter what adventure your life was meant for, follow God's dream for you, and when it comes to a close, you can rest satisfied in His loving arms.*

Go ahead open up the pages, see where life has taken you, then open your eyes to where he wants you to go. Appreciate the dream you're living, then look for the adventure in the future. Oh, yes—and be sure and thank God for the one he has given you to share it with. You may never get to Paradise Falls, but life is a great adventure. Live it.

Scripture: Psalm 37:4: "Delight yourself in the LORD and he will give you the desires of your heart."

Prayer: Dear Lord, help us to appreciate the life you give us, to find satisfaction in the little things and to seek the adventure that lies for those who follow you with all of their heart. Thanks for walking with us through this journey and for awaiting us in the next. We ask these things in the name of Christ, Amen.

Looking Behind the Curtain

I saw a set of eyes this week that were truly beautiful, but I could not tell you what color they were. I looked inside a heart and watched it beat. It was an amazing sight. I watched someone move from side to side, trying to avoid all the attention they were getting.

I even looked inside their body and saw their blood pumping through their spinal column. It was truly unbelievable.

The heart, it beats inside my wife, and it is not hers. You see, my wife is expecting our seventh child, and with the technology of the sonogram, we were able to peek behind the curtain and watch the true Master at work.

The Scriptures say in Psalm 139:15, "My frame was not hidden from Thee, when I was made in secret, and skillfully woven in the depths of the earth." It was as if we were in on a secret. We were looking in on a sacred event, the knitting together of a human soul, a creation of God. I believe, in those moments, my wife and I were looking as close to heaven as a person on this side ever can.

This world has great artists who can paint pictures, architects that can design buildings, musicians that can compose beautiful music, but who is like our God? Who can knit together a human heart and give it a soul? In our greatest moments of advancement in science and art, we will never be able to recreate the human soul. Creation is God's business, and I felt uncomfortable watching Him work.

In the first chapter of the book of Jeremiah, beginning in the 5th verse it reads, "I chose you before I formed you in the womb; I set you apart before you were born. I appointed you a prophet to the nations." Before Jeremiah was born, God called him to be a prophet. Psalm 139:16 repeats the thought: "Thine eyes have seen my unformed substance; And in Thy book they were all written, The days that were ordained for me, when as yet there was not one of them." Before we took our first breath, saw our first sunrise, or felt the touch of a loving mother, God knew us and knew the days before us.

Man can create sonograms and x-rays that can see inside the womb, but there is something going on there, something ordained from the Highest of places that no amount of x-ray vision can see. There is the work of the God of the universe who knows every hair on your head and every day of your life before it ever takes place. I have but one word for a God like that: unbelievable!

Around our house we call each baby, be they twenty or new-born, *special*. How could you not be special in the sight of God? When an artist creates a beautiful picture, they want others to see it; otherwise, what good would it be? When a musician composes a beautiful set of music, what good would it be if only he heard it? When an architect designs a great structure, it is no good until it is built for the world to see. You are *special*, created by God for the world to see.

God created you just like he did that little heart that beats inside my wife. He has a plan for your life; you are *special* to the creator. It says so in the Bible in Jeremiah 29:11, "For I know the plans I have for you, plans for your welfare, not for disaster, to give you a future and a hope."

Perhaps you are a long way from the womb now and your days have gone on, and no one is telling you that you're special any longer. You may not be feeling too special today, but you are. Each person has a place in this world, each person counts, and today I want you to know that if somebody has not said it to you lately, you are *special,* and God loves you. How could He not love His very own creation?

What? You don't believe me? Trust me, this week I peeked behind the curtain and saw the Master at work. Unbelievable, my friend. Trust me, you must be *special.*

Scripture: Psalm 139:13-15: "For Thou didst form my inward parts; Thou didst weave me in my mother's womb. I will give thanks to Thee, for I am fearfully and wonderfully made. Wonderful are Thy works. And my soul knows it very well. My frame was not hidden from Thee, when I was made in secret, and skillfully woven in the depths of the earth."

Prayer: Dear Lord, help us to marvel at your creation, to take time to praise you for your creation. Help us to live out the plan you have for our lives each day. Put your arms around us, and help us in our moments of weakness to know that we are in your sight if not in the sight of anyone else. We thank you that you know us, and we ask all these things in the name of Christ. Amen.

8 Days, 12 hours, and 31 Minutes

I am trying to be patient, really I am. Normally, patience is not a real problem of mine, but at times like these, I get a little anxious. I know it is not right to worry, but I do it anyway. I know it is not good to be inpatient, but I do it anyway. You see, my wife is expecting our 7th child in 8 days, 12 hours, and 30 minutes—but, really, who is counting?

You may be thinking to yourself, "Goodness, Richard, you have traveled down this road before; it should be no problem." Go ahead and think that, but it is not reality. The reality is that just like every other person who has ever had a child, the fear of the unknown can get the best of you.

We have seen the sonogram; it gave us a very good report. Kim has heard the heartbeat often, even just a few days ago, and that little heart is just beating away. Kim's reports are all good, and except for the difficulties that accompany the final days of pregnancy, she is doing great.

So why all the anxiety? Why all the worry? I believe it is simply the unknown. Though you know the child is well from all the doctor's reports, you just want to see it for yourself. Though you know technology can help solve many issues of childbirth, still in the back of your mind, you never know what might happen, not to mention the unknown of when this baby is going to decide it is time to make its appearance. Thank goodness for cell phones. The unknown is killing me.

Doctors like to control things, but honestly they have little knowledge of what is happening inside the womb. We can peek behind the curtain, but our view is limited. Doctors do not even know what starts the process of labor.

Let's face it—God is in control, and that is a good thing.

As our excitement grows (it is now only 8 days, 12 hours, and 7 minutes), our desire to control things grows with it. While expecting children, as with all other aspects of life, we may know that God is in control. We may say that at church, hear it preached, and see it countless times in scriptures, but our human nature still has trouble letting go. Knowing is one thing, while trusting is a whole other subject.

Learning to trust God is one of the great spiritual disciplines of life. It is called faith. When you trust someone, you are able to release whatever you need to them. You have faith that the job will get done, and that it will be done in the best possible way with the best results. That faith helps you to relax and enjoy the journey. Personally, I love it when someone else is in control. It takes the pressure off. God is there to take the pressure off. Trust Him.

What causes us trouble is when we show a lack of trust. We want to hold on, we want to do it ourselves, and we want to control each issue. When it comes to life, micro-managing only leads to things like anxiety, depression, worry, sickness, irritability, and utter loss of joy. God never meant for you to live that way.

God has a plan for your life (see Jeremiah 29:11). He is in control, and His ways are best. Have faith, trust God, and live it up (see John 10:10).

I will let you know how I handle the journey. Just 8 days, 11 hours, and 45 minutes to go. But who is counting?

Scripture: Hebrews 11:1: "Now faith is being sure of what we hope for and certain of what we do not see."

Prayer: Dear Lord, help us in our moments where our trust is low, where we are tempted to take control. Help us to release our lives to you. Drive home to us the fact that you are in control and your ways are best. We thank you that you are in control and that you are a gracious God. We ask all these things in the name of Christ, our loving Savior, Amen.

A Busy God

Life does not always go as you plan. You may like to set your own course, but God has His own agenda. You may plan to be a businessman in a big company, but He may have planned for you to teach children in an inner city school. You may have planned to teach children all your life, but God may plan for you to be a missionary in a far away land. Who knows? God does.

My plan over the last nine months was to celebrate the birth of my seventh child somewhere around the first of February. In order to make that plan work, we did all we could do. My wife had a sonogram that showed a perfectly healthy baby, perfect being the key word. She took care of herself the best she could. The pregnancy went as planned, really without flaw. We had done this six times before and my mind was at ease that this time would be no different. And then…

We went to the hospital around 10:30 pm January 26th. The family joined together in the waiting room as we always have. The excitement grew and after several hours, at 5:25 in the morning, little Gracie Harris was born into this world, just as planned. And then…

The nurses joined around little Gracie, and I knew something was not right. They said little and went right to work. After a few minutes they told me they would be taking her up to the Intensive Care Unit. This still did not make me too nervous; I had been there before with another baby. After everyone was settled in, a doctor entered my wife's room and delivered the news that our new child had several serious health issues and was born with Down Syndrome. Life does not always go as planned.

This started the longest day of my life. My emotions took every turn possible as we struggled with the unexpected news. There were phone calls to make, a family to worry about, and a child's sudden needs to concern myself with, both long and short term. My mind raced, my stomach had a knot in it and my eyes were wet with tears. And then…

God got busy. First he sent someone from the hospital, a fine Christian woman to talk to us. She had a sweet spirit, a calming voice and helped bring us back into the light. She gave us information, but did not overwhelm us. She listened to our questions and set about working to answer them. I will never forget her smile. Without a doubt, God sent her our way. And then...

We walked into a room with a child filled with wires; standing next to her was a young woman named Glennis. She had a good spirit, a friendly smile and was working hard around our child. Her words were comforting, informative, and caring. She, too, will not soon be forgotten. But God was not through. He just kept sending nurses to baby Gracie's side that were just like Glennis. They all were the best, and it gave us comfort as we left our child in their hands. A group of servant angels sent to care for God's little children. They were a Godsend, no doubt. And then...

He kept right on working. God sent a Filipino nurse who loved God for my wife. She missed Kim at first because she was with our baby. But she kept coming back until the third time she caught my wife in the room. She had been on the floor for 25 years. She brought with her experience, but more importantly than that, she dripped with sincerity and a love for God. She had a message for us. She told my wife through tears that she knew we had a special family because she had never met a family gifted with a Down syndrome baby that was not very special and close. God gave her the words and she delivered them, right on time. She continued to come back with more words of encouragement, more smiles, more hugs, and more tears until my wife was discharged. A little angel, with special tears and a beautiful smile. And then...

God wouldn't let up. He sent a young chaplain our way with a listening ear, a sweet spirit and strong prayer. He delivered more than a pink Bible; he delivered a spirit of peace. As I listened I was reminded of how good God is and how He has a plan for our lives and Gracie's as well. And then...

God wouldn't stop. As I made phone calls to relay the message of Gracie's long-and short-term health issues, each call was a 'gut-wrencher.' But with each call, words were said that should have been said years ago. Closing words like "I love you," words like "whatever I can do." There were quiet moments of tears during some, but strong words of encouragement from all, words of prayer, love, and peace. Each phone call was another visit from God.

Life does not always go as we plan, but God is always in control. He is not surprised by the turn of events in our lives. He is ready for them, and just when we need Him most, He gets busy. And you see Him like you never have before.

A perfect sonogram revealed a perfect baby. The world may think differently, but God has His plan. As I look back over the last six days, I am sure the sonogram was right on the money—a perfect baby, planned and placed by a perfect and busy God. Thank you God, for your grace and for Gracie.

- I realize that I am not the first person, nor will I be the last, that God has changed the course of their life. Each of you has faced sudden changes. Today take a moment to recall how God worked in those moments. Maybe there is a card of thanks that needs to be sent, or a phone call, or just praise offered up to God thanking Him for being there in a critical moment.
- Perhaps you are in the process of that sudden change: your emotions are raw; your life seems to have lost its balance. Know this: God understands. He is there. Though circumstances change, God never does. That's good news. Fall in His arms this day. There is safety there.

Scriptures: Psalm 34: 17 – 29: "The righteous cry out, and the Lord hears them; he delivers them from all their trouble. The Lord is close to the brokenhearted and saves those who are crushed in spirit. A righteous man may have many troubles, but the Lord delivers him from all."

Same verses in *The Message*: "If your heart is broken, you'll find God right there; if you're kicked in the gut, he'll help you catch your breath. Disciples so often get into trouble; still, God is there every time."

Lamentation 3: 21-23: "Yet this I call to mind and therefore I have hope; Because of the Lord's great love we are not consumed, for his compassions never fail. They are new every morning; great is your faithfulness."

Proverbs 16: 9: "In his heart a man plans his course, but the Lord determines his steps."

Prayer: Dear Lord, though we do not always understand your ways, we are thankful for your presence. Help us not to worry about tomorrow but to lean on you for strength each and every day. Indeed, great is your faithfulness, and no doubt it is fresh and new each and every morning. We praise you for that. We ask all these things in the name of our loving Savior, Jesus Christ. Amen.

From Tears to Joy—It's a Short Ride

When I received the phone call from my wife that our little girl had Down syndrome, I leapt from my bed and started for the hospital. Before I could get out of the house, I had to stop and tell my two oldest children. After that I took two steps toward our door, put my hand on it, and cried. I was frozen in tears. I just stood there and cried.

As I drove to the hospital, there were more tears. I cried for our baby; I cried for the fact that she was in the NICU. I cried for my wife; I cried for the rest of the children. I cried for myself. I was in grief and probably did not know it. Dreams had been dashed, and before new ones could form, the old ones had to be grieved over. I know that now, but I did not know it then.

I cried as I called my parents and other friends and family I needed to tell. After a while, I could call no more; it was just too much. Over the next few days, as a new way of life at the hospital took hold, there were still tears. During the weeks in the hospital and right up until we cried tears of joy to take her home, weeping was a way of life.

As I look back of those days now, I am reminded that you never really know how you will respond in certain situations. It is easy to talk about how you will respond as opposed to how you will really act. Those days taught me much about myself. I will never forget them, and they will shape me for the rest of my life. I am certain of that.

Now I find myself asking one question—why the tears?

If I had known then what I know now about God's mighty hand, the tears that flowed would have been for joy. In just six short months, God has taken our Gracie and turned our world upside down.

No one in my world smiles more than Gracie, and there is nothing I love to see more than her smile. She has the sweetest disposition, one I wish I could pass on to myself and all the others in this world who find it hard to muster up a smile.

No one, and I mean no one, I know has been prayed for more than Gracie has. In just six short months, people have been praying for her all over the world. Everywhere I go and everyone I see has asked about Gracie. They have told me of their own prayers and of those they had asked to pray for her. Old friends and family I have not seen in months or years have all asked my parents or me about how she is doing. I am certain the Lord has been overwhelmed with the prayers of His people for this little girl.

I was sitting in a wedding the other day, and an aunt I had probably not seen in years turned around, looked at Gracie, and declared to me, "She is an angel." I could only smile and agree. By sheer force of God's love, He has brought a family, friends, and a church together for one cause—Gracie.

Then there are the phone calls from people that I love dearly who I had not talked to in quite a while. They have brought tears to my eyes just at their thoughtfulness and kind words. Let's don't forget the cards and letters that still keep coming. These cards are filled with words of encouragement that force us to read them over and over again.

I pause and think that many marriages might fold under the stress of the last six months, but I find that God has worked in reverse here. I have found myself loving my wife more and wanting to take care of her needs more than ever before. Even seeing her needs has been a great step of progress for me. For things she used to do alone, she now has a partner, as I always should have been. I have found myself loving her more and seeing her in a different light.

Stronger love in my marriage, better relationships with my family, a bond to a church, prayers lifted up daily, new friends made, a better appreciation for good health, seeing God meet financial needs—and the list goes on and on; all because of a sweet-spirited girl with a golden smile.

What great love the Lord has shown me. Just thinking about it brings a tear to my eye.

Remember—what we see with tears for the moment, God can turn to joy in His time. His plans are always bigger and better than we can imagine. God has a way of showing love in the most unlikely ways. Today you may find yourself struggling greatly. If so, fall into the arms of a loving God and trust Him, even with your hurts. Especially with your hurts.

Scriptures: Ephesians 3:20: "Now to him who is able to do immeasurably more than all we ask or imagine."

2 Corinthians 12:9: "But he said to me, 'My grace is sufficient for you, for my power is made perfect in weakness.' Therefore I will boast all the more gladly about my weaknesses, so that Christ's power may rest on me."

Prayer: Dear Lord, we thank you that you love us so, that you take our weak moments and make us strong. Help us to release all things to you, the little and the large. Help us to see your strength in weak things, help us to be weak things. We ask these things in Christ's name. Amen.

Tears—They're Welcome Here

The Neonatal Intensive Care waiting room is a nice place. It is a place with lots of room, a good television, and a phone in case you need it. It is a place where you go to get away for a few moments from the room where your child is. It is a place to go to catch your breath from the intensity of it all, a place to just sit alone or visit with your family. This week, it has been a place of tears.

It started one night when I walked in and found a young man, 19 years old, with tears in his eyes, unable to speak to his family. His first child had been born in another city, but transferred to our hospital due to complications. The coming days would hold surgery for his young child, and he was breaking under newfound pressure and apprehension when he had expected this to be an exciting and happy time in his young life. The family gathered around him and gave encouraging words, words like, "It will be okay." As I watched the young man, one thought came to my mind. Let him cry. Yes, sure, encourage him, but let him cry for now.

Then, the next day, my wife and I were talking when we looked up and found a young lady wiping tears from her eyes, silently crying alone. Our hearts broke for her, and we hated to see her cry alone. We talked to her and found she had a young baby that had been born prematurely. Things had been going well, but all of a sudden, today, everything took a turn for the worse. She lived miles away. So she sat in a distant city, worried about her newborn, and she cried.

Later on in the evening a young mom came back to the waiting room after seeing her child, and she, too, is suffering pain. She simply wants her baby, and she is having trouble looking at her in a hospital bed. Though her baby will be coming home, for her it is not soon enough. Her family helps with words of comfort, but still the tears flow.

One room, a safe haven and a place filled with tears. Watching the world around me, and knowing that I, too, have shed a tear or two in that room, I realize that we all need a place for tears. My thought is, "why not church?" We live in a world of religion that sings happy songs, we have smiles on our faces, but where can a person go for a good cry? Is everyone in a church having a great day or great life? I seriously doubt it. We do damage to the word of God and to His people when we enforce some kind of "happy code" within our churches.

I am reminded that some of my most meaningful days of worship have been on days I have shed tears, days I have cried tears of repentance and brokenness. As a matter of fact, I cannot think of a day of meaning at church that did not contain tears. Sure, it is good to be happy when we worship our Lord, but there needs to be a balance. For an example of the balance of emotions involved in scriptures, you need read no further than the Psalms.

A simple room, a place called "a waiting room," but honestly that name does it little justice. It is a place filled with many different emotions and budding relationships, a safe place to share how you feel, to sit alone, to say a prayer, or hold a friend while they cry. Yes, that place in a hospital is called a waiting room. My prayer is that a simple place filled with similar feelings in the hurting world in which we live is called "a church."

I pray the world knows that tears are welcome there.

Scripture: Watch the emotion flow in this Psalm. Psalm 13: "How long, O Lord? Will you forget me forever? How long will you hide your face from me? How long must I wrestle with my thoughts and every day have sorrow in my heart? How long will my enemy triumph over me? Look on me and answer, O Lord my God. Give light to my eyes, or I will sleep in death; my enemy will say, 'I have overcome him,' and my foes will rejoice when I fall. But I trust in your unfailing love; my heart rejoices in your salvation. I will sing to the Lord, for he has been good to me."

Prayer: Dear loving heavenly Father, help us to be honest in our emotions to you who knows our every thought. We praise you, God that you are there for us that you will never leave us or forsake us. Help our places of worship to be filled with praise, joy, love, and tears. Help us to be compassionate people wherever it is you send us. Thank you Lord, for your Psalms and the emotions that are shared within in them. We ask these things in the name of Christ. Amen.

Put a Steeple On It

What goes on at church? If it is a good one, then, of course, Christ is mentioned often, and He is worshiped. That should be a given. But there are other things that make a church strong.

Let me name some. Things like people sharing freely with one another, each member being able to share without any fear that they will be looked down upon for what they say. Fellow members should mourn with their brothers and sisters in Christ when sad moments come and celebrate with them during the joyous ones. There also should be a commonality between the members; they should be able to relate to one another's feelings. A good church knows no prejudice against people of any race, education level, or social status. All should be working for the common good of each other, selflessly putting others before themselves.

Having said all that, let me lead you to a wonderful church. Where is this church? It is on the 7th floor at Baylor Hospital in the Neonatal Intensive Care waiting room. I have been a member for a month now and have grown to love it and its members. As much as I love it, I must admit I am looking forward to moving my membership back to my previous church just as soon as possible.

So why, you may ask, am I calling a waiting room a church? Because it has operated as one, and perhaps even better at times. First, all of us current members have one thing in common. We have a sick baby that needs critical care. This fact alone is enough to create a bond that has helped us to build friendships that will last in our memories forever. This bond starts conversations over things like, "How is your baby doing?" "How long have you been here?" "When are you going home?" "How is the other twin doing?" "Where do you live?" There is one subject and one subject only that is a priority—our babies.

With the subject in focus, we have learned to pray for one another. The name of Christ comes up often. Here, there has been no question of God, only the mention of His name when we talk about praying for one another, or thanks to Him for his provisions during a difficult time. Funny, but on the 7th floor, denomination is rarely mentioned, but Christ often is. Barriers of religious politics and denominational fighting do not exist when you are a member of the 7th floor church.

I am a preacher, and I must admit that I have talked more about God to strangers in the last month than in any other period of time in my life. By the way, who needs preachers here? Everyone has a testimony; everyone has a word to say. At times, it is said through tears of heartache, and at others, through tears of joy. Let me tell you, I have no trouble staying awake for their messages, either.

You might think this is a sad church filled with misery. Think again. Though our focus is on our babies, we have had a great deal of time to share with one another about our lives. There have been moments of laughter. God has used this church to cut through the pressure with moments of joy. Amazing? Not really. When God is involved, when there is freedom of sharing with one another, laughter seems to follow.

Now any good church needs a good outreach leader. We have the best; he is my 20-month-old son. This guy will walk up to anyone at anytime, no matter what age, race, or gender. And of course, he is so cute (writer's prejudice) they cannot resist him. He has created more conversations and more smiles than I ever could have imagined. With him as our outreach leader, we have been able to meet all kinds of different people and welcome them into the 7th Floor Church Of The Waiting Room.

For one reason or another, churches in this day and time have become show-oriented, more concerned with the personality than the person. Rarely does real fellowship develop. Deep, meaningful conversation is a rarity. Until that changes, churches will be cold, lifeless places where few lives are changed.

If you're looking for a good example of church done right, visit the 7th floor. I am thinking of putting a steeple on it before I leave.

Take a look at how you do church today. Are you a surface person, only going through the motions of playing church? Staying on the surface is safe, but it is not church as it was intended to be. Who knows—you may be the engine God uses to get a whole new church started: one that reaches and changes lives for Him.

Scripture: Jude 20-22: "But you, dear friends, build yourselves up in our most holy faith and pray in the Holy Spirit. Keep yourselves in God's love as you wait for the mercy of our Lord Jesus Christ to bring you to eternal life. Be merciful to those who doubt; snatch others from the fire and save them; to others show mercy, mixed with fear-hating even the clothing stained by corrupted flesh."

Prayer: Dear Lord, we thank you for your church and how it ministers to believers and to the lost. Help us to be faithful members, motivated by the love of Christ as we live out the remainder of our days here on earth, awaiting your soon return. In Christ's name, Amen.

Cap'n Crunch versus Cheerios

I am a very simple guy, not real complicated, and I like it that way. As a matter of fact, you can pretty much break down my theological life this way: some days I am Cap'n Crunch, and some days I am Cheerios.

From childhood to today, my all time favorite cereal is Cap'n Crunch. I love what the Captain has to offer. Not the new stuff with berries or peanut butter—I am talking about the original, sweetened corn and oat cereal. I love what the box says—"Crunch-A-Tize Me, Cap'n." Amen, brother.

Now that I am an adult (or close to one), I understand that a person my age is not supposed to eat cereal like Cap'n Crunch. I am most reminded of this when I go to the doctor or check out my blood pressure. This is where Cheerios comes into play; I like them, they taste good, and they are good for me. Unfortunately in the enjoyment category, they are well below Cap'n Crunch.

Thus my dilemma: eat for enjoyment or eat what is good for me. This situation mirrors my spiritual issues. Will I live with a short or long term perspective on pleasures and their benefits in this life? I suspect many of you can relate.

You can tell which of these cereals is better for you by looking at the side of the box. The Cap'n advertizes his three great flavors while Cheerios advertizes a healthy heart. Advertizing is very important with cereal and sin. The world tells us to go for it: the drug will make you feel great, sex no matter what the circumstance is awesome, or go ahead and take it—no one will ever know. Lots of sugar, but nothing good for you, I assure you.

God's advertisement team is a bit different. It sells self-control and right living; the Bible calls out the short-term rush of a drug and would warn about the long-term addiction; it declares sex as a spiritual relationship between a husband and wife, while warning of the pain and heartache caused by using the gift carelessly; then it declares that work is the way to acquire material goods as opposed to taking what others have earned.

On both boxes of cereal, there is a whole portion dedicated to nutritional facts—cold, hard numbers that do not lie. If you simply looked at the numbers on the side of the box and were looking for what would be best for you, Cheerios is a no-brainer. Who reads that stuff! Check out the cool picture on the box, and then make your decision. My guess is that Cap'n Crunch eaters don't read the side of the box much.

Cereal companies know that children often determine what cereal is purchased. So they advertize the box in such a way as to appeal to the less mature. Lots of pizzazz, little facts; the devil does the same thing. He advertizes sin toward the spiritually immature, the weak, or the distracted, and his plan works much too often.

Look no further than movies, television, or books, and you see an emphasis on short-term pleasure with no mention of any long-term consequences. They sell an individualistic attitude or "getting yours because you deserve it" mentality while ignoring the long-term pain of addiction, divorce, separation from those you love, failing health, or even financial ruin.

I would love to tell you that spiritually I am a Cheerios man all the time, but that would just not be fact. Too many times in my life I go for or have gone for the Cap'n Crunch. In my physical life, I come back around after a swift kick from a doctor or the bathroom scales. In my spiritual life, I come back around after a visit from the Great Physician with great conviction. Thank God for His grace!

The choice is ours in both our physical and spiritual life; will we live a Cap'n Crunch life or a Cheerios one? Trust me here, take the whole grain in both the physical and spiritual sense, you won't regret it!

Final Emphasis: I talked about pleasure during the devotional. Make no mistake: living for God is pleasurable. The evil one sells a cheap, short-term pleasure while God sells one that lasts a lifetime without regret. We choose!

Scripture: Proverbs 10:23: "A fool finds pleasure in evil conduct, but a man of understanding delights in wisdom."

Prayer: Dear Lord, let our hearts find pleasure in pleasing you. We thank you that on this earth you allow us to enjoy life and to be blessed by you. Guide us to use self-control and to consider you in choosing the ways to live out our live. We ask these things in the name of Christ, Amen.

A Great Contradiction

Aaron Burr is a famous American who fought in the Revolutionary War and eventually would become Vice President under Thomas Jefferson. He had famous spiritual roots in a father who was a Presbyterian minister and the second president of Princeton University. His grandfather on his mother's side was even more famous: Jonathan Edwards, the great preacher of the Great Awakening in America.

During the war, for a time, he served under General Israel Putnam who had taken him under his wing. While serving with General Putnam, Burr helped save an entire brigade by his vigilance in a retreat from lower Manhattan to Harlem. One of the officers in the brigade he helped save was Alexander Hamilton.

Burr would become a national hero along the way, and he used this status to move up the political ladder later in life. In a different election system than we have today, he and Jefferson would end up tied for President in the election of 1800. The final election had to be moved to the House of Representatives and there, on the 36th ballot, Jefferson would win, moving Burr to Vice President.

Alexander Hamilton and Burr would be friends until politics began to drive a wedge between them. In the election of 1800, Hamilton was a Federalist and Burr was a member of the Democratic-Republican Party, and each would be the chief campaigners for their respective parties.

Let me move quickly to avoid making this a complete history lesson. Burr and Alexander's once-good relationship would deteriorate to the point that they got into a war of words. Hamilton at one point called Burr a "dangerous man, and one who ought not to be trusted with the reins of government." They then would get into an argument at a dinner party where Hamilton said he could express a "still more despicable opinion" of Burr. Burr demanded Hamilton recant what he had said about him over a period of years, but of course we all know that did not happen.

The war of words went on until Burr (mind you, Vice President at the time) challenged Hamilton to a duel. This duel occurred on

July 11ᵗʰ, 1804, and ended with the death of Hamilton. Twenty years earlier in one war, Burr had saved Hamilton's life, only to later take it because of another war: a war of words.

We need to be very careful we do not end up as these two former friends did—ruining their lives over words. The war of words has been going on for thousands of years, and that is exactly why the scriptures tell us quite clearly to be careful how we use them.

We say things in a moment of anger that hurt others deeply and mortally wound relationships. We kill those we love because of words we said and sometimes simply in how we said them. In a moment, a lifetime of friendship is over, never to be repaired because of stubborn hearts and careless words. Let's examine the Bible's message about words:

1 Peter 3:9-10: "Do not repay evil with evil or insult with insult, but with blessing, because to this you were called so that you may inherit a blessing. For, 'Whoever would love life and see good days must keep his tongue from evil and his lips from deceitful speech.'"

James 3:9-10: "With the tongue we praise our Lord and Father, and with it we curse men, who have been made in God's likeness. Out of the same mouth come praise and cursing. My brothers, this should not be."

Ephesians 4:29: "Do not let any unwholesome talk come out of your mouths, but only what is helpful for building others up according to their needs, that it may benefit those who listen."

Hamilton and Burr—two great Americans, intelligent men both, but they allowed their words to consume them and eventually to even kill. Let us be careful today to take the spoken word seriously, treating the words as a matter of life and death.

Prayer: Dear Lord, teach us this day to take seriously the words we speak. Guide us to use words wisely to lift others up instead of bring them down. Let us use words to heal and not hurt. We ask these things in the name of Christ, Amen.

A Solid Anchor

I worship and serve at a small church with an aging building. Some worry about its stability, but I have seen below and have complete faith. When it comes to structures, our building is not what we are known for in the community; we are known by the three white crosses standing in our field.

As we minister in our neighborhood and people ask what the name of our church is, many give a puzzled look after I tell them. Then I ask them "do you know where the three white crosses are by the highway?" and most, if not all, know right where I am talking about.

We have a field we bought many years ago to replace the aging building, but God has used it in other ways up to this date. On the back of that property, close to a major highway and its service road, sits three crosses twelve feet off the ground for all to see as they pass by.

These crosses are set in what seems like two feet of concrete. One thing for sure is that the wind might blow, but it is not going to blow these crosses over. Those crosses are on solid ground: unmovable and unshakable.

The other day I was in the field working with some children playing soccer. For a moment I glanced around the area and saw two people resting underneath the crosses. This moved me to ponder these crosses' significance to the world around it.

My first thought was what a nice place to rest. In a world going a million miles an hour, it is nice to know there is something that will never change, and best yet is a place at which you can find peace and rest. Needless to say there are not many places like that around anymore. We all need a place of rest and God provided it at the cross.

The next place my mind took me was that the people sitting underneath this cross came from a different country, a different culture, and spoke a different language than I did. Yet, we are both welcome and equal at the foot of the cross. In a world that defines people by how they look, where they are from, and how much they make, it is nice to know the cross is a place that welcomes all people and calls us all to a place of peace.

The last thought I had was that these crosses are more recognizable than the church in the neighborhood, and I thought that is a good thing. We make a mistake as Christians when our buildings and programs overshadow the cross.

There is something simple yet unavoidable about our three crosses. They stand like a beacon to a world rushing by. In regards to the cross, it seems like little has changed in the last 2000 years. It's still an unavoidable, unshakeable beacon of hope to a lost world rushing by.

Scripture: Matthew 11:28-29: "Come to me, all you who are weary and burdened, and I will give you rest. Take my yoke upon you and learn from me, for I am gentle and humble in heart, and you will find rest for your souls."

Hebrews 12:2: "Let us fix our eyes on Jesus, the author and perfecter of our faith, who for the joy set before him endured the cross, scorning its shame, and sat down at the right hand of the throne of God."

Prayer: Dear Lord, let us go to the cross where it is safe in time of danger, have us visit the place or rest when we are busy, and let us cling to the cross when all else fails. We thank you for your love and ask all these things in the name of Christ, Amen.

A Friendly and Timely Reminder from the Lord

This past weekend I was blessed to coordinate a group of generous people in helping a family reestablish themselves in a mobile home. After the weekend we still needed to make a couple of deliveries to the home: one being a bed and the other a portable heater, but for the most part our work was complete. I was not in a big hurry to complete the task because I understood the family would not be living there at night until later in the week.

Tonight I was looking for a book with my wife and kids while one of my other kids practiced basketball. During that time I received a phone call from a neighbor of the family we helped, and she was telling me they had moved in earlier than expected and that if I had the heater for their house, they were ready. I told the lady I would be by tomorrow to give it to her, hung up the phone, and went back to my family.

I remember looking in my car and being surprised the temperature was 51 degrees. I also remember thinking while on the phone that it had almost warmed up since nighttime hit and that it wasn't too bad to be outside. This impacted my decision to just wait until tomorrow to deliver the heater.

We arrived home late in the evening so I gathered myself in my nice, warm house, with our children and grandchildren. They were having a nice time baking Christmas cookies, and we were getting to hold the new grandbaby. I decided at this time to check my emails. In the process, I did what I always do—I checked the on-line newspaper for the latest news.

As I looked at Obama's plan for jobs and checked on the Cowboys loss to the Giants, I took a moment to check the weather. I was in shock as I read that tonight the temperature was to get down to 22 degrees. Immediately my mind went to the family sitting in the house in need of another heater! I had wondered why the neighbor called, and now I knew.

I grabbed my coat and hat, headed to some generous friends of mine who had the heater, picked it up, and headed for the mobile home to make the delivery. There was no way I was going to sleep tonight with that family in need of a heater I could have delivered. My memory is the reason why.

Because I remember; I remember what it was like to sleep under as many blankets as possible with only a small electric heater and stove for heat. I remember what it was like to "blow smoke" with your breath in your own house. I know what it was like to dread the news when it would report a cold front was coming. I remember feeling guilty to be at a nice warm place of work while the rest of the family was in a cold house. I remember what it was like to drive in a car with little or no heat and wishing for spring to come.

I haven't lived that way in a while, but I remember. Some who are reading this devotional lived through the Great Depression and remember what it was like to scrape for food on the table. Others of you might remember a home where a single mom did her best to keep the electricity going and to keep food on the table. Those are things you never forget. It affects the way you live.

As I drove over to the mobile home by myself, I had a lump in my throat, and I spoke to God. During those quiet moments, I asked God to never ever let me live in a nice warm house and forget those who are cold. I asked him to never let me forget the hungry because my belly was full. I thanked him for letting me deliver the heater this night and for his reminder of how he has blessed me.

Perhaps you, like I, need to bring your heart in out of the cold and be reminded of the warmth of God's love and provisions.

Scripture: 2 Corinthians 1:3-4: "Praise be to the God and Father of our Lord Jesus Christ, the Father of compassion and the God of all comfort, who comforts us in all our troubles, so that we can comfort those in any trouble with the comfort we ourselves have received from God."

Prayer: Dear Lord, help us to not be so comfortable in our world that we forget those in need. Help us not to be judgmental of those in need but to remember our days of need. We ask these things in the name of Christ, Amen.

Undeserved Daffodils

I love my flower bed, and twice a year, I change it out, once just before winter and another right around Easter. When I arrived at my current home almost two years ago, the flower bed was set and in great shape. It was mid-May.

As that year passed and we came to the end of our first winter, I noticed some green shoots coming out of several places in the flower bed. At first, I could not figure it out. Then it hit me. These were annuals that lay dormant for the winter and come up unannounced in the spring. Sure enough, in a few days, I had nice daffodils blooming in several places. They were a very pleasant flower bed surprise. I loved them.

As the spring moved forward, they died and disappeared just about the same time the heat arrived. This explains why I did not know about them. Their season of life was completed before we moved in, and as we arrived, they were again laying dormant.

Just this week, I looked in the flower bed, and amongst my winter flowers were green sprouts. This time, it did not take me by surprise. I had just about forgotten about them, but just as faithful as last year, there they were again, right on time. I announced to Kim that my daffodils were back. She smiled.

Now every day I come in from the front yard with daffodils in full bloom I declare, "I love my daffodils." The other day I came in and declared my love for the daffodils while Kim was talking to my daughter. She smiled and turned to Sadie and said "He calls them his daffodils, and he did not even plant them." Good point.

There, in my flower bed is a picture of grace. I had nothing to do with these flowers, I had no knowledge that they were even there, and I have no idea how long they have been around. None of that matters. They still come out each year. Through no effort of my own, I get to enjoy them.

God's grace comes undeserved to me as well. I know who I am, a stubborn sinful person who deserves nothing but punishment from a perfect God, yet His grace comes to me none the less. I don't deserve it, didn't do anything for it, yet I still get to enjoy it. Grace: it is good.

One last thought: the daffodil comes just after the coldest part of the year. While everything is still dead, up come these beautiful blooms seemingly out of nowhere. Grace is the same way in our life. Just when you think all is lost, just when everything seems dead in your life, seemingly out of nowhere, God's grace blooms, giving you a new outlook and hope like only grace can.

Grace, like the daffodil, can be trusted, though it can't always be seen, and is oh-so-beautiful when it blooms.

Scripture: Ephesians 2:4-5: "But because of his great love for us, God, who is rich in mercy, made us alive with Christ even when we were dead in transgressions—it is by grace you have been saved." (Check out 2:6-9)

Prayer: Dear Lord, we acknowledge our sin to you this day and thank you for your forgiveness and grace. We also thank you for the grace to make it through each day. We ask these things in the name of Christ, Amen.

16 Words That Make a Big Difference

My wife teaches my children at home. Thus, she gets to choose what curriculum they use and what special books they might read. This year, for one of their books, she chose *Holes* by Louis Sachar.

With the need for this book, we went to the trusty used bookstore to see if they had some gently used editions. Just as we had hoped—they had some books that were in good condition and at a really good price. Mission accomplished.

As we started home, Kim was reading through the back of the book and checking each book out a little further when she saw a note in one of them. Evidently, this note was from a teacher to a student. Here are the contents of the note:

Michelle,

You are so wonderful! I will miss you very much! Stay sweet and come see me!

Love,
Mrs. Schultz

Sixteen words of pure encouragement; sixteen words that say you are special; sixteen words providing worth and love. Mrs. Shultz, wherever you are, I tip my hat to you!

Did she have to write this note on the inside of the book for Michelle? Of course not! She could have simply handed out a book, given an assignment, and went on her way. But Mrs. Shultz proved to be one of those special people that takes the time to lift up instead of ignore, one who builds up instead of tears down. She is a special breed; but she does not have to be alone.

There is much to learn from this teacher. Here are just a few lessons:

- It only takes a few minutes to lift up with words. Take the time.

- You can always find fault; find the good.
- Words have great power; use them carefully.

Positive words from people of influence are very important. A good word from a parent, teacher, grandparent, or supervisor goes a long way toward building the self-esteem of others.

Let us learn from the teacher today. Let's use our words wisely.

Scripture:
Proverbs 10:19: "When Words are many, sin is not absent, but he who holds his tongue is wise."
Proverbs 12:18: "Reckless words pierce like a sword, but the tongue of the wise brings healing."
Proverbs 16:21: "The wise in heart are called discerning, and pleasant words promote instruction."
Proverbs 16:24: "Pleasant words are a honeycomb, sweet to the soul and healing to the bones."

Prayer: Dear Lord, help us to speak good words, to watch our tone, and to be people who encourage instead of destroy. Forgive us when we fail in this area. Always have our mind to be on guard for the evil and angry words and help us to focus on the positive and loving ones. We ask these things in the name of our Savior, Jesus Christ, Amen.

23 Flavors

We here at simple/truths want to keep our readers informed, so it is my duty to let you know that Dr. Pepper in the two-liter bottle is on sale for 88 cents at Wal-Mart. Being the wise shopper that I am, last night I picked up three.

As I walked out, I was checking out the label and noticed this 23 flavors deal they were advertising. Thus being the inquisitive guy that I am, I decided to go to the computer when I arrived at the house and see what this was all about. Were there really 23 flavors and if there were, what were they?

Let me back up just a second and let you know that I am not a huge fan of the Dr. Pepper, but it is a distinctively Texas drink so it can't be all bad. I normally like it with the pure cane sugar and in a bottle. I have also been to the original plant in Dublin, Texas, so I have a little Dr. Pepper history. The purchase was for others who might like it more than me—just shows you what a great guy I am.

Now back to the 23 flavors. It only took a second to find that indeed there are 23 flavors. I always keep in mind that not everything I see on the internet is true, but I confirmed this in a couple of different places. So I am somewhat confident of these flavors. So what are they? See below.

Here they are in alphabetical order: Almond, Amaretto, Black Licorice, Blackberry, Caramel, Carrot, Cherry, Clove, Cola, Ginger, Juniper, Lemon, Molasses, Nutmeg, Orange, Pepper, Plum, Prune, Raspberry, Root Beer, Rum, Tomato, and Vanilla.

The secret to what makes Dr. Pepper taste like it does is not in the flavors but how they put them all together; how they mix them, and when; how much they put in; and what temperature all of this happens at. I am sure there is a lot more to it than that. I will leave the mix for a chemist to figure out. The bottom line is that all of those flavors mixed together make one distinctive taste. It is the same with the church: many different people and personalities, one distinctive body.

It is a disservice to God for those within the church to expect everyone to be the same. Cookie-cutter Christians are just not what

God had planned. God created us not only in His own image, but also with our own distinctive personality and gifts. These personality traits and gifts were created to be used within the body of Christ to lift up, to encourage, to teach, and to serve the world around us.

For a church to work right, it needs many different ingredients (personalities). Sure our differences cause us to be uncomfortable at times (we like for everyone to agree with and be somewhat like us), but God knows just the right mix of people and personalities that will work to get His purpose fulfilled. Think of Him as the Great Chemist who knows the secret formula.

Now keep in mind that Dr. Pepper is not the same if even one ingredient is missing. Same with the church: if we are not in our place doing what God gifted us to do, then the body does not have all the flavors He desired for it to have. Sure the church will get by, but it does not taste exactly as it should.

Are you in the mix? If not, jump right in—the Great Chemist is waiting to use you in just the right way at just the right place.

Scripture: 1 Corinthians 12:12-14: "The body is a unit, though it is made up of many parts; and though all its parts are many, they form one body. So it is with Christ. For we were all baptized by one Spirit into one body—whether Jews or Greeks, slave or free—and we were all given the one Spirit to drink. Now the body is not made up of one part, but of many."

Prayer: Dear Lord, guide us in our relationship with you so that we can be used for the greater good. We ask these things in the name of Christ, Amen.

1982/2009

I have lived through four recessions in my "working" lifetime. Through each of the previous three, I was able to keep my job. My only struggle was making sure I was able to take care of the young family I had been blessed with, which was nothing new.

In 1982, I was young and just starting work with a power utility. While inflation was going crazy and people were losing their jobs, I was getting raises and had a steady income. My job was insulated from job reductions because everyone needs electricity. Life was good.

On top of the utility job, I worked part-time at two other jobs to make ends meet. So when everyone else was struggling to get one job, I had as many as three. Needless to say, I had a little trouble relating to the world around me.

The recession of these last couple of years started off just like the others for me. I had a good contract at a large corporation I had been at for 27 years. I enjoyed the people I worked with, and on top of that, I had a part-time job that was my true passion. Life was good.

Once again, as the world crumpled around me last fall, I could not relate. But, things change.

Midway through this year, I lost the job of 27 years at the large corporation. All of a sudden, I moved from the ranks of the employed to the unemployed. With that, I moved into a world of unemployment insurance battles, resumes, job filings and reduced income. Life is good, but boy is it different.

Guess what—I no longer have trouble relating to the world around me. Isn't that great! It is always good to understand what the other guy is going through. Too bad we have to go through a recession for it to happen.

There are four quick lessons for us in this:

1) **Be thankful.** In the midst of a world crumbling around you, remember how good you have it. Nothing is more insulting to

those hurting than to listen to someone who things are going well for bellyache about some insignificant aspect of life.

2) **Be aware.** Don't be trapped in your sunshine days and miss an opportunity to minister to someone who is struggling because you did not notice. Almost every day God sends someone our way we can minister to. Normally their problem is one we can relate to. Keep your head up, your eyes open and your ears listening.

3) **Be careful.** We want to say something, but we need to be careful with what we say. Don't say you can relate unless you can, and even at that, each situation is different. Stay away from the temptation to compare someone's situation to your own. Most of the time just listening is plenty.

4) **Be available.** Don't just say the words "can I help?"; help. Most people are not going to ask for help. Pride gets in the way. If you see a need, meet it.

God is good. He was good in 1982, and He is still the same God in 2009. Remember, God does not waste any experience on us. He will use it for His good and glory—even if it comes during a recession.

Scripture: Psalm 145:8-9: "The LORD is gracious and compassionate, slow to anger and rich in love. The Lord is good to all; he has compassion on all he has made." *Let's practice being like God!*

Prayer: Dear Lord, help us to be more like you; good listeners, eager to serve, and compassionate to all. Help us to see you in each circumstance, to have joy when good days arrive, to appreciate the simple things of life, and to lean on you during difficult days. You are indeed a good God, and we ask all of these things in the name of Christ, Amen.

Hope Springs Eternal

Here in Texas the weather has just been wonderful. I can hear the birds sing outside my window in the mornings, the grass is getting green, and the warmth reminds me that very soon spring will be here. When it comes to spring, my mind goes to hope and new beginnings.

I am a baseball fan and have lived in Dallas all my life. I sat on the third base line of the second game the Texas Rangers ever played in Arlington. I have been a fan for over 30 years now. I pull for them no matter if they win or lose. They are my team. Of course, if you know anything about baseball, you know with the Rangers there are a lot more losses than wins.

The Rangers have never won a championship and have rarely ever gotten close. Yet every year at this time, new hope arrives. The Rangers head out to their spring training destination in Arizona with a new set of players and some different coaches, and well, everything looks so very good.

Each new player is going to add the piece of the puzzle that will get them to a championship. We fans just believe that. Everyone involved with the team is upbeat and positive. Their record is 0 and 0. They have yet to lose a game. Of course they have yet to play a game, but that's beside the point. That is the beauty of it all. Last year's record, as miserable as it might have been, is gone, cleaned right off the slate. That is old news. Everyone now is looking ahead. Nobody really knows what the future holds, but everyone involved thinks it will be better than last year, and who is to tell them differently?

Let's face it. We all need a little "spring" in our life every once in a while. We need to be able to wipe the slate clean and start all over again. For some of us, it has been years of losses and bad records. You don't have to try to remember your seasons of loss do you? Most people are glad to remind you of what a poor record you have. As the losses build up, so does our discouragement. As we grow more discouraged, our ability to put the past in the past diminishes, and we end up thinking we are, well, for a lack of a better word, losers.

Perhaps we're losers in the world's eyes, but not so with God! He is the King of Spring! He looks out there and He sees you—and

I am telling you, he sees a champion. He sees potential. He knows what your strengths are. Goodness, He gave them to you. Does He know your losses? Sure. He was there. Nothing got by Him. For Him, they were not losses but lessons. He was using those to teach you, to prepare you for your coming days, or even to get your attention. God wasn't looking for the winter. He was looking to the spring when all things are new again.

Let me ask you something. Are you living in the ditch of past seasons of defeat? If so, let me ask you another question—why? If there was sin in those defeats, repent and move on. He is the God of second chances. If there was a sudden turn of events that seemed to be a loss, turn the events over to God and look ahead. God is there. What's done is done. God has a purpose and plan. Stay busy with Him as you watch the plan unfold. You might just be surprised how God will use your loss. Last time I checked, God was still undefeated. His plans and purposes always come to be.

Right now, on March 6, the Texas Rangers are in first place, and so are you if you have turned your life over to the King of Spring, Jesus Christ.

Scripture: Philippians 2:12 & 13 and 3:13 & 14: "Therefore, my dear friends, as you have always obeyed - not only in my presence, but now much more in my absence—continue to work out your salvation with fear and trembling, for it is God who works in you to will and to act according to his good purpose."

"Brothers, I do not consider myself yet to have taken hold of it. But one thing I do: Forgetting what is behind and straining toward what is ahead, I press on toward the goal to win the prize for which God has called me heavenward in Christ Jesus."

Prayer: Lord, help us to follow the path to you that lead us from discouragement to hope, from defeat to victory. We thank you for your love and we ask these things in the precious name of Christ. Amen.

Bomb Throwers Cause Casualties

In the late 19th century, the mood and relationship between workers and their employers was tense to say the least. With the Industrial Revolution well under way, workers were just starting to unite for better working conditions. One of the improvements they were seeking was for an 8-hour work day.

On May 1, 1886, gatherings were held in many different cities all over the country in order to rally for the 8-hour work day, with the largest of these gatherings being in Chicago. On May 3, a group of striking workers would end up in a confrontation that would lead to at least two workers being killed by police.

These events led to a meeting at Haymarket Square in Chicago the next day. This event started calmly, so calmly that the mayor of Chicago who had come to witness the event, went home early. As the last speaker was finishing, the police ordered the crowd dispersed. Trouble quickly followed.

As the police began marching toward the speaker's wagon, someone threw a pipe bomb into the policemen's line, immediately killing one policeman and setting off a riot that would last five minutes but would end up with the deaths of 8 policemen and 4 civilians. Other reports indicated as many as 50 deaths, 60 wounded policemen, and untold civilian injuries—civilians who never reported those injuries because of fear of being punished for being at the riot.

A trial was held for the killing of the policeman and 8 men were found guilty, with seven of those given the death penalty. Before it was all said and done, four were hanged and one committed suicide the night before he was to be hanged.

During the trial, no one argued the fact that none of these men threw the bomb. The person who threw the bomb was never established. He walked away free; they often do.

In life, some people use their words and actions much like a bomb tossed at the police line at Haymarket Square. They cause emotional injury, spiritual chaos, and in the end, many innocent people are hurt by what they do.

We all know these people. They dwell within our families, our neighborhoods, and even unfortunately our churches. Their deeds are aptly timed to cause the most damage. They say or do them at family gatherings like weddings or reunions, but one of their favorite times is while a family grieves at a funeral.

They say their hurtful words or perform their irresponsible acts in the midst of church meetings and neighborhood gatherings. They care little for the group they have hurt and the people who are affected. What they are looking for is attention, and they will grab it any way they can regardless of the adverse effects on others. Chaos is their friend; evil is their intent.

There is little you can do about others who are out to hurt. The most important thing for us is to be certain we never are the ones who carelessly throw bombs:

1) Make sure your words are always seasoned with grace and your actions reflect your love for Christ. Don't be an unintentional "bomb thrower" by saying things carelessly or doing things without thinking through the consequences.

2) "Bombs" are often found in information you know about others that came to you through gossip; shut it down! Gossip often explodes; make sure it stops with you. Or better yet: do what it takes not to hear it. Gossips are one of the top "bomb throwers." Stay clear!

3) The Bible says to "not be overcome with evil, but overcome evil with good." One of my favorite all time verses. People seeking revenge often throw bombs; don't get hung up on getting back at someone. Leave them in the hands of God who is just and who will handle all situations. Revenge can overcome you and have you act in ways you never thought possible. Instead of giving back evil for evil, do a good thing instead. You would be surprised at how many bombs are diffused by following this verse.

4) At Haymarket, it was reported that many of the wounds of the policemen came from friendly fire. In the dark they turned and just started shooting. Unfortunately, they hit the people on their side. Friendly fire hurts because it hits those we love

the most. Often we hurt those closest to us in stressful times. If you are under a great deal of stress (for example, you're unemployed, you have a big project due, you have a wedding approaching, or someone you loved just passed away), be careful to make sure you keep in mind the feelings and personalities of others. Friendly fire can be fatal to families and churches alike.

If you are ever tempted to drop bombs in the lives of others, remember Haymarket Square where one bomb destroyed the lives of many.

Scripture: Romans 12:19: "Do not take revenge, my friends, but leave room for God's wrath, for it is written: 'It is mine to avenge; I will repay,' says the Lord."

1 Timothy 5:13: "Besides, they get into the habit of being idle and going about from house to house. And not only do they become idlers, but also gossips and busy bodies, saying thing they ought not to."

Prayer: Dear Lord, guide our hearts to be like yours. Help us to care for people and to not be ruled by our emotions but by your leading in our life. Help our words to be filled with grace and love for those we come in contact with. Forgive us where we have used words and actions in the past to hurt. We ask all these things in the name of Christ, Amen.

The 960th Try is the Charm

They are going to miss Cha Sa-soon at the driver's license agency in Jeonju, South Korea. The 69-year-old had been almost a daily visitor ever since April of 2005. But they won't be seeing her anymore. She finally got what she came for: her driver's license.

"Perseverance" and "persistence" should be Cha Sa-soon's middle names. She has plenty of both, and finally, last month her persistence paid off. In South Korea, you have to pass a written test before you can get your driver's license, and on her 960th try, she finally passed it.

The news agency quoted her as saying she wanted to get a used car so she could go and visit her son and daughter as well as use it for her small vegetable business. My only hope is that she drops by the driver's license agency to visit the friends she must have made while spending time there over the last five years.

Let me confess that I would have given up somewhere around try number 14, and I would have been very close to a mental break-down no later than try number 29. I tip my hat to Cha Sa-soon. In a world that encourages you to give it up, she kept her head up and reached her goal.

You may be a teacher working hard to make the world a better place and give kids a bright future. It may seem like there is more bureaucratic hassle and parent apathy than positive results, yet you stay at it. Look again, positive results are out there. Perhaps you are a parent of a preschooler, and it just does not seem to be getting through—the days are frustrating and the nights tiring, yet you lovingly stay at it.

Maybe you're a minister of a small church among mega churches. The results seem small or nonexistent. Don't fall into the trap of comparison, and don't be fooled—

God is in it, and good things are happening. Maybe you had a dream to start a business, but it has been slow going at first, and most months, the bills outnumber the income. Hang in there.

Perhaps you're raising a teenager while caring for a parent, or you're waiting for the right mate, or working hard to get through school while raising a family. You may be up to your ears in frustration and heartache. Remember our friend Sa-soon and her persistence, but more importantly, lean on God to see you through.

Failure can affect your self esteem if you are living by the world's standards. Don't do it. Lay your self worth at the feet of the Savior who gives way more than 960 chances (thank goodness). He is the one who created you with a purpose and plan. The Bible holds many examples of those who stayed the course in spite of delay or disappointment. Here are just two:

1) Moses stood in exile for 40 years before returning to lead the people out of captivity at 80 years of age.
2) David's heart's desire was to build a temple for God, but he was not allowed; instead he made preparations for his son to build it.

Not buying all this "don't give up stuff?" Life getting on your last nerve? I understand. Trust me, the one behind the keyboard has seen plenty of failure. Frustration, failure, and disappointment are best understood in the light of the Heavenly Father and His word.

1) *God has a purpose*: **Jeremiah 29:11**: "'For I know the plans I have for you,' declares the LORD, 'plans to prosper you and not to harm you, plans to give you hope and a future.'"
2) *God's desire for us is greater than we can even imagine*: **Ephesians 3:20**: "Now to him who is able to do immeasurably more than all we ask or imagine, according to his power that is at work within us."
3) *What God starts, He finishes*: **Philippians 1:6**: "being confident of this, that he who began a good work in you will carry it on to completion until the day of Christ Jesus."
4) *You are a wonderful creation of the living God*: **Psalm 139:14**: "I praise you because I am fearfully and wonderfully made; your works are wonderful, I know that full well."
5) *God had a work planned for you before you were even born*: **Ephesians 2:10**: "For we are God's workmanship, created

in Christ Jesus to do good works, which God prepared in advance for us to do."

6) *Stop doing it on your own*: **Philippians 4:13**: "I can do all things through Christ who strengthens me."

Prayer: Dear Lord, Help us to believe your Word, in Christ's name, Amen.

Falsely Accused

I made my way to the mailbox the other day and among all the enjoyable things I always receive was a letter from my Homeowners Association. I rarely hear from them, so I was interested in what they might have to say—until I opened it.

Along with a note telling me all the things they do was a notice that my garbage cans were seen out on days that my garbage was not to be picked up. This is not only a violation of the Homeowners Association's rules, but the city I live in doesn't like it either. I was advised to get this situation resolved in ten days.

This will not be a problem because my garbage cans are never out on a day when the garbage is not being collected. My day is Monday. When I come home from church on Sunday night (and normally that is somewhere around 10 pm), I put them out. Then on Monday afternoon, I bring them back up to the house. So unless they were driving around my neighborhood at 11 pm on a Sunday night (highly unlikely), I was falsely accused. It bugged me a bit, but then I promptly filed the letter in the appropriate trashcan to be taken out at the proper time.

Later that same day, I was heading out to check the flowerbeds, and as I did, I noticed something attached to my door that looked like a notice. Again, this is unusual, so I took a peek. There, in my hand, was a notice from the police code enforcement agency that I had ten days to get the carpet out from behind the house.

That sounded interesting since I have not done anything with carpet, ever, at this house. I went to the back and found nothing in my alley or at the back of the house. As I walked back to the house I found that the address number on the ticket was 5005, and I live at 5009. The notice was for my neighbor—not me. They had put it on the wrong door. I quickly informed the fine city of their mistake. They were apologetic, and the issue was resolved.

Trust me—in my life, you could safely accuse me of a lot of things, and that is bad enough, but nothing seems to bother me more than when someone says I did or am something I am not. In the two above cases, the issues were quickly resolved; that is rarely the case. False accusations can destroy. Let's pause to make sure we are not guilty of making false accusations. Below are some friendly reminders.

1) If you are tempted to accuse someone of something, ask your-self this simple question, "Why?" Your motive will reveal a lot about your spiritual and mental status.

2) Make sure you have all the facts. I will let you in on some-thing: if it is in regards to another person, you probably don't have all the facts. Very rarely do I find one side of the story to be the absolute truth. When it comes to differences between people, or in descriptions of events, everyone has their slant. The truth is almost always somewhere in the middle. *Note to self: even I have a slant. Ouch.

3) Ask yourself another very short question, "What good is it going to do to bring this to light or to make the accusation?" This is when our spiritual life should kick in. Understand that the Bible, from start to finish, is concerned about redemption, forgiveness, and bringing a person back to a right relationship with God. If our concern is about those things, then good, the risks are worth it. If it is about getting even or jealousy, then not so good, stay away from it.

Let me identify what harm accusations, especially false ones, can do. These in themselves should make us very careful about what we say or who we accuse:

1) Once something is said, it can never be retrieved, and even if the truth comes out, the damage has been done. Some people will always have doubt or see the person as guilty.

2) Be prepared for the accusation to drive a wedge between you and the accused. Families, friends, co-workers, and church members are separated forever when someone is wrongly accused or accused with the wrong motive in mind.

3) You become attached to the accusation yourself; if done for the wrong reasons or found to be false, then it sheds a nega-tive light on you that will not go away either.

I am still good friends with my city and HOA. I like the job they do. Don't count on being so fortunate with others if you join them in the false accusation business.

Scripture: Proverbs 6:16-19: "These six things the LORD hates, yes, seven are an abomination to Him: A proud look, a lying tongue, hands that shed innocent blood, a heart that devises wicked plans, feet that are swift in running to evil, a false witness who speaks lies, and one who sows discord among brethren."

Prayer: Dear Lord, help us to be wise in how we handle the truth. Guide us to seek your wisdom as we deal with relationships and the words we use. Have us to seek the best in all circumstances. We ask these things in the name of Christ, Amen.

Bill Buckner

I was having a baseball conversation with a fellow fan the other day when he started telling me about a team making a bunch of mistakes on easy plays. He made this statement, "They were missing ground balls just like Bill Buckner." Why this bugged me, I have no idea, but it did.

The name Bill Buckner means little to you unless two things: you are a big baseball fan and/or a fan of the Boston Red Sox. Since numbers mean everything to baseball fans, let me give you some numbers on our friend. He played for over 20 years, which is a long time; he had 2,715 hits overall, and, just for a point of reference, 3000 hits gets you into the Hall of Fame. One year he won the batting title (the best hitter), and he played in 2,715 games, which again says he was good enough to be around a while.

All of that means nothing until you come to October 25, 1986. Bill Buckner was playing first base for the Boston Red Sox. They were ahead in Game 6 of the World Series, and all they needed was one out to win their first World Series in ages. With the game tied and a runner on second base, Mookie Wilson hit a grounder to first base where Bill Buckner was playing. Instead of fielding it and ending the inning as he had hundreds of times before, the ball went right between his legs into right field, and the runner scored from second base, thus ending Boston's chances that night to win the World Series.

For Red Sox fans, it was a hard pill to swallow; for Buckner, it defined an otherwise fine career. Twenty-one years later when people think of Bill Buckner, they do not think of the great career he had, they bring up October 25, 1986. Too bad. And it brings me to my point, or really points, of the day. In honor of Bill who now lives in Idaho, let's call it lessons to learn from a slow roller:

1) One is that it only takes one bad choice to ruin an otherwise solid life of good choices in the eyes of others. How many of us know the truth of that statement? Be very careful to stay in a good relationship with God, keep good company, and be

busy about serving others. If a choice seems questionable, take it to good, Godly people for review.

2) On the other hand, one bad choice, though it may change your life, does not end your life. Buckner did not simply walk off the field and never play again; he played for four more years. One bad choice, no matter how bad, does not end your life. God still loves you, He seeks to forgive you, and for us to learn from our mistakes and, more than anything, to find grace from him for our sins. He is a redeeming God.

3) Don't put yourself in bad situations. Buckner had two bad ankles and really had no business out there that cold Boston evening. Who knows why the coach had him out there. Likewise, do not put yourself in situations you are not spiritually able to handle. Who knows why we put ourselves in bad situations? But when we do it almost always leads to failure.

4) That fateful night in Boston, the entire team failed. When that last inning started, the Red Sox were ahead by 2 runs. It should have never come down to that slow roller toward Buckner. The game should have been over long before that, but it was not. Why? Because others failed around him. This note is for everyone: we need to make sure we understand that our bad choices affect others. Especially as parents, we need to remember that when we make bad choices, it puts our children in a position to fail, not succeed. No parent wants that. Just as it takes a team to win, it takes a team to fail. We need to make sure as a family of God we are in the right place taking care of business the right way.

** One last side note on that. Teams fail, churches do the wrong thing, and Christians do not always make the right choices. Don't make it worse by continuing to make wrong choices. Seek forgiveness from those that were hurt. This will help build a stronger team (church).

Life hits us slow rollers every day. Nine times out of ten, we have no issues; we make the play. But when we don't, God is still there, loving us and teaching us. There will be other grounders. We just need to make sure the next one doesn't get by.

Scripture: Ephesians: 2:6-7: "And God raised us up with Christ and seated us with him in the heavenly realms in Christ Jesus, in order that in the coming ages he might show the incomparable riches of his grace, expressed in his kindness to us in Christ Jesus."

Prayer: Dear Lord, we thank you for your forgiveness when our choices are wrong, when they lead to sin. We are thankful for your grace. Help us to do the things that lead to proper decisions and a righteous life. We ask these things in the name of Christ, Amen.

Be Careful—Life Can Be a Wreck

Today I was doing some driving, and at a busy intersection I came very close to having a wreck. For a moment, this event really shook me up, and then it led me do some thinking.

The first thought that comes to mind is that if you drive long enough, especially in a busy area, you are more than likely to be involved in a wreck at least once in your life. The law of averages comes into play here. With that thought in mind, I went to the National Highway Traffic Safety Administration to see just how many wrecks there are in a year.

The site had a lot of staggering and depressing numbers, so let me just stick with the number of police-reported wrecks there were in the United States last year. That number is 5,811,000. That number is big, and my guess is that there were a lot of unreported wrecks that could be added.

The bottom line that we don't like to admit, though, is that unfortunately during our driving life, we will likely be in a wreck. The other news of the day is that in our personal lives, we are going to find ourselves in a few wrecks as well. Let's think about those for a second.

- Sometimes personal wrecks are our fault, but they can be the fault of others. The less time spent pointing fingers and the more time spent dealing with the real issues before a loving God, the better.
- The real question is not "are you going to be in a wreck," but "what are you going to do after it." Be prepared. And just as in a car wreck, get in touch with the authorities (God) as quickly as possible. This will minimize the damage and get things on the road to recovery much quicker.
- Insurance companies will take a look at your car and on occasion will call it a total loss. **There are no total losses in the sight of a loving God!** Things might change in your life, people are sure to be hurt, but believe me: there are no totaled lives. If you do not believe me, simply read your Bible. It is

full of people who made wrecks of their life but were used by God afterward.

- If you happen to be the person at fault, don't pass the blame. Take responsibility for your part in the accident. If you can, address the pain of those hurt, ask for forgiveness, repent, then seek God's help in making sure that particular wreck does not occur again, then move on. There is nothing more you can do. Don't let others keep accusing you by taking you back to the scene of the wreck. God does not do that. We do that to ourselves, sometimes with the help of others. Don't go there.
- Final thought on this is if you can stay away from that intersection in life, do it! Car wrecks have a tendency to happen at the same place. It's the same with our personal wrecks. Keep your head up for dangerous intersections, and STAY AWAY from them.

There was a point in my life where I had three wrecks really close together, and each was my fault. Needless to say, my insurance company did not think I was a very good risk, and I had to find another one. Thankfully, I did find an insurance company that was willing to take me on, and I have survived for a good while without any crashes.

If we took a good look at our personal lives, most would say we are not a very good risk; thankfully we have a God that is willing to take the risk to truly and unconditionally love us. The next time you find yourself in the midst of a personal wreck, remember that most of all!

Scripture: Isaiah 57:15-16: "For this is what the high and lofty One says—he who lives forever, whose name is holy: 'I live in a high and holy place, but also with him who is contrite and lowly in spirit, to revive the spirit of the lowly and to revive the heart of the contrite. I will not accuse forever, nor will I always be angry, for then the spirit of man would grow faint before me—the breath of man that I have created.'"

Prayer: Dear Lord, lead us from sin and guide us in the way ever-lasting. Help us in our times of hurt, lead us to do what is right and help us to seek your healing. We ask these things in the name of Christ, Amen.

9 Minutes and 23 Seconds

Every great athlete loves a challenge, so it was with that Olympic Spirit in mind that I offered to take three preschoolers to the grocery store. Okay, maybe I am not such a great athlete, but with the speed and moves I made, I should be one.

Today I set a new world record in the event of "speed shopping" at 9 minutes and 23 seconds. Before we move forward with the play by play you need to know all the participants by name; there is Caleb, the mature one coming in at five; Gracie right behind him at four; and Trevor, the rookie, bringing up the bottom of the line up at not-yet-two.

In order to set any record or overcome great challenges, you need a plan; for the sake of public service, below is my plan:

- Park by the baskets. This works out great because you can move the little ones from the car straight to the basket. Remember every minute counts.
- Get popcorn and coke. This does take some time, but it keeps little hands busy for about two minutes. It does cause all kinds of sharing trouble with preschoolers, but it still is good for some kind of diversion, and quite honestly by the end of it all, I need a stiff drink (Mountain Dew).
- Move quickly and do not stop for anything or anyone. Woe be to the unsuspecting person who stands in my way as I dash from the bread aisle to the hot dogs back over to the chip aisle. For you older readers, think of O.J. Simpson running through the airport going for a Hertz rent-a-car. Speed is everything here.
- Always check the basket—do not take your eyes off of it. "Why?" you might ask. Because if you do, someone is going to stand up, or someone is going to grab the coke, and the other one is not going to like it. You must have your eyes on all the moving parts at all times. The last thing you want is a preschooler doing a flip and a half off the back of the basket.

- You must be ready and able to talk and think on your feet. Encouragement is important. For example, here is a piece of the conversation during my trip to the store: "Sit down, Gracie...Great job...Caleb, give Trevor the coke...thank you...Trevor, sit down...good job...Trevor, give Gracie some popcorn...Gracie, sit down...look out for the buns...ooopps we'll pick some more that aren't crushed...Caleb, stay by the basket...Trevor, you and Gracie sit down...thanks...we are almost done..." Repeat that several times, and you have my conversation.

- Make sure you are ready to pay at the checkout line and never—and I do mean never—take a phone call on your cell phone. These are two moments that preschoolers sense that you are not paying attention, and they will seize these moments to do all kinds of unruly things. For example, they might make a run from the basket or tip over the coke onto the checkout counter. This is the most critical stage if you are going to get out in record time or even just with your sanity. Don't take your eye off the prize too soon. If you do, you are sure to pay for it.

Here is the course to victory: It is all about having a plan and the proper focus! Never lose focus, get a good plan, and stay with it.

Such it is with our spiritual life; it is all about having a plan and keeping the proper focus. Each day is a challenge. The day might start off simple enough, but you never know what stands before you. In order to reach the final goal we must keep our focus on the Lord and follow a prearranged plan. That might mean short prayers for peace of mind or recalling scriptures you are familiar with. It certainly means setting aside a time of quiet to be with Him alone. Whatever and whenever works for you is best, but the key is staying rightly focused.

We live in a world of distractions and challenges; it's easy to get outside of God's plan if we don't keep our eyes on the Lord. Trust me. Just one moment without focus can doom an otherwise successful time.

Scripture: Philippians 3:8: "Finally, brothers, whatever is true, whatever is noble, whatever is right, whatever is pure, whatever is lovely, whatever is admirable—if anything is excellent or praise-worthy—think about such things."

Prayer: Dear Lord, help us to keep our minds focused on you and what is right. Help us to find a plan and to follow it in such a way as to bring glory to you. We ask these things in the name of Christ, Amen.

What? It's Not All About *Me*?

Today, Monday morning, July 24, my wife and I, along with the rest of my older children, took our sweet Gracie in for surgery on her heart. On our way, there little was said. I was focused on my little girl and me. I was in my own world. For some reason, I thought when we showed up for surgery early in the morning it would be just my family in a lonely waiting room.

It was all about me and my situation, but that quickly changed. As we showed up, my first steps within the door gave me an indication how wrong I was. The room was packed full of children coming for some kind of surgery that day. Within those first few moments, I recognized some of the children we had seen the day before in pre-op. As I sat holding my own girl, I gazed at the people in wonder that so many children would be in need of surgery.

There were some that had obvious physical needs, and it broke my heart to think of all the surgeries they would need in the coming days and years. I looked in the eyes of parents whose hearts were in every bit as much pain as mine. In that room, I believe there was almost every kind of pain and suffering that could be had by children and their parents. It was a sobering moment, one filled with much perspective.

As I type this, I have been in the hospital for two days and God has used each moment of it to remind me that it is not all about me. One such moment was when I stopped to use my computer and found myself having a conversation with a young lady with a year-old child in the hospital for chemotherapy. Her spirit and resolve were an inspiration, but it still did not stop my heart from aching for her and her child.

The halls, the waiting rooms, the cafeteria, and the patients' rooms all served as constant reminders that perhaps my situation is not so bad after all. Or at least, that I was not alone in my pain.

Let us leave the corridors of a children's hospital and look out to the world that surrounds you and me. I would dare say that all around us each and every day there are people who are struggling with great pain, if not physically, certainly spiritually. From the 11th floor at this hospital, I can see much of Dallas, an area full of millions of people. Imagine if you can the amount of suffering among so many.

Yet often I walk by and think little about it. Often I am so caught up in my own world that I fail to notice the hurt in others' lives. While God surely wants to comfort you and me in our times of hurt, I believe He also wants to use those painful moments to teach us to look outside our little world and see others as He does. When Jesus saw the hurting multitudes and their lostness, it says in the scriptures that He had compassion on them. I suspect He wants us to do likewise.

God does not wish to waste your pain, if that makes any sense at all. He wants us to use our experience to teach us to hold the hurting hands, to love those who are broken, to listen more intently, to pray with more fervor, and to recognize each opportunity to share His love with someone.

Early Monday morning, God woke me up again to the realities of this world.

- Look around you today; make a list of those you know who are having some kind of pain. Leave no one out—your friends, your family and even those you do not think so highly of. Then look for ways to meet one of their needs, even if it is in a small way.
- Do not limit yourself to church friends; the world around you has droves of hurting. Keep your eyes open in your neighborhood, local club, or sports team as well as when you're at work. Opportunities are limitless.

Scripture: John 13: 34-35: "A new command I give you: Love one another. As I have loved you, so you must love one another. By this all men will know that you are my disciples, if you love one another."

Prayer: Dear Lord, we thank you that you are there for us when things hurt. Help us to share the comfort, joy, and peace you give us with those we come in contact with. In Christ's name, Amen.

Her Heart—His Hands

I am in the middle of a lesson on trust. Trust is at the heart of everything we do and think of in our faith. If we trust God, we will allow Him to use us any way He pleases. If we trust God, we will step out in faith when we feel His urging us out of our comfort zone. Then, of course, if we trust God, we will put things in His hands and have faith that He knows best.

The last sentence is the one I am dealing with at this moment. As you read this, my little, almost six-month-old Gracie will be having open-heart surgery. Gracie has taught me a great deal about love and care over her short life. She has taught me much about priorities and the importance of the family. At this moment, she is giving me a Master's degree in what it means to really trust God.

At approximately 7 a.m. on Monday, we will hand our little girl off to a team of very talented and gifted doctors and nurses. By handing her off, I will be saying to them, here is my prize possession. I trust you with it. That is a very difficult thing to write, and I cannot imagine what it will be like to do it when the time comes.

For something between four and five hours, this team of medical professionals will hold my little girl's heart in their hands. They will make it beat. They will have machines to do the work of the heart while they seal two holes. Then, task finished, they will place everything where it belongs and set her heart to beating for what I hope is a hundred years.

To do this, it will take all the trust I can muster. First, I have to believe that this even had to be done. Many tests and the confirmations of about 15 doctors made the decision easy. Then, I had to trust that these doctors knew what they were doing. You ask questions like what kind of experience do they have, where were they trained, what hospital will the operation be done at. To put the heart of someone you love into someone else's hands, you must trust them.

She lies beside me as I type this, the most pleasant baby we have ever had, sweet, with a smile for everybody who speaks to her. The thought of losing her hangs heavy on my mind. Though the surgery, to them, is almost routine, it still comes with risks, and nothing is

133

routine when it comes to my girl's heart. I am trying to trust, but it is not coming easy.

Just as many of you who have walked these kinds of roads before me have found, I am finding that when it comes to trust, you must have an Anchor. His name is Jesus. To walk dark roads, you must know that Jesus has a plan and that His plans do not fail no matter what the outcome (tough one to write). You must know His history; He has never broken a promise.

You must know His credentials. He is the Son of God who died for the sins of all mankind. You need to know the Anchor cares for you. He does. Jesus loves you and me. Gracie, too. You must know He has power to work miracles; Jesus has the power of the entire universe at his fingertips.

Do we know all things? Of course not. That is where trust comes into play. We as humans want to know, and it just flat out scares us when we don't. Jesus came to cast away all fear and give us peace.

When I think of trust, I think of the father standing in the water and his young child on the side of the pool. He calls out to him to jump though the water is way over his head. The child runs and jumps without any hesitation into the loving arms of his father. No fear, total trust.

Tonight as I write, I am standing on the side of the pool; my Jesus is standing in the rough waters. In a few short hours, He will hold his hand out, and I will jump. He will be there—I trust He will.

"How can I do it?" I have asked myself many times over the last two weeks. I can do it not because of the nurses or doctors and certainly not because of machines. No, although those things are important, the only way I can hand her off is......

I will hand my girl off, because her heart will be in His hands.

Scripture: Psalms 139-1-2 and 23: "O Lord, you have examined my heart and know everything about me. You know when I sit down or stand up. You know my thoughts even when I'm far away…Search me, O God, and know my heart; test me and know my anxious thoughts."

Prayer: Dear Lord, it is good to know we can jump into your arms, and you will keep us safe. We praise you because you are a loving God, there for us all times, knowing each need. Help us Lord to trust you with our very lives and the lives of those we love. In Christ's name, Amen.

Yvette—Putting God's Wheels in Motion

It has been almost 7 months since we left the hospital with Gracie by our side. Over that period of time, I have had many opportunities to reflect back on that time of life. With reflection comes perspective, and as the days go by, that perspective has made one thing perfectly clear: God was in it all.

We had many nurses during our one-month stay, and we came to love almost each and every one of them. There were a few, though, who were extra special in our eyes, and Yvette was one of them. Yvette was a fun, loving, dedicated nurse who loved Christ and our Gracie. She met us early in our stay and played a special part of what has been an extra-special year.

Yvette could read our emotions well and when we were dissatisfied, confused, or upset with the events of the day, she would take the time to explain things to us or get someone who could. She took us under her wing of experience and walked us through some difficult days. To put it best, she became our advocate, and it was in this role that I can look back now and see how Yvette put the wheels of God in motion.

At first, we were not pleased with one doctor's bedside manner or with his seeming lack of concern for Gracie. Yvette picked up on this, and before we knew it, she had Gracie moved over to another team of doctors that she thought would be the best fit for us. She was right on the money. From there, the ball has just never really stopped rolling.

Because she made that move for us, we ended up with a different cardiologist, one that communicated well and showed a real concern for the patient as well as the parent. We have just fallen in love with her. This cardiologist found the problems with Gracie's heart, which eventually led to her heart surgery. She took us into her office, explained things to us, and then, the next day, she took the issue to several other doctors that suggested the surgery. Our trust in her made the decision for surgery an easy one, though not one we really wanted to make.

We did not meet the surgeon who would do Gracie's surgery until the day it was performed. We had talked to him on the phone once and met his nurse but had not seen him personally. Knowing nothing about heart surgery or heart surgeons, we had to trust our cardiologist's recommendation. He turned out to be a very gifted surgeon who repaired Gracie's heart and knew the right procedures when she struggled a bit in the operating room. No doubt he was the right man for the job.

There was no coincidence that Yvette was a nurse on the second night we were there. It was no coincidence that she suggested our new doctors, no coincidence that our doctor suggested our cardiologist, and no coincidence that our cardiologist recommended our surgeon. God's hand was in it all.

It took one floor nurse to put God's wheels in motion, one Christian lady who loved Him and cared for people, one person willing to take a stand for one scared and confused couple. The world needs fewer theologians and more Yvette's.

Where are you at as you read this? Is there a co-worker who needs a helping hand or one friend who needs a listening ear? Is there a young mother at the grocery store that needs a smile and a word of encouragement? God is the God of details and little things. You never know how even the slightest decision or encouraging word or action will affect someone's life.

What a great privilege we have to be a catalyst for God. Today, Gracie is a healthy and happy eight-month-old, and I owe much of that to Yvette who cared enough about a family and a baby girl to put God's wheels in motion.

What will you do today to put God's wheels in motion?

Scripture: John 13: 34-35: "A new commandment I give to you, that you love one another; as I have loved you, that you also love one another. By this all will know that you are My disciples, if you have love for one another."

Prayer: Dear Lord, teach us to be mindful of our actions and their effects on the lives of others. We thank you that you see fit to use us. Remind us each day how your hand is in on all the activities of our lives. In Christ's name, Amen.

Give 'Em Another Chance

There are some things I just do not like to do. On the top of that list is going to Wal-Mart. There are only two reasons to go there as far as I am concerned: they are the only ones who have what I need or they are the only people in town open at 2 in the morning.

Today was a day where they fell into category one. They were the only ones who had what I needed. So off Gracie, my trusty side-kick, and I went. I did not enter into this field trip with an open mind. Let me be honest with you—I was dreading the crowd, dreading the long lines, and not looking forward to my experience at all.

As I arrived, I noticed the crowd was low, and I was able to go straight to the first thing I needed. That was easy. The next venture was where I figured I would run into my problem. I was not familiar with what I was looking for and had no idea where it would be. My only hope was to find someone who would help, and that is not always so easy. Today it was.

I found a nice person, and she showed me right where I needed to go. Just like that, I was able to find my item, and I even took the chance to ask her another question, and she was still helpful. Mission accomplished. But now was the hard part—paying for it.

I just knew they would have one lane open, and I would be there forever, standing in line amongst thousands with two items in my hand and a three-year-old by my side.

I was wrong again. We were met in a short line with a friendly checker. She actually talked to us while we checked out and another checker came over and had a word with Gracie. We were out in no time and she wished us a good day. I think she might have even meant it.

Lesson learned? Always give someone a second chance. Good idea at the local store, great idea in life.

Here are some thoughts on giving people a second chance:

1) Remember we are not always the best person in the world, and we do not always make the best first impression.

2) My guess is you, like I, did or said some pretty silly or even bad things in your life, things you are sorry for. Thankfully, you have grown from them. Give someone a chance to grow from their errors as well.

3) Never forget circumstances shape people's attitude. On any given day, they might be going through a difficult time in life. When we give people a second chance, we allow them time to come through their difficult season. Your understanding spirit might be just what the doctor ordered for them today.

4) God has given us many second chances. The least we can do is extend a few to others.

Second chances: if Wal-Mart deserves one, surely the people around us do as well.

Scripture: Colossians 3: 12-13: "Therefore, as God's chosen people, holy and dearly loved, clothes yourselves with compassion, kindness, humility, gentleness and patience. Bear with each other and forgive whatever grievances you may have against one another."

Prayer: Dear Lord, help us to be understanding toward others, to be people who give others a second chance. Help us to be kind and compassionate toward all. We thank you that you care for us and have given us a second chance; we ask these things in the name of Christ, Amen.

More Than a Ceremony

I enjoy going to weddings, especially to weddings where I do not perform the service. I just sit back and take in the moment and use it as a time of worship and reflection.

There is something for everyone who attends a wedding. For those who are already married, it is a wonderful time to recall your own marriage and the vows you took years ago. For those who are thinking "someday," the words speak to you about the commitment that you will be undertaking and how serious it is.

I believe if you go to a wedding just to show up, then you have missed a grand opportunity to both worship God and to learn something about yourself in the process. If you just show up, you have not only wasted your dry cleaning bill, you have wasted some precious time as well. Please allow me the next few moments to share with you some precious reminders and lessons I learn at weddings, because it is more than just a ceremony.

❖ Your vows are serious. Be careful what you say in front of God and your family. Listen to your vows. Find the ceremony performed by the pastor. Most pastors have them around. Read through it again and remind yourself of what you promised your spouse and God on your wedding day. (If you have failed in any area, it is never too late to ask for forgiveness from God and your spouse and recommit to live those vows out for the remainder of your marriage.)

❖ There are a lot of friends standing around you. Most are very careful about whom they ask to be in a wedding. We should be just as careful that in our lives we pick the right friends who are going to support us and keep us accountable after we are married.

❖ By the way, if you are chosen to be in someone's wedding, then take that seriously not only for the hour you are a part of a ceremony. Always make yourself available for this couple. Consider yourself a part of the marriage, not just the wedding. You were a good enough friend to be in the wedding.

That makes you a good enough friend to be there for them in the years to come.

❖ A wedding is always well attended by family. A marriage should be as well. I look around and there is the mom, dad, brothers, grandparents, and the list goes on. Family is a must at a wedding and a must afterwards. This is your support system; hang onto it as best you can.

❖ No wedding I have ever been to has gone off perfectly even though, let me assure you, most expect it to. No marriage will ever go off perfectly either even though most expect it to. When it goes wrong, keep on going. I tell most people whose ceremony I perform that if you miss a word keep right on going; no one else will know but you. It is the same for the rest of your life. If you make a mistake, take care of it, but keep on going. Few will know, and even if they do, it does not matter. Shake it off and keep on going. A wedding is not ruined by a couple of mistakes and a marriage is not either if you have the proper attitude.

❖ Celebrate with one another. The receptions I go to that last a long time are always the most fun. Family and friends gather together for a meal, dancing, and lots of laughter. It is great to celebrate; let's don't just hold it to one day. Learn to celebrate with others and share their joy.

Married or not, a wedding teaches about love, commitment, joy, friendship and God. It definitely is not just a ceremony.

Scripture: Ephesians 5: 31-33: "For this reason a man will leave his father and mother and be united to his wife, and the two will become one flesh. This is a profound mystery—but I am talking about Christ and the church. However, each one of you also must love his wife as he loves himself, and the wife must respect her husband."

Prayer: Dear Lord, for those of us who are married, we pray to pay close attention to you and to our spouse. Give us the power to also take care of that relationship. For those who are hurt through the pains of divorce, separations, abuse, or who just long for someone special, I pray that God will touch you with His spirit and you may know the significance of your life and His love for you. For us all, may we learn to celebrate with one another, to hold each other accountable, and to see God in the goodness of love in all of our relationships. We ask these things in Christ's name, Amen.

Executive Worship

I enjoy exercising; it gives me energy for the day and makes me feel better. I am a different person when I have had time to get out and have a good sweat. Of course, living in Dallas right now, having a good sweat just means you walked to your car.

With my schedule, I have to be a little creative to make time to exercise. I have had a membership at a local gym for 20 years, and it is both inexpensive and convenient. One of the gyms is near where I work, so I can take my lunch, work out and be back within an hour. It works out great.

There are some days when I just want to get away from the office but really do not want to exercise. Then there are times when I plan on running after work, so working out at lunch is not that big a deal. But I still want to get away from the office, so I make my way to the gym.

On those days, I normally just put on my swimsuit and go sit in the wet sauna. Oh my, I love that place. It's hot and steamy, and when I sit in there, all my troubles just melt away. I get a good sweat going and never have to lift a finger. Then I can make my way to the pool and cool off before heading back into the Dallas heat. I get lots of sweating going on and feel better without exercising one bit. I call this my executive workout.

As much as I enjoy my executive workouts, they do little good. Other than sweating out some water and relaxing, nothing is being done to help my body be in better shape. My heart does not get the exercise it needs, my muscles are not toned in any way, and really nothing is getting firmed up at all. The executive workout, in reality, is not a workout at all.

In today's church society, I believe there are a lot of people who are having executive worship. Here is how executive worship works (and by the way, I believe there is an epidemic of it these days). We go to church and sit in our pews; we listen to wonderful music, are blessed by good prayers, and then are challenged by a good sermon. We sit there and work up a good spiritual sweat.

Then the problem arises. We walk out of the church and put nothing into practice we have heard. We do not pray ourselves; others have done it for us. We do not sing anything to the Lord; others have done it for us. We do not open up the Bible; others have done it for us. And then, we practice nothing of which the pastor challenged us. We have worked up a good sweat, but our heart hasn't started beating fast for God.

Sunday we sit in the sauna of worship soaking in all the good stuff, but on Monday through Saturday our lives never get the exercise they need to practice the faith and worship in God we declare on Sunday. In the end we find ourselves out of shape spiritually because we depend on others to do our work.

Sitting in church is a good thing. It is what we should be doing. Like sitting in the wet sauna for me, it is nice and relaxing, but also like my executive workout, it does my body little good. For me to make progress, I must exercise, get up off the couch, and move my body. It is as simple as that.

Exercise in a nutshell is getting the heart pumping a little faster for a period of time, thus making your heart muscle stronger. Spiritual exercise is the same. It is making your heart beat faster as you serve, study and deal with the things of God.

In order to have real faith and real worship, you have to get your heart beating for God. You can't do that sitting down. So how is your worship? Is it executive, or is it executing?

Scripture: James 2:14-18: "What good is it, my brothers, if a man claims to have faith but has no deeds? Can such faith save him? Suppose a brother or sister is without clothes and daily food. If one of you says to him, 'Go, I wish you well; keep warm and well fed,' but does nothing about his physical needs, what good is it? In the same way, faith by itself, if it I not accompanied by action, is dead. But someone will say, 'You have faith; I have deeds.' Show me your faith without deeds, and I will show you my faith by what I do."

Prayer: Dear Lord, help us not only to hear the Word, but be doers of it as well. We ask these things in Christ's name. Amen.

Where Is A Good Friend When You Need One?

John Daly is one of the best golfers in America and has been for some time. He is also one of the most popular golfers and has drawn millions of dollars from simply making appearances over the last decade.

I can imagine at these appearances that people come to him, shake his hand, get his autograph, and generally just let him know how much they admire his golf game. I can imagine these appearances could leave a fellow thinking he is well liked and has lots of friends, at least on the surface.

John Daly is not only one of the most popular golfers, but he is also one of the saddest stories in sports. For over a decade he has battled alcoholism, has suffered through embarrassing divorces and split ups, and has been known to dismantle a locker room in anger. He probably, for one reason or another, has never lived up to his potential.

Today I read an excerpt from a book that details another of Daly's struggles, this one with gambling. He speaks in this book of going to Las Vegas and loosing $600,000 in 30 minutes! Then losing $1.5 million in 5 hours. That boggles the mind. It boggles *this* mind anyway.

I first heard this report on the radio today, and one thought jumped to my mind right off the bat: "Does this man have one friend in the world?"

There he is, sitting there at the slot machine or the black jack table, and no one says, "Hey, John, don't you think you ought to slow down a bit?" Or, "Hey, John, let's leave this place while you still have some money in your pocket." Did he not have one good friend by him who would grab him by his coat and get him out of there before he self-destructed? Where were his real friends?

That is a sad story of millions lost, but I wonder—how good of friends are we to those around us? Sad stories happen every day that real friends might have been able to prevent. When our friend gets in a relationship at work, and we see it heading the wrong direction, do we step up and say, "Hey watch out. This is a trap." When we see the books being manipulated, do we step in say, "Hey this will get you in jail. Bail out while you can." Just simple stuff like, "Hey you're spending too much time at the golf course or fishing hole while your kids are growing up. Go home and stay there a while."

People lose their families, jobs, position, freedom, and their relationships with people they love every day. They make decisions that they later regret with all of their heart. Most of the time, someone close to them can see the train coming but never blow a whistle of warning.

As believers, we need to step in and say the hard things when they need to be said. We need to lovingly confront someone when we see them making destructive choices. We need to try more than once if we have to.

Which is better—trying to help someone avoid unnecessary pain in their life or helping them pick up the pieces of their broken life?

Experience has taught me this—a good friend cares enough to speak up, take charge, and do whatever it takes to keep a friend from harm's way. For John Daly, the silence of those around him has cost him millions. For our friends, it may be far more costly than that.

What kind of friend are you?

Scripture: Proverbs 27:6: "Wounds from a friend can be trusted, but an enemy multiplies kisses."

Proverbs 13:14: "The teaching of the wise is a fountain of life, turning a man from the snares of death."

Proverbs 18:24: "A man of many companions may come to ruin, but there is a friend who sticks closer than a brother."

Prayer: Dear Lord, help us to be wise and knowledgeable friends. Help us to pray for those we love and to have courage to speak the truth in love when we see pain on the horizon. For us this conflict is often scary. Have us to lean on you for our very strength. We ask these things in Christ's name, Amen.

When Mission Control Changes the Plan

The Apollo years of space travel were some of the most glorious and proud our nation has ever known. We were challenged with a goal of putting a man on the moon by the end of the '60s, and then worked to achieve that goal, finally achieving it with less than six months to go in the decade.

In all, twelve men touched the moon over a span of seven missions, though the number was supposed to be fourteen. Jim Lovell and Fred Haise were scheduled to walk on the moon in April of 1970. On April 14, at 10:06 pm, during a routine procedure an explosion occurred that changed the plans for the mission from landing on the moon to survival.

Over the next several days, all of the world watched and prayed as NASA and the astronauts worked around the clock to bring the injured spacecraft home. Finally, after a long and difficult trip, with many twists and turns, the spacecraft landed safely on April 17. The world, and NASA especially, breathed a collective sigh of relief. Their mission was called a "successful failure" in that they did not accomplish their original goal, but did succeed on getting the men home.

We do well if we see our life's mission in the same light as NASA saw their ill-fated Apollo 13. When something unexpected happens, instead of quitting or becoming bitter, we should refocus on the new mission and make it work. So how do we make our life a successful failure? Let's use NASA as our example as we point to God.

- When the explosion first occurred, they had to deal with the crisis at hand. The future was put on hold while they dealt with the present issue. We need do the same. When a crisis occurs, we must focus on getting through each day. A baby born premature, an accident occurs, a serious health issue arises, or you lose you source of income. It is here that we learn to walk with God one day at a time. It is during these moments, when we have nothing else to hold on to except God, that we learn to truly trust Him. Lean on God, walk with him one 24 hour shift at a time, and soon you will have weathered the explosion.

- When the explosion occurred, they first had to come to grips with the reality that their dream of walking on the moon was dashed. They had to grieve over the loss of their goal before they could move on. We must do the same. You expect a healthy, normal child, but find out you have one with special needs. Your job, it's nice and secure until the manager calls you in his office. You think your retirement is set, but the stock market crashes and leaves you with little. This one is very important: when you lose a dream or a goal is lost because of a sudden explosion of life, take the time to grieve that loss. There is nothing wrong with it, and it is a must before you can move on to the next mission of life.

- They trusted their support team to help them accomplish the new goal and land safely. God provides for us support in family and friends. When you are forced to change directions in life, lean on those people who love you who have your best interest in mind, and let them, along with the guidance of God, lead you in getting life back in order. Each person can play an important role in your life. Let them. We can be prideful people. We think we can handle the big issues of life on our own. That kind of pride is foolish and a waste of the recourses that God provides. God sets people in our life for a reason. Use them. Also remember to be available for others when they need you for support. Think of it as a God calling, because it is.

- A new mission is not a bad mission—it is just new. God often, if not always, uses the explosions of life to get our attention, to get us on the move, and to get us right where He wants us. He uses them to help us grow and to depend on Him more. He uses them to wipe away our pride and self reliance. Most of all, He can use them to place us in positions that are best for our lives that we would have never, ever gone to on our own. After each shift in life, there often comes a new and exciting mission. Be ready for it.

Be certain of this: after a long and difficult journey of life, filled with many twists and turns, God's main goal has never changed. He wants to bring you home and give you a safe landing in His loving arms. When that occurs, we will have truly had a life that was a "successful failure."

Scripture: Proverbs 19:21: "Many are the plans in a man's heart, but it is the LORD'S purpose that prevails." NIV

Proverbs 19:21: "We humans keep brainstorming options and plans, but God's purpose prevails." *The Message*

Proverbs 3:5-6: "Trust in the LORD with all your heart and lean not on your own understanding; in all your ways acknowledge him, and he will make your paths straight."

Prayer: Dear Lord, help us when we are weak to lean on you, to trust you, and to follow your paths though they may seem dangerous or scary to us. We thank you that you love us enough to walk with us and that you provide safe havens. We ask these things in Christ name, Amen.

Getting In and Out of Shape at the Same Time

If you took a good look at me (most of you can be pleased that this is something you do not have to do), you would never know that I work out at a gym about three times a week.

This week, as I am driving to the gym, I see this 50+ year-old guy walking out, and something he was doing caught my attention. First of all, he looked like he was in really good shape for a guy his age. He looked fit and trim, a picture of what we should look like when we really take care of ourselves.

As I glanced his way, I saw something in his hand, and I had to do a double take to make sure I was seeing things correctly. I looked again and sure enough, there, in his hand not carrying his workout bag, was a cigarette. It just really caught me off guard; it was the last thing I expected to see.

The last thing I expected to see in a guy's hand coming out of a workout gym was a cigarette. Having just spent time working on his health, he comes out doing one of the worst things someone could do for their health. The contradiction was striking.

I wonder if God does the same double take when we come out of church. He sees us come out of a place where we are doing the very thing He created us for, worship. Yet we head off into the world and do some of the worst things we could ever do for our spiritual life. I am sure the contradiction is striking for Him.

We have become a world that is full of spiritual exercise. We have our church, and then we head off to our separate prayer meetings. We read untold Christian books, and the airwaves, both of television and radio, are packed full of great preachers and teachers. We feed the poor and give like nobody's business to different mission activities all over the world.

All of this is good, just like going to the gym and working out for an hour. But if you follow the good with something destructive, then you have really accomplished nothing. If you walk out of the gym with a cigarette, then you have just wasted your time, wouldn't you agree?

If you walk out of church with malice, hate, gossip, and lust in your heart, then you have just wasted your time, wouldn't you agree? Yet we do it all the time. We go through the exercise, we feel good, and then we walk out into the world with the same bad habit or sin that we walked into the church with.

When we came to Christ, we were meant to be transformed. Take a good look at yourself and ask yourself this question: "If God saw me outside of church, would the actions of my heart make Him do a double-take and wonder why I ever went in the first place?"

This I know—physical exercise without a change in what you eat and how you live transforms little concerning your health. Likewise, spiritual exercise without a transforming of the inner soul changes little concerning your relationship with God.

Scripture: Psalms 119:1-3: "Blessed are they whose ways are blameless, who walk according to the law of the Lord. Blessed are they who keep his statutes and seek him with all their heart. They do nothing wrong; they walk in his ways."

Prayer: Dear Lord, lead us to avoid the duplicity of life that creates a confusing message to those that surround us. Have us to seek your ways with all of our heart. Help us not to only do spiritual exercise for the sake of doing, but lead us to proper actions with proper motives. We ask these things in Christ's name, Amen.

Your Sentence—Community Service

If you are found guilty within our justice system, the judge has many options as to what your sentence will be. You can serve time in prison, you can get probation, you can be fined, or you can be sentenced to community service.

Let's talk about community service for a bit. For some, that sentence means picking up trash on the side of the road while others clean and repair parks and public places. Then there are those who have been found guilty of things like doing drugs or driving while intoxicated. There are times the judge makes these folks go to schools and community centers and tell young people the dangers of committing such crimes.

The judge is thinking that young people will listen to people who have faced the judgment of making such wrong decisions in their lives. He hopes the young people will learn from others' mistakes. Some of these speakers can be very effective. Who knows how many lives have been spared the dangers of these sins by the words of these people doing community service?

When it comes to sin, we all stand before the Judge, and that Judge is God. Of course, He is a grace-giving God, and when we seek His forgiveness and repent, He forgives our sins. But guess what He does after that? Yes, you guessed it; He sentences you to community service.

One of the great mistakes we make in church is this thinking that we should all be perfect, and that if we are not, we are not worth anything for God. In reality, it is our guilt that makes us worthwhile.

One of the great opportunities we have as Christians is to help others who have the same temptations and weaknesses as us. We can stand up and say, "That is a pit from hell; don't go there." We can share what it was like to be out of the will of God. We can say, "Hey, follow me. I know how you feel. I have been there, and I am never going there again." They can learn from our sins, and it can save people from horrible decisions that can destroy their life.

Of course, it would be great if we never sinned, and holiness is something we should always be working toward. But the fact is we all have sinned, we are all guilty. That is what is so great about God. He knows our guilt, takes on the penalty of death we deserve, and then sends us out to help others avoid the same crime we committed.

There is one very big difference in someone being sentenced by a judge and one being set free by one. When a judge tells someone to go and do 40 hours of community service, they do it because they have to. When someone does it just because they have to, they deliver the message with little passion.

When we share the grace given to us by God and tell how sin hurt our relationship with God and the pain it caused us and those we love, we do it with a passion. Not because we have to, but because we want to. When set free by the Judge, we know we owe Him a great debt that can never be repaid. The least we can do is to go out in the community and tell of the great grace-giving God we have.

Yes, we are all judged. When the verdict comes in, we are all guilty, but thankfully the Judge says, "I will take your guilt upon me." What a verdict! But with it comes community service, and we need to be busy about living out our sentence.

Scripture: Romans 6: 20-22: "When you were slaves to sin, you were free from the control of righteousness. What benefit did you reap at that time from the things you are now ashamed of? Those things result in death! But now that you have been set free from sin and have becomes slaves to God, the benefit you reap leads to holiness, and the result is eternal life."

Prayer: Dear Lord, We seek your help as we attempt to lead holy lives knowing we cannot do it on our own. We also seek the power of your Holy Spirit when we share with others we come in contact with the evil of sin and the brokenness that comes with it. Help to share your grace with all we come in contact with, sharing how you brought us from death to life. We ask these things in Christ name, Amen.

Vanity

Thomas A. Kempis was a monk some 600 years ago. In 1427, he wrote a handbook called *The Imitation of Christ* on Christian growth for other monks. What he wrote, especially in the area of humility and Christian devotion in 1427 for a group of Monks, still rings true for us who live today, and so I wanted to share a portion of it with you:

> Indeed it is not learning that makes a man holy and just, but a virtuous life makes him pleasing to God. I would rather feel contrition than know how to define it. For what would it profit us to know the whole Bible by heart and the principles of all the philosophers if we live without grace and the love of God? Vanity of vanities and all is vanity, except to love God and serve Him alone.

There is more I want to share with you from this book:

> It is vanity to wish for long life and to care little about a well-spent life. It is vanity to love what passes quickly and not to look ahead where eternal joy abides.

Vanity is a word not used very much in the English language today, so let me help you out. In *Webster's*, vanity is defined as something that is vain, empty, or valueless. Perhaps that helps to clarify what Kempis was trying to tell us so many years ago.

We tend to give value to many things in this world; our position in society, our bank accounts, the house in which we live, our relationships, etc. But he tells us that all of those things are empty and valueless compared to the riches of serving and loving God.

One point he makes that I find interesting is where he asks what good it would do us to know the entire Bible and all kinds of philosophies and live without grace and the love of God? In a world that puts a great deal of emphasis on knowledge, we need to hear that knowledge without the love of God is empty.

Church people need to hear this message, keeping in mind that Kempis himself was writing his handbook to a group of monks. We must be careful not to live empty lives filled with knowledge of God and about God, but without the grace of God.

Let's be honest for a minute. Some of us are living empty and valueless lives. We are searching in vain for anything that will give value to our lives. The world stumbles in darkness in search of purpose. Unfortunately, many find things other than God that keeps them bound to the darkness and still feeling empty at the end of the day.

Today your soul may feel empty; you may be religious but still not feel close to God. You are valuable to God, and He, He alone, can fill the emptiness in your heart.

Knowledge is not bad, but without the love and grace of God—well, it is vanity.

Scripture: John 8:12: "Then Jesus spoke to them again, saying, "I am the light of the world. He who follows Me shall not walk in darkness, but have the light of life."

Prayer: Dear Lord, be with us as we seek to follow you. Help us to find true meaning with you. Help us to serve and love you with all of our hearts. Help us to find the balance between knowledge and action. Have us to represent you well, and may you find us on our knees as we seek forgiveness where we have failed you. We ask these things in Christ's name, Amen.

After It All, There is Hope

Perhaps no news event in my lifetime has affected me quite as much as the news of the horrific murders of little girls at a school-house in Pennsylvania. The more I read about it, and the more I heard, the more my heart broke for all concerned. To get more information, I watched *Nightline* on ABC; I could only watch ten minutes. As the reporter closed his report from in front of the schoolhouse with tears in his eyes, I could watch no more.

There is much to think of when you look at this sad story. Let's think of those things and then close by taking a closer look at God.

❖ We live in an evil society, unbelievably, unthinkably evil. We not only live in the middle of it, but as fallen humans in the world today, we are capable of evil ourselves. That is hard to tell ourselves, but it is the truth.

❖ Evil affects everyone's life. Without question, the children in that room and those sent out of it were affected. With little doubt, the family and community were affected, but also the family of the man who committed this horrible act was affected as well. As the day wore on, they sent out a statement telling of their sorrow and deepest of regrets for what happened but also requesting prayer for their own family. The statement said their lives were "shattered." I see that as perfect wording. Evil shatters lives, all lives that cross its path.

❖ Anger always leads to evil, not normally on this scale, but always it leads to sin. This man was angry with God. Anger leads to bitterness. He had suffered the loss of a child in 1997 and evidently from all accounts had grown bitter during that time. There is a proper saying that goes like this, "hurt people *hurt* people." It is true.

In dark moments like this, I look for God, for some glimpse of Him in any place I can. With events like this, there are no easy answers, and so I do not wish to give you any. I just want to turn your eyes toward Jesus. No matter how dark the night you will find Him.

I found Him with the Amish neighbor who went to his neighbor's house, which happened to be the house of the killer's father. He held this father in his arms for an hour and said, "We will forgive you." Dwight Lefever, a witness of this moment, said that the Amish "extended the hope of forgiveness that we all need these days." Words like that do not come easily and actions like that cannot come at all without the presence of the Holy Spirit to give courage, strength and peace.

I found him in Sam Stoltzfus, a 63-year-old Amish man who lived just a few miles from the school. He declared that they will be sustained by their faith. He said that for them, a funeral is a much more important thing than the day of birth because they believe in the hereafter. "The children are better off than their survivors." What a different perspective than provided by most in this world, and honestly even myself, at times. Yet I find a final thought in his words.

My thought is this: we have a habit of falling in love with this world and the things of it. This is not all bad. As a matter of fact, we can fall in love with good things like our spouses, children, and family. We can love our churches and how we serve the Lord there. The bad thing is that when we fall in love with this world, we tend to take our eyes off the big picture that some day they will all go away, that some day Christ will return and this world, with all of its evil will end as we know it.

That is not said by someone who wants to bury his head in the sand and just ignore the hardships of this world by saying, "Well, Jesus will be coming soon." I do not know when He will come, but I know that He will, and that gives me hope. This is not pie-in-the-sky thinking. It is Biblical fact as spoken clearly in several books of the New Testament.

The thought that these girls were welcomed to heaven by a heavenly Father brings me some comfort. The fact that the Lord hears the cries of the families and children brings me another sort of relief. Having a belief that most of these families, if not all of them, were believers in Christ gives me the comfort of knowing that someday there will be a reunion of some sort in heaven.

When I first heard of this event, I was not around a television, but I was around a computer. I looked up a news outlet and clicked on a video of what was going on. A helicopter was flying around the area shooting scenes of the school and surrounding farms. My sound was not up on my computer, so I watched in total silence. I watched the helicopters fly in and out with the wounded. I looked at a farm just a mile or so from the school filled with children and parents waiting for word on the wounded. I watched men begin to come to this house and speak with one another. I could only wonder what they were saying.

Then I saw a scene unfold in my silence. A man walks up to the gathering at the house; a little girl sees him and begins to run to him. She jumps into his arms and he holds her tight. She has a hold on him like she will never let him go, and he has a hold on her that says him letting her go is something she will never have to worry about. At that moment, I was given a picture of what heaven looked like an hour earlier—innocent girls thrust into the Father's arms who will never let them go. Home at last.

Let us live our lives to the fullest in the world He has given us while never losing the hope He provides with the knowledge of His imminent return. The Bible closes with these words, "He who testifies to these things says, Yes, I am coming soon." Amen. Come, Lord Jesus." I could not agree more.

Scriptures: 1 Thessalonians 4:15-18: "According to the Lord's own word, we tell you that we who are still alive, who are left till the coming of the Lord, will certainly not precede those who have fallen asleep. For the Lord himself will come down from heaven, with a loud command, with the voice of the archangel and with the trumpet call of God, and the dead in Christ will rise first. After that, we who are still alive and are left will be caught up together with them in the clouds to meet the Lord in the air. And so we will be with the Lord forever. Therefore encourage each other with these words."

2 Corinthians 5:1: "Now we know that if the earthly tent we live in is destroyed we have a building from God, an eternal house in heaven, not built with human hands."

Prayer: Dear Lord, we pray for all throughout this world who are hurting at this time, we pray for the hungry and afflicted, we pray for the soldiers at war, we pray for the innocent hurt by violence and their families. We pray for the heroes who go in during dangerous moments and who must witness the worst kind of scenes. Ease their minds, and give them peace. We pray for your quick return, and we thank you for dying for us, sinners that we are, so that we would spend eternity with you. We ask these things in Christ's name, Amen.

Calling on God, Waiting for the Answer

The journal of a person of prayer holds within it petitions offered up by someone who loves the Lord and her family. One such journal I recently had the chance to see revealed prayers for one prayer warrior's children and grandchildren, their needs, and her desires for each one. A certain entry in March of 1998 requested a home for one of her children. *No recorded answer sits next to this prayer.*

Two years later in March of 2000, the day arrives when no more entries will be written into this journal—this saint goes onto to be with her Lord. Still, no answer sits on the March 1998 entry requesting a home for her child; her prayer never answered.

Some ten years later in the spring of 2008, the daughter of this prayer warrior sleeps on a hide-away bed in the living room with her husband and two of her younger children. Her house sits in a form of disrepair, needing heating, new plumbing, and a new roof, to name only a couple of the needed repairs. Few things work as they should. Nine people live in a house of less than a thousand square feet.

The home is a happy, but small one; the warrior's prayers for a home have not been answered.

In May of 2008, an event occurs that no one would have imagined. Unexpectedly, and in unlikely form, the daughter and her family receive a gift. The gift? A home—and not just a home, but one two times larger than the one she lives in. Not just a home, but one with enough rooms for all to have a one, with space enough for an entire family, including grandchildren, to eat at the table. The heating works, the water flows, and the roof doesn't leak—a home filled with the finest of furnishings, a palace for her family. All a gift from heaven.

Ten years and two months after the prayer journal entry was written, eight years after the saint has been in the presence of God, the prayer is answered, and in grand style.

This prayer warrior saint: my mother-in-law.

Scripturally I cannot find anywhere that tells me God has told her of His grand scheme, how he used Godly people to answer her prayer and did it in such a way as to make it unavoidably a God thing. But in my heart, I am sure she knows.

Often in our prayer life, we become frustrated with what we see as a failure to answer. But I have found in this journal friendly reminders that there are some aspects of prayer we should always keep in mind, and they are as follows:

1) **God has his own timetable.** We like results quickly; God knows when the time is right. As in the case of this gift, God answered the prayer but years after the first prayer was lifted up. I might add, knowing Muriel as I did, the first prayer was lifted up long before 1998. In the spring of 2008, my father-in-law said, "It just does not pay giving up waiting on the Lord." A better truth has never been spoken.

2) **God has his own agenda.** He is always at work in the lives of His people. He is busy about shaping relationships and setting things in place. Though we don't see the big picture, He does. Looking back, we can see clearly how God set things in motion, how he used people, and how he brought glory to Himself, giving hope to a multitude of others through His big plan.

3) **It is not about the house, but about our faith.** While we focus on the perceived need, God has our spiritual development in mind. His desire is not to give us things but to give us Himself. He wants us to know Him more intimately, and He uses each event in our life to build upon our faith and to lead us to trust Him more with each passing day. This takes time and a strategic plan. God has both. His plans never fail.

As I look at God's blessings (not only the house, but a thousand others), I am thankful for people who care enough to really pray and for a God who loves enough to really answer. Each day as I walk the house, it is a reminder that God answers prayers: in His time, in His way—and His ways are always best.

Thanks, Muriel, you would love the place you prayed for!

Scripture: Colossians 4:2: "Devote yourselves to prayer, being watchful and thankful." *NIV*

Colossians 4:2: "Pray diligently. Stay alert, with your eyes wide open in gratitude." *The Message*

Prayer: Dear Lord, guide us in our faithfulness to pray and never give up. We thank you for those who love us and pray for us; may we follow their example of faith. We praise you for how you answer our prayers in both big and small ways. We thank you for your loving kindness and ask all these things in the name of Christ, Amen.

Your Mug Shot

Recently, in a county near where I live, the sheriff released all the mug shots that were in the county's files. I am not too sure how far back he went, and I am really not too sure why he did it, but this sheriff has a long history of good work, so I am going to imagine it was all for a good reason.

The only reason I know this occurred is because of an interview I saw on the local news. They were talking to a man who is in his late 30s now, but 11 years earlier, he had been arrested for a DUI. He paid his dues to society, and now he is a well-respected member of society and the owner of his own company.

The only way he knew about the mug shot being on the internet was when he received a call from a friend telling him he was looking at his mug shot. Needless to say, this caught him off guard. He thought that DUI and that mug shot were old news, packed away in his past, never to be visited again.

After all, he had done all the right things. He took care of business, got his life together, and put the event in his past. He moved on—that is, until someone else, for whatever reason, brought it back up.

Obviously, he could not deny it; it was there for the world to see. He could not run from it; he had no control of the internet site. By the way, they have now taken those pictures off the internet, but the damage was done.

Here is what really hurts. Eleven years ago, he made a mistake (sin), paid the price, and took care of business. The people he loved most, his parents, never found out. How good he must have felt to get his life right and never to have hurt those he loved the most. But one punch of an internet button changed all of that.

The key moment of the interview for me was when he looked in the camera and told his parents he was sorry. He had hoped never to have to tell them, and though I am sure they forgave him (what parent wouldn't), I know he wishes and thought he would never have had to do it.

For just a moment, imagine that in heaven there is a mug shot with your picture on it. Underneath it, there on a long list, are all the sins you have ever committed. Every bad word spoken, every lustful thought, every lie uttered, every bit of hatred toward someone else there on the paper, every distasteful joke laughed at, every prejudice, all etched under your picture. The list goes on and on there for all in heaven to see. Nothing hidden. I don't know about you, but for me that is a scary thought.

Now go back to the day you accepted Christ as your personal Savior. No more religion, no more hiding from God, you really saw your sin for what it was and you asked God for forgiveness; you fell on your knees and really made Him your Lord. What a great day that was.

Now, on that day, God walked over to the computer and He pulled up your name. There was your mug shot with that long list below it. He took a look at it, and He remembered His own shed blood on the cross for each sin committed. He smiled as He recalled the moment you asked for forgiveness. He looked over at the right hand side of the computer, and He saw the delete key.

Without pause, he punched the key and there under your mug shot the list disappeared. No more long list, no more guilty pleas, no more sin to answer for, it was all gone. As a matter of fact, when he pulled up your name and your mug shot appeared, under it was just two words: **NOT GUILTY**.

The world may remember, but He never will. Praise God for that.

Scripture: Psalms 103:8-13: "The Lord is compassionate and gracious, slow to anger, abounding in love. He will not always accuse, nor will he harbor his anger forever; he does not treat us as our sins deserve or repay us according to our inequities. **For as high as the heavens are above the earth, so great is his love for those who fear him; as far as the east is from the west, so far has he removed our transgressions from** us. As a father has compassion on his children, so the Lord has compassion on those who fear him."

Prayer: Dear Lord, we come humbly this day and know you do not give us what our sins deserve, but you give us grace, and we simply say thank you. We ask this in Christ's name, Amen.

A Closing That Speaks

Each and every day, I deal with hundreds of emails, and each has a different closing. I can tell who and what kind of attitude each person has by how they close the email.

For instance if it is all business, the closing is, "Regards." For someone who knows me at work, but still wants to be businesslike, the closing is usually, "Thanks and regards." When someone is not quite so businesslike, there is always the standard, "Thank You" closing.

When you receive a personal greeting, it is always interesting to see exactly how they close out their email. If it is a church friend, many times the closing is, "God Bless." For family members, the closing might be, "Love." I have a good friend who sometimes closes it with, "Hugs." I like that one a lot. The list could go on and on, but there is one I really like and that is the purpose of this devotional, so let's get to it.

One friend of Loaves and Fishes closes out her emails with, "Make yourself a good day." I absolutely love that one. Now let's take a closer look at that statement. First, you might think you cannot make yourself have a good day. I respectfully disagree.

Let me make the point by going the other direction. Many people make themselves have a bad day every day. For them everything seems to go wrong. Nothing is right and is only getting worse. I label these folks the Eeyore people in honor of the Winnie the Pooh character who always had a rain cloud over his head and spoke in a low, monotone voice. Nothing went right for him, and each day held out to be a bad one. There are millions of people like that out there; each day holds 24 hours of misery.

Many people think like this: "I will have a good day if the circumstances fall my way. If the traffic is good, if the boss is in a good mood, and if work is not too busy, then I will have a good day. If the weather is right, and the kids are all in good spirits, and I receive no bad news, then today will be a good one." If that is what you are waiting for, then I fear you rarely will have a good day.

Each day holds its own set of unfortunate circumstances. It is how you approach them that will determine if you really make for yourself a good day. Attitude is everything, and having a strong relationship with Christ will only help you make for yourself a good day.

With Christ at the helm of your life, you can have the confidence to handle the unfortunate parts of each day. But also with Him leading the way, you have an acute awareness of the good that happens each day. Though each day has its own set of unfortunate circumstances, each day also has its own set of good events.

It's all about the little things. How do we approach the little things that build up during the day to help make it good or bad in our eyes? Rarely do days hold pay raises or job losses. Those are big things. It's the little things like traffic, talks with the spouse, someone cutting in on you at the grocery store line, or someone asking you to do something last minute at work. It's how you handle those things that will determine what kind of day you have.

Paul certainly had his difficult days, but we find from the scriptures that he was able to be content in whatever circumstance he found himself. In reading the fruits of the spirit, I do not find grumpy, angry, or hard-to-get-along-with in them. Instead, I find joy, love, peace, and patience to name just a few. We believers in Christ can have a good day no matter what goes on, because we know who is in control and that He loves us.

So let me say in closing—make yourself a good day!

Scriptures: Philippians 4:11-13: "I am not saying this because I am in need, for I have learned to be content whatever the circumstances. I know what it is to be in need, and I know what it is to have plenty. I have learned the secret of being content in any and every situation, whether well fed or hungry, weather living in plenty or in want. I can do everything through him who gives me strength."

Galatians 5:22 & 23: "But the fruit of the Spirit is love, joy, peace, patience, kindness, goodness, faithfulness, gentleness and self control. Against such things there is no law."

Prayer: Dear Lord, help us to allow you to control all aspects of our life, including our attitude. Have us to find your presence in each day. Let us each display the fruits of the spirit for both our own good and for the good of those who live and work around us. We thank you for being God of the circumstance and we ask all these things in the name of Christ, Amen.

Who is in Charge?

Being the man of the house, as we all know, means I am in absolute control of my home. The dog sleeps by my feet as I read the paper and the kids all come to me for sage advice that only a man in control like I am would know the answer to.

My wife brings me my coffee in the morning and refills my tea glass while I sit comfortably at the table awaiting my home-cooked dinner. When I talk, the kids all listen, and there is never any back talk. Life is good when you are in charge like I am.

From time to time, the kids remind me where I stand in the pecking order. The truth hurts.

Just the other day, Caleb my very cute and wise five-year-old son, asked me if he could take a bath. Of course I gave him the good fatherly go-ahead. I thought, "he can always use a good bath." That was the end of it as far as I was concerned.

But before he could get in the tub, he had one more thing to do: confirm the go-ahead with his mother! Much to my shock, just after I told him yes, Caleb walked by his mother and asked her the exact same question. Seems he was not confident that my answer was safe enough to move forward. Sort of like you asking your direct supervisor for an answer and then taking it one step forward as you walk by the owner, asking him the same question. We all know the direct supervisor hates that stuff!

When those things happen, it shows who the boss really is. Obviously to Caleb, I am somewhere in mid-management around the house. Stepping back and looking at things realistically, he probably is more correct than I care to acknowledge.

Like me in the first two paragraphs, many of us live in a dream world that has us in total control, when in reality, that is false. Living in that type of dream-world is dangerous.

Knowing who is in charge is very important; realizing it is not you is a must. One of the first steps in Christian maturity is acknowledging and allowing God to be in control. That can sound negative, but let me unload some positives on you this day concerning God's control in our lives.

- *It takes the pressure off.* Think of God as a supervisor. He tells you what to do, you follow. The plans are God's, and the results are left up to Him. We get in tangled-up messes when we try to tell God what to do.
- *Who better to lead our lives than God?* We think we're smart. Really? Think of the God of the universe, the creator of all things, and I mean *all* things, leading your life. Having confidence in who is in control is critical.
- *You get to be a part of God's work!* All of us want to be a part of something special, something that lasts long after us. I have met few who did not have that desire. If you are following God's lead according to His plan, you get to be a part of what God is doing in the world today. Do you have something better going on? I doubt it!
- *In order to know the plan, you get to communicate with God.* How good is that? As we take our life to God in prayer, He reveals the plan for our lives. Imagine communicating with the same God

Caleb knows who is really in control of the house, thus he makes sure all things go through the proper channel. How can I blame him for that? When we do the same with God, we, like Caleb, get the right answers.

Scripture: Jeremiah 29:11: "'For I know the plans I have for you,' declares the LORD, 'plans to prosper you and not to harm you, plans to give you hope and a future.'"

Prayer: Dear Lord, help us to release our lives into your capable hands. Deal with our pride and arrogance in such a way that we become humble in your sight. We thank you that indeed you are in control and that your plans for us are good. We ask these things in Christ name, Amen.

Helpless in Wal-Mart

This week is the week before Vacation Bible School at the church I attend. My wife, Kim, is a big player in that. Kim spends a great deal of time at the church this week, and that means one thing for me—fatherhood.

Let's just say this: I depend a great deal on my wife, and this week always is an eye- opener for me in the area of understanding all Kim deals with on a daily basis. With one of my older children now married and two others living at a camp for the summer, it leaves me with the four youngest, Matt (10), John (8), Caleb (3), and Gracie (16 months). I love my children, and really it is no problem for me to take care of them. I enjoy it.

But for some reason, when we go anywhere, we attract quite a bit of attention. I am not sure if it is the fact that I am a man walking around with four children. I am not sure if it is the age of the children. I just know when we are doing business, people take notice.

The other night we took a little trip to Wal-Mart, just me and the little guys. With Gracie in one arm, Caleb holding my hand (most of the time), John pushing the basket, and Matt hanging around, we went to work. Really, I thought we did quite well with no major incidents. Sure, we almost took out a couple of people with the basket, and Caleb did perform a few break-a ways, but for the most part everything was in check, until…

Until I ran into my greatest nemesis: the self-check out. Oh, how I long for the days when someone would check me out, take my money, and send me on my way. Normally I will do anything to find a human to check me out, but I was in a hurry and feeling pretty good about myself. Not to mention the fact that a friendly lady was telling me how easy it was. So, I took the plunge.

It was at this moment when I started attracting attention. Holding Gracie in one hand, I attempted to scan my goods. This left Caleb free (never a good thing) while John and Matt tried to figure out what I wanted them to do with the basket. Things weren't clicking. Chaos ensued. Fortunately, the friendly lady was making friends with Caleb as he crawled under the basket. This did not look good, but at least I knew where he was.

While everyone watched, I kept one eye on Caleb, held onto Gracie, scanned, and paid for my products while calling out commands to Matt and John. It was a bit of a helpless feeling. I felt a little out of control, but one thing got me through it: my new employee friend at Wal-Mart. Something tells me she has seen things like this before.

This is what I know—not just from Wal-Mart, but also from other events in my life: when you are helpless and you need a friend, God is good to send at least one.

Using my Wal-Mart friend as an example, let's pause and do two things this morning: one, acknowledge how friends operate; and, two, see if *we* are a friend:

- Friends do not judge you in the midst of your helpless moment. The employee at Wal-Mart simply took charge and helped me through it. She never said anything like "Where is your wife?" or, "Why did she let you out of the house?" though those would have been good questions!
- Good friends take action; they jump in where they can. My helper talked to Caleb and kept him at bay while I handled the rest. She did not try to do too much; she did what she could, that is always enough.
- Good friends do not make you feel bad for being helpless. They do not say words like "I told you so" or, "You should have done it this way." They just help.
- Good friends have a good attitude about helping. They do it willingly, with a smile. Recently another good friend of mine, knowing I was in a helpless state, simply asked me this, "What can I do to serve you?" Enough said. Normally when you are feeling helpless, you're not feeling too good about yourself. A smile and friendly attitude goes a long way toward allowing you to accept the situation.

- A good friend expects nothing in return. Sure, my buddy at Wal-Mart was getting paid, but believe me, just because someone is getting paid does not mean they have to be friendly. There was no raise in it for her, nothing extra, just doing her job, helping out a guy who needed it before moving on to her next customer.

We will all find ourselves in helpless situations from time to time. God knows that and it will not catch him by surprise. He will be ready to send a friend to your side. Fortunately for me, my friend was in a blue Wal-Mart vest.

Thank God for the friends He sends your way, then keep your eyes open and look to be a friend when given a chance.

Scriptures: Proverbs 17:17: "A friend loves at all times, and a brother is born for adversity." *NIV*

Proverbs 17:17: "Friends love through all kind of weather, and families stick together in all kinds of trouble." *The Message*

Prayer: Dear Lord, we pause and thank you for our friends. They love us when we are helpless and when we are hard to love. We thank you that they stick with us. Heavenly Father, help us to be good friends, to jump in when needed, to have a good attitude about what we do. We ask all these things in Christ's name, Amen.

Without Carrying a Gun

War veteran Desmond T. Doss, Sr. passed away at the age of 87 on March 23. Though you would have had to dig into page 8 of the newspaper to find his story, it is worth recalling.

Mr. Doss was a conscientious objector and refused to carry a gun during WWII. A veteran friend said in the paper that Doss wanted to serve; he just didn't want to kill anybody. It was more popular to serve during WWII than it has been in recent wars; thus, being a conscientious objector was not very popular.

Patti Parks said of Mr. Doss that he had to endure ridicule for his beliefs, but that he "remained true to his convictions even when it was not the most popular thing to do."

His convictions said he didn't want to kill anyone, but his heart wanted to serve his country and serve he did. While under fire on the island of Okinawa, Mr. Doss carried 75 wounded soldiers to the edge of a 400-foot cliff and lowered them to safety. A later story tells of how during another attack, he was seriously wounded in the legs by a grenade. But as he was being carried to safety, he saw a more critically injured man and crawled off his stretcher, directing the medics to help the other wounded man.

For his service to his country, he received the highest military honor from President Truman in 1945. He was the only conscientious objector to be so honored during WWII.

A man objected but still found a way to serve. I find that refreshing in a world filled with plenty of objectors but few servants. No matter if you agree with Mr. Doss' philosophy on carrying a gun, at the very least you can appreciate the fact that, though he disagreed, he still found a way to serve.

The Christian community would be well served by people who find ways to serve even though they may disagree with some aspects of leadership and the decisions that are made. It is rare, if not impossible, to agree with everything one human being does. We need to work our way past the thought that everything must go our way before we can serve.

We need to keep in mind that there is still a battle going on, and there is still a place for us to serve in that battle. There are still people wounded by the heartache and hurt that this world has to offer. We need to jump in the battle and start carrying people to the safety of the cross. No matter if we agree with the order of service, the style of music, or how our Sunday School teacher teaches.

Perhaps in America we have lost our witness because we have become so "objectable." What we have become known for is what we disagree with, not what we do. In the headlines, you see more about how we feel we are mistreated than about any service that we do.

The world is not looking for that, and surely there is little impact in an "objectable" attitude. For one minute do you think those 75 men who were carried to safety by a man not carrying a gun cared that he was a conscientious objector? No way! They just wanted to be saved, and that is exactly what the world is looking for.

Disagree if you must, there is a right way to do that. But never let it stop your service for your Lord. There is a high honor in heaven awaiting those who overcome the objections and obstacles of service and willingly give their life to the Lord.

Got convictions? Good. Sick to them. But remember—you don't have to carry a weapon with you while you do.

Scriptures: Proverbs 15:33: "The fear of the Lord teaches a man wisdom, and humility comes before honor."

Proverbs 20:3: "It is to a man's honor to avoid strife, but every fool is quick to quarrel."

Prayer: Dear Lord, give us the desire to serve you and the willingness to do that in spite of the obstacles we face. Give us courage and help us to point a lost and hurting world to you. We ask these things in Christ's name, Amen.

Stop Looking, It's Right There!

I have a ritual every morning. I guess that is what makes it a ritual, huh? I get up, take my shower, throw on my clothes, and then I start to look for my glasses. Being that I am 43 years old, you would think I would be smart enough to put my glasses in the same place so I could find them more easily. If that is what you think, then you would be mistaken.

I have found my glasses in all kinds of places. To name just a few, I have found them on the back of the couch, on the night stand next to my bed, under the kitchen table, next to the computer, on top of the TV stand, and on the floor within inches of being stepped on by either me or my children. It seems as though wherever I happen to be or walk by is where my glasses land.

Looking for them is not one of my favorite things to do. Many mornings I get frustrated with my lack of common sense in putting them where I can find them. The best place for glasses is on the table, and that is where I found them today, but only after having looked in several other places first.

You see, I was looking in all the wrong places for my glasses when actually they were right in front of me the whole time. If I had just looked down at the table (actually, I did, I just didn't see them— I guess that is why I need glasses), I would have saved myself a lot of time and frustration.

I am convinced a lot of people are looking for something in their life, and it is sitting right in front of them. They look for peace, so they buy pills, drugs, or alcohol. They are looking for love, so they look for a physical body to share it with. They find sex but not love. They are looking for fulfillment, so they throw themselves into a dizzying amount of activities and what they really find is exhaustion. They look for financial freedom through hours of extra work and find instead bondage to their job.

When I think of someone looking for something and it being right in front of them, I can't help but think of Mary standing at the tomb, crying, looking for her Lord that Easter morning. She has come out of devotion and love; she finds Him missing and is broken-hearted in fear that the authorities have taken His body.

She turns from the tomb to find what she thinks is the gardener and asks if He has taken away her Lord, and if he has, she wants to know where so she can go and get Him. What she fails to see through the pain, tears, and heartache of the moment is that she is speaking to her Lord.

Jesus simply calls her by name, and her eyes are opened, and she sees that it is indeed the One she has been looking for all along.

The world is full of people looking for something that is missing in their lives. The shame of it all is that, like me looking for my glasses or Mary looking for her Lord, it has been in front of them the whole time. His name is Jesus.

Are you fearful? Are you low on hope? Are you looking for real love? Are you beating yourself up with failures of the past, not forgiving yourself? Have you found yourself in bondage to things of this world?

The answer to all these questions and worries is right in front of you. Stop looking all over the place. Stop wasting your time. Do what Mary did and grab hold of the Savior and call out His name.

Scripture: Luke: 24: 4-6a: "While they were wondering about this, suddenly two men in clothes that gleamed like lightning stood beside them. In their fright the women bowed down with their faces to the ground, but the men said to them, "Why do you look for the living among the dead? He is not here; He has risen!"

Prayer: Dear Heavenly Father, We praise Your holy name for sending your Son to die on the cross for our sins, and we give glory to You for His resurrection that gives us hope for the future. Please help all those who are lost without you to see you clearly this day. We ask all these things in Christ's name, Amen.

The Perfect World

We are imperfect people living in an imperfect world; there are times we forget that, but God always seems to shine a little light of revelation our way when we get our expectations out of line. Such was God's work in my life this week.

I have a friend at a funeral home that, from time to time, will need some help if a family does not have a pastor. This week, he gave me a call, and I was glad to help. A husband had just lost his wife, and when I called the gentleman, I could tell he was upset. So I made a visit to his home, and while there, I found that the adult son was deaf. As I continued the conversation, I found that others within the house were as well. It turned out that at the funeral, there were three rows of deaf people in front of me.

My grandfather was blind, so people with handicaps such as that do not disturb me. More recently, I was blessed with a daughter with Down syndrome, so people with disabilities are also something I am familiar with. For the funeral, there was a person skilled in sign language to handle the first three rows and one of the pallbearers as well. She did a wonderful job and had a sweet spirit to her.

After the service, I struck up a conversation with her. One of my first questions was what got her started in this service. She told me that her parents are deaf, her husband is deaf, and their child was deaf. She called sign language her first language and I could understand why. I could also understand what led her to the job she had.

She went on to tell me that they were looking to adopt another deaf child soon, which moved the conversation toward adoption. I told her that my wife and I also had been interested in adopting another child born with Down syndrome. We had looked at a great many web sites, and it had broken our hearts to see so many children in need of adoption, children unwanted in many cases.

She, too, shared our concern for the many unwanted disabled or mentally challenged children. She spoke of how they had been given a chance to adopt a different deaf child than the one they were adopting, but they were already committed. Her statement was, "there are just so many—you can't take them all." I agreed and stood there in the cold for a moment with my thoughts whirling around me, and then I said, "yes, the world wants the perfect child." We smiled at each other and nodded our heads.

As I have thought about that conversation, I thought of the service we had just been a part of. There we were, two imperfect people sharing a message of hope from a grace-giving God to rows of imperfect people. *Unfortunately, only three of those rows know they are imperfect.*

When you are around those who have outward handicaps, you are reminded of how difficult those handicaps make life. As I look at it though, it gives them one advantage on our "perfect people" world: at least they know theirs.

We attempt to cover up our imperfections with a façade of "we have it all together" smiles and "everything is fine" conversations. These only lead us down the path of frustration and trouble instead of redemption and reconciliation with the loving and living God.

In a world that loves the perfect, isn't it good that we have a God that knows our imperfections and loves us anyway. The only true handicapped people in this world are those who have yet to admit their handicaps. Where do you stand?

Scripture: 1 Corinthians 1:26-28: "Brothers, think of what you were when you were called. Not many of you were wise by human standards; not many were influential; not many were of noble birth. But God chose the foolish things of the world to shame the wise; God chose the weak things of the world to shame the strong. He chose the lowly things of this world and the despised things—and the things that are not—to nullify the things that are."

Prayer: Dear Lord, reveal to us where we are weak and drive us to you for our daily needs of grace. We ask these things in the name of Christ, Amen.

God's List

Everyone has a list out these days. David Letterman has his top ten every night; newspapers have their top 25 best teams in the nation every week. I recently read a story about the top ten most hated sports figures in the world. Wouldn't you love to be on that list? I can't forget the recent list of the top five mistakes made by Presidents.

These lists tell you a lot about the person who makes them up. So just for fun, let's look at some things on Richard's lists. How about my top three favorite foods list:

1) Anything Tex-Mex—and it must have great hot sauce to go with it.
2) Chinese food. I have no idea what I am eating, but I like it anyway.
3) Hamburgers—especially grilled outside in my backyard.

Or how about my top three Bible characters outside of Jesus:

1) David—a flawed man, honest with God, and had a heart for God.
2) Peter—another flawed man, but zealous for God, and overcame.
3) Elijah—one wild dresser, who with God's help performed some wonderful miracles.

Okay, here is the last one, my list of favorite little people in the Bible:

1) The Samaritan woman at the well—lost and lonely, found God and started a revival in her city.
2) Lazarus—Jesus brought him back from the dead. What a story he could tell.
3) Father of the prodigal son—he had great love, kept looking for his son to return, and threw a big party when he did.

Now, there are my lists. What might you know from them? Well, you would know I am a Tex-Mex loving guy who enjoys reading about flawed people who overcame obstacles and kept on loving God.

But what about God's lists? Does he have any? Well, yes, he does. Let's take a look. *Proverbs 6:16-19* gives a list of things God hates. "There are six things the Lord hates, seven that are detestable to him: haughty eyes, a lying tongue, hands that shed innocent blood, a heart that devises wicked schemes, feet that are quick to rush into evil, a false witness who pours out lies, and a man who stirs up dissension among brothers."

So what does this tell us about God? It tells He hates prideful people who are quick to do evil things and stir up trouble. Now that is my paraphrase; yours might be different, but I assure of this—we would do well to stay away from the things that God has on His list.

For an exercise, let's break the list down and see where we stand:

1. Are you prideful?
2. Do you tell the truth at all times?
3. Do you hurt the innocent?
4. Are you always scheming about how to get the next guy?
5. Are you quick to fall into sin?
6. Do you tell the truth when under oath?
7. Are you a troublemaker?

Now think about the above list. Don't just assume you have it all together. What real believers would want to find themselves on a list of doing even one thing that God hates? It's called sin. God hates it; we need to avoid it.

Now God has other lists. Check out the Ten Commandments, for one popular example. Some lists you want to be on, and some you don't. But the list of names in the Lamb's Book of Life is a list we all wish to be on. Those people will find themselves in heaven with the living God. (See scripture below).

Scripture: Revelation 21:27: "Nothing impure will ever enter it, nor will anyone who does what is shameful or deceitful, but only those whose names are written in the Lamb's book of life."

Prayer: Lord, help us to hate what you hate. Help us to repent from our sinful ways. Father in Heaven, we thank you that you sent your Son to die for our sins that our names might be written in the Lamb's Book of Life. Help us to live changed and grateful lives because of that sacrifice. In Christ's name, Amen.

What Can You Live Without?

When I was a teenager driving around my hometown and I needed to call my parents, I had to stop at a pay phone, drop in a quarter, and call the house. For us, a mobile phone was a gadget on a James Bond movie. Never could we imagine that it would be a necessity of life just 30 years later. People today cannot live without them.

I know people who did not purchase their first new car until they were well into their 50s. They had never had the money to buy a new car until then, and they had to make do with used cars. This amazes me when I look around the parking lot at work and look at all the brand new cars parked there. Some people buy a new car every couple of years; they just cannot do without it.

Some people absolutely must have every minute of every day filled with some activity. They are addicted to speed and activity. They spend every day bouncing from jobs, to clubs, to sporting events. They can't stop; they can't live without activity.

What is it that you can't live without? Perhaps it is money, your boat, your cable television, your home, or your job. I could blame our consumer spirit on society, but really, if you look at the past, I believe you will see that people have always been obsessed with "things" they cannot live without, especially the wealthy.

This reminds me of the rich ruler in the gospels. He was a righteous man; he knew the commandments and had kept them since his youth. I find it interesting that the title for this story in most translations calls him the "rich young ruler." I do think there is a correlation between being young and going for things and being older and satisfied with what you have in life. I guess you could call it spiritual maturity.

During his conversation with Jesus, the Lord confronts him with the *one* thing he can't live without. The one thing for him was money. Jesus said in order to follow Him, he needed to give his money to the poor then come and follow Him. The young man turned and walked sadly away. He was not able to give up his one thing, thus he was not able to follow Christ.

What about you? What is your one thing? The one thing you can't give up that is hindering your relationship with the Lord?

Phillip Yancy remembers reading the account of a spiritual seeker who interrupted a busy life to spend a few days in a monastery. "I hope your stay is a blessed one," said the monk who showed the visitor to his cell. "If you need anything, let us know, and we'll teach you how to live without it."

Are you a spiritual seeker or a thing seeker? Are there things you just cannot live without? Ask Christ. He will show you how.

There is really only one thing that you can't live without, and that is Jesus. Seek Him and He will not only show you what you need to give up, He will show you a life filled with great things that soon you can't live without.

Scripture: Philippians 4:11: "I am not saying this because I am in need, for I have learned to be content whatever the circumstance."

Prayer: Dear Lord, Help us to hold nothing back from you. Keep us free from the temptation to desire things over our relationship with you. In Christ's name, Amen.

It Is Never Over

I have some hard and fast rules in my life. These rules are what I stand by without fail, and they make me who I am. One of those rules is never, and I mean never, leave a sporting event early.

Now all of my hard and fast rules come with good reasons behind them; no doubt, this one does as well. First, many times when I am at a professional sporting event, it is because someone has given me tickets. This year my company gave me and my 9-year-old tickets to a game in a luxury suite. Well, we got there early and stayed until they turned out the lights. It was the best seat in the house, and I sure was not going to leave early. Hey, I ate their food, drank their cold drinks, and generally was big-timing it. You know how it goes. How often does the little guy get to big time it? I would have been nuts to leave one minute before my time was up. Cinderella did not leave the ball until the stroke of midnight. I wasn't either.

My second reason, and the main reason for this rule, is that I have played enough sports to know that anything can happen. One bounce of the ball, one great play, one serious mistake, and a sure loss can be turned into victory. It happens all the time.

This week I am watching a game with a group of friends from the church, and our team is just getting whipped up and down the field. Slowly the crowd starts to dwindle down until there are about four faithful fans left with about 15 minutes to go in the game. We watch a little longer and decide this is hopeless, so we all agree, myself included, to go home. So, I say my good-byes and get in the car. I listen to the game in the car, and it is the same hopeless situation. By the time I get home, there are just 5 minutes left, and I don't even bother turning on the TV. The next morning, I get up, head to work, and start listening to the radio, and much to my surprise—that team that was hopelessly defeated, with no chance for victory, had won the game.

I was disappointed in myself for giving up on my team. Where was my faith? I at least should have been a good enough fan to watch them to the finish. You see, I know this: the game is not over until the final buzzer sounds.

185

I know this about life as well: it is not over until the Lord calls us home. We as humans tend to write people off, declare that they will never be used for God. We see the losses keep mounting up, the bad decisions they keep making, and we declare that they will never be good for anything. We even write ourselves off sometimes. That's too bad.

After a while, we start to lose faith in people. We tend to think people are always going to be how they are and will never change, and though many are like that, it does not give us an excuse to give up on folks. There is a God that can do miraculous things!

The thought today is don't give up. Not on other people and not on yourself. One softly spoken word, one requested prayer, one hand reaching out in love, or one word of encouragement, and God can turn it around in a heartbeat.

We miss out on so much when we give up. We miss out on the opportunity to be Christ to people who really need it. We miss out on seeing God do wonderful works that only He can do. We miss out on growing our faith by seeing God keep his promise to always be faithful.

The great ones play the game to the finish. God is the greatest of all. Let's give Him and others a chance. Stick it out to the end, and enjoy the victorious finish.

** You may feel like you are hopelessly defeated today with no chance of victory. Remember, today is just one day. The game is not over, and God is not through with you or your situation. Remember that God has some hard and fast rules as well, and one is—He never gives up on you.

Scripture: Philippians 1:6: "… being confident of this, that he who began a good work in you will carry it on to completion until the day of Christ Jesus."

Prayer: Dear Lord, help us to hang in there with others and ourselves. When we are tempted to quit, help us to lean on You. Perhaps today there is a friend who is reading this who needs to feel your love in an extra special way. May they feel your loving presence right now. In Christ's Name, Amen.

Just the Facts

My older preteen kids have shown great wisdom in their television-viewing lately. During the lunch hour, they have been watching Adam 12 and Dragnet. Those kinds of decisions are what really make a dad proud.

Adam 12 and Dragnet are two of the best police shows of all time. They may not be as realistic as shows today, and they may be from a period of American life long since gone, but they are some good, clean entertainment.

My favorite character of these two shows is Sgt. Joe Friday. Let's say this about Joe: he didn't talk much. The man never met a run-on sentence, let me assure you of that. The other day, I counted most of his sentences and few ran past six or seven words. Yes, you need to get a life if you are counting the length of Joe Friday's sentences, but my lack of a life is a topic for another day.

Often, Joe and his partner (he had a few—the one I remember most is Officer Frank Gannon) would interview potential victims or suspects. When Joe interviewed you, the question was clear, and you would do most of the talking. A famous phrase from Sgt. Friday was, "just the facts, ma'am." Actually, in early shows, the phrase was "all we want are the facts."

Joe didn't talk much, and he was not real interested in listening to you talk a whole bunch either. All he really wanted were the answers that would help him do his job. Don't get me wrong, he listened to your answer, but he was not looking for anything extra.

Joe Friday is not a guy you would think that you could learn a lot from in the communication world, but I am thinking he is just the guy. I have the Bible to back him up. Let's take a look:

We get in lots of trouble when we talk too much; preachers are you listening? The more you say, the more likely you are to say something wrong, or at least for it to be taken the wrong way.

Proverbs 10:19: "When words are many, sin is not absent, but he who holds his tongue is wise."

We do best when we give just the facts and don't go off trying to explain everything. One thing I have learned is people are going to make their own judgment anyway. That may sound cynical, but it is how people are. Try not to be so concerned with what people think of you that you have to explain every move. Just give them the facts; the rest is between you and God.

Psalm 34:13: "Keep your tongue from evil and your lips from speaking lies."

Be a good listener. Joe would shoot straight and then sit back and wait for the victim or suspect to talk. They may have talked longer than he wanted, but he always listened. As a matter of fact, this one is the key: talk less, listen more. That is what we learn from Joe Friday.

Proverbs 18:13: "He who answers before listening—that is his folly and his shame."

Be clear with who you are. One of Friday's sayings was "My name is Friday—I carry a badge" or in earlier shows it was "My name is Friday—I am cop." Let people know who you are. You don't have to give them a sermon or speech. Just be clear on what you stand for and why. It is up to the other person to decide what they want to do with who you are.

John 14:6: "Jesus answered, 'I am the way and the truth and the life. No one comes to the father except through me.'"

It is amazing the insight you can gain when those kids make the right lunchtime television choices. Fortunately, you can learn the same things from the Bible, without ever having to turn on the television.

Let's close with an example of what we have learned. I am Richard Harris; I carry a pen. See how easy it works.

Scripture: Proverbs 21:23: "He who guards his mouth and his tongue keeps himself from calamity."

Prayer: Dear Lord, Help us to be careful how we speak and be caring in how we listen. We ask these things in the name of Christ, Amen.

I Choose Us

I have a yearly routine: if a book or movie inspires me, I read or watch it annually. For example, I read *Holy Sweat* every year for spiritual motivation, I read *Isaac's Storm* for its historical drama and skillful writing, and I read Philip Yancey's *Soul Survivor* for its spiritual and personal insight into the church and the people that influenced his life.

As for movies, I watch *Apollo 13* for its teamwork, crisis management, and inspiration. Then I watch *Facing the Giants* for its spiritual lessons and encouragement. I also watch *It's a Wonderful Life* for obvious reasons. The last two years I have added another movie, *Family Man*.

Family Man starts with Jack and Kate at the airport. Kate is asking Jack to stay and not go overseas to work. Evidently they had a plan, but she was worried the plan would lead them apart. She basically says her peace and then points out they could do the plan or stay together, then she looks him in the eyes and says, "I choose us." He doesn't, and thus the story begins.

The movie picks up 13 years later with Jack Campbell's life. He is rich, successful in worldly terms, can have any woman he wants, and basically has everything he will ever need at his fingertips. One night an angel, or something like an angel, gives him a glimpse of what his life would have been like had he made the choice to shuck the plan and "choose us."

Needless to say, it was a very eye-opening experience for him, and for me every time I watch it. In the "glimpse" time period, he ends up with two kids, a mortgage, a wonderful wife, a minivan; he works in retail; and he has limited success in worldly terms. During that time, though, he sees what he missed and finds what real love and success truly are.

If only he would have "chosen us."

The next few moments are aimed right at those married, thinking of getting married, or who want some day to get married. Let me first make sure you understand you are not going to get a "glimpse" or a second chance. In life, we have to live with the choices we make. To avoid a life of regrets, I have one sentence of advice:

Look yourself in the mirror every day and say, "I choose us."

Every day, the world is going to offer you choices. You can choose other relationships; instead, "choose us." You can choose your job over your family; don't be fooled, "choose us." You will be tempted to escape with friends, games, computers, sports, or hobbies. These are not bad when used correctly, but dangerous when they overtake your most important relationships at home; remember, "choose us."

Jack Campbell's life revolved around him. He was selfish. Basically, that is what happens when we don't "choose us." We do the opposite: we choose "me" instead. "Me" never works in marriage. I believe most of us struggle with "me" over "us" at one time or another in our life. You must never drop your guard; you have to make the right decision each day.

Because if you don't, you will likely wake up years from now and wish you would have said, "I choose us!"

Scripture: 1 Corinthians 13:4-6: "Love is patient, love is kind. It does not envy, it does not boast, it is not proud. It is not rude, *it is not self-seeking*, it is not easily angered, it keeps no record of wrongs. Love does not delight in evil but rejoices with the truth."

Prayer: Dear Lord, help us to make the right decisions each day, and if we fail, have us to quickly seek your forgiveness. Guide us to work hard at the most important relationships and use the power of your spirit to overcome the temptation to think of ourselves only. You are a good God, and we ask these things in the name of Christ, Amen.

The Repairman

I am not a fix-it guy, so I depend on the repairman heavily. Outside of God, you need to have some people in your life that you trust: a mechanic, a plumber, and in Texas, someone who can fix your air-conditioning. If you have these guys in check, then your life is going to go pretty well.

The problem is: finding people you can trust in this area can be difficult.

You know as well as I that there is no better time to start praying then when you are looking in the Yellow Pages or on the internet for someone to come fix an appliance. That is a fine time for Godly intervention.

Seeing repairmen from a spiritual perspective (believe me, there are times that is a stretch even I am not eager to make), they are a lesson in trust. Since we could all use such a lesson, let me provide for you some thoughts:

- In order to have someone you trust, there has to be that first time you put your faith in them. If that first time they do a good job and treat you fair, then the foundations of trust are created. With God, there comes that first step, that first time you put your faith in God that He is going to get you through some experience. When it happens, and by the way it always does, then the foundations of real trusted are created.
- In order to trust a repairman of any kind, you have to feel comfortable that they have a working knowledge of what they are doing. If they can come in and quickly diagnose the issue, explain it to you in terms you can understand, while correcting the problem, it puts you at ease. Let me put you at ease right now: God is the creator of all things, has a working knowledge of how we work, and can communicate with us well through prayer if we allow him to.
- In order to build a good trusting relationship with your local handy repairman, you have to believe he is being fair with you. They have to make a living like everyone else, but you have to

trust that they will not take advantage of your lack of knowledge and charge you for work not done or work not needed. We have all been here before—fairness is a key to trust. With God it is very simple. He deals justly with all people. There is no prejudice. He has your best interest at heart. He will never, and I mean never, let you down. **In a world that chooses sides, God always chooses yours.**

• The repairmen you love the most are those who love what they do. I always enjoy watching someone that loves their job work on something. You can just tell a difference in someone making a living and someone working on their passion. Here is the best and final word on this: **you are God's passion!** He created you, loves you, and knows when you are broke and how to help you repair the hurts of your life.

If you have something that needs to be fixed, your personal life, your health, your broken heart, no matter. Stop looking around for the right person, book, or magazine; trust God. His record of customer satisfaction is unmatched.

Scripture: Psalm 9:9-10: "The LORD is a refuge for the oppressed, a stronghold in times of trouble. Those who know your name will trust in you, for you, LORD, have never forsaken those who seek you."

Prayer: Dear Lord, help us to have the courage to trust you with each aspect of our life and then to acknowledge you when we see you work. Remind us of the ways you have delivered in days gone by. We ask these things in the name of Christ, Amen.

Going Fishing

Jesus and I do not have much in common, but one thing we do have in common is we have friends who love to fish. Fishing is not my favorite activity, but I do it from time to time because much of my family enjoys it.

I have a well-defined role when it comes to fishing, and I think some of them can be used to define the roll of Jesus in our life. Let's take a look.

- When it comes to fishing, I bank roll the whole deal. I buy the pole, I purchase the bait, I buy the tackle, I buy the entrance into the park, and most importantly, I buy the snacks. It is all on me—no matter what I think of fishing. Do I mind? Of course not—that is what fathers do. Jesus is the same way. When it comes to our life, He created it, He watches over it, He takes care of the provisions, provides the blessings, and paid the ultimate price of His life on the cross to take care of our sins. He did not mind at all. After all, that is what Saviors do.

- Fishing preparation is important. It is another of my jobs. I put on the weight, find the proper hook and get it on the line, and then I make sure the bobber is in working condition. I do a test throw to make sure the tension is correct, then hand the pole over to the very patient fisherman. No pole goes out until dad has prepared it. Jesus has a very similar role in preparing us for our purpose in life. He brings people our way who love us enough to teach us, he provides opportunities for us to grow, and then he throws a few tests our way. After that, He determines if we are ready for our purpose in life. No one goes out for their task until the Lord has prepared them. That is what Heavenly Fathers do.

- Repairing broken equipment is a major task. It is all mine. No one can tangle fishing line like a 9-year-old. It is at this time that I have to put down the snacks and get to serious work. I hand new equipment over to the young fisherman and get to work on the broken pole. I patiently take the tangled mess and begin to remove the tangles, one at a time. This is very tedious work and could be avoided by following some simple rules of fishing, but none of that matters when the line is tangled. All that matters is someone I love has gotten themselves in a mess, and I am the one to get them out of it and back fishing; that's what fathers do. Repair of life is one of Jesus' major tasks. We often find ourselves in trouble that could have been avoided by following some of His simple rules. But to Jesus, none of that matters. All that matters is someone He loves is in a mess, and He can get them out of it and back in the flow of life. That is what Heavenly Fathers do.

- My favorite task is taking the caught fish off the hook. After all of my other tasks have been completed, fish are to be caught. There is nothing like the smile on a kid's face after he has caught a fish, no matter how big or small it is. First, we cheer and congratulate the great fisherman, and then we take their picture holding the mighty catch; we enjoy the moment thoroughly. After all the fanfare is completed, I take over the task of removing the hook from the fish and getting it back in the water. My role can get a little messy, but few notice because they are basking in the glow of the moment. I don't mind because someone I love has received a blessing; that is what fathers do. Jesus loves for us to catch the fish of our life. He loves the moment children are born, grandchildren learn to walk, seniors graduate, young couples are married, and hard workers receive promotions to name just a few. He was very much there through the process, but He allows us to reel in the blessing and then lays low to allow us to stand in the spotlight for a moment. It is not about Him; it is about us. He does not mind because someone He loves has received a blessing; after all that is what Heavenly Fathers do.

As Jesus walked on this earth, He probably saw a lot of great catches, but even more tangled lives. Nothing has changed in 2000 years; He still sees the value of a good catch, and He is there for us to straighten out our tangled lives. That, after all, is what Heavenly Fathers do.

Scripture: 1 John 3:1: *"How great is the love the Father has lavished on us, that we should be called children of God! And that is what we are!* The reason the world does not know us is that it did not know him."

Prayer: Dear Lord, we come to you today simply to say we love you, we thank you, and we praise you that you indeed love us as your children. We give all this praise in the name of Christ, Amen.

Grumpy, Sleepy, Doc, Dopey, Happy...

When you are 47 with a four-year-old, your Friday nights are not spent out on the town but in town, often watching a four-year-old movie. Such was the case this past Friday when Gracie, Caleb, and I settled in for private viewing of Snow White and the Seven Dwarfs.

I will not bore you with a story you already know, but needless to say, the beautiful princess ends up running for her life and finds herself living with seven little guys with funny names. These guys are doing some work in a pretty serious diamond mine, and when they arrive home, they fall in love with Snow White—well, all except Grumpy, who acts like he doesn't love her. We all know better.

Each of our bearded miners had a name that matched a trait they possessed. For example: *Grumpy,* well, he was grumpy; *Happy* had a good disposition; *Dopey,* well he was not always so smart, but always good-natured; *Doc,* he was the wise one of the bunch; *Bashful,* well he of course was shy; *Sneezy,* well he sneezed all the time; *Sleepy,* he looked like me on a Sunday afternoon sitting in my easy chair all the time. Snow White loved 'em all, no matter their trait, even Grumpy.

As a matter of fact, it was her love for Grumpy that got my attention. Her first night there, she kneeled down to pray before going to bed and at the very end of her prayer she made a special request for Grumpy. It was then the thought came to mind; Kim Harris is married to the seven dwarfs. Allow me to explain.

My name is not Grumpy, but sometimes I am. There are days that I am kind of Sleepy and just can't get it going. There are some days I am on top of my game and am Doc, the leader of the family, while there are others days, more than I would like, that I am Dopey, not using my head. Sometimes I am kind of shy like Bashful (not often), while other days I am in good spirits like Happy. Then there are the days I am not feeling so well, and I am a bit like Sneezy. Actually if I worked real hard, I could come up with a lot more than seven different personality traits for myself, but I am certain you get the picture. As a matter of fact, I am certain if you are married, you, like Kim, are married to the seven dwarfs.

When we stand before God and commit our lives to someone, we are committed to everything that person has to offer. At times, that may be heavenly bliss, while at others, it may take everything you have to stick it out. *I say: "stick it out."*

How exactly do you do that? Follow Snow White's lead and fall to your knees in prayer. Prayer works. Allow it to. Below are some prayer tips:

1) Prayer leads you to God in regard to your relationship. Go there often.
2) Thank God for the good traits as well as asking for help with the not-so-good ones.
3) **Be sure and ask God to deal with you. We all have issues.**
4) Ask God to bind you closer together as a couple, that nothing or no one would come between the two of you.
5) **Ask God for forgiveness for when you fail in the relationship and for a forgiving spirit when the other fails.**
6) Thank God for your special loved one He has blessed you with.

Keep a good hold of your prayer life, and the prospects are good that you, like Snow White, will live happily ever after with the prince or princess that God has given you.

Scripture: Colossians 4:2: "Devote yourselves to prayer, being watchful and thankful."

Prayer: Dear Lord, lead us to our knees in regards to those we love; provide for us your Spirit in abundance that we may enjoy the gifts you give us. We ask these things in the name of Christ, Amen.

Holding on for Dear Life

For each of us, every day holds the possibility for immense good or devastating tragedy. We never know what the next ten minutes will hold. The one thing we all know is that life is unpredictable. Change can come quickly.

For Barbara Wilkins, a simple ride home turned into a moment she will not soon forget. It started with her husband calling her, suggesting she come home early. It ended in the midst of a storm.

As she drove, the storm picked up, and as she described it, hail began to fall that sounded like her car was being beat on with a baseball bat. With her husband encouraging her on the phone to attempt to outrun the storm, she made the decision to find refuge in a nearby gas station.

Right thinking, wrong place. She drove past a Phillips 66 for some reason and pulled into a Love's gas station. Soon she found herself holding onto the metal railing on the wall of the bathroom. When that wall began to shake and appeared to be coming down, she then reached over and grabbed the sturdiest thing she could find, the toilet, and hung on while a tornado ripped the building to shreds.

Fortunately, she walked away from the event, but she was mentally shaken and physically sore. I asked what had made her sore, thinking something might have hit her, and she corrected me with this statement: she was sore from "holding on for dear life." Storms in life have a way of making you feel that way.

All of us, at one time or another, will find ourselves holding on for dear life in the midst of a storm that is tearing into the walls we have placed in our life for security. For some, it is the wall of marriage that comes tumbling down. For others, the security of a job is ripped out beneath us. Often, our health or the health of those we love rocks our world. No matter when the storm comes, all we can do is hold on for dear life. Let us use Barbara's experience to point us to God for some tips on how to handle the stormy days of life.

- **Listen to the Godly advice of others.** Had Barbara left a bit earlier as her husband suggested, she might have missed the storm. We need to listen to Godly words when offered. Often, they help us avoid great tragedy in our life.

- **Be careful where you find refuge.** For Barbara, it was Phillips 66 or Love's—it was a guess. For us, we have more clear choices—it is God or the world. Many choose the short-term escape of recreational drugs or destructive habits instead of the more solid, never-wavering hand of a loving God. Think of the world's escapes as Love's, and think of God as the Phillips 66. (By the way, it still stands today, while the Love's—not so much.)

- **You can't outrun a storm.** Storms are bigger than us, faster than us, and very unpredictable. Don't take chances—deal with it as soon as you can by finding the proper place of refuge. Don't get caught running unprotected from trouble. It can be disastrous. Go to God immediately!

- **Be certain what you hold onto is not going anywhere.** Again, Barbara, in desperation, grabbed the most solid thing she could—the plumbing. That was wise. We need to be equally wise in what we choose to hold onto for dear life. The storm is coming. Barbara could not control that. What she could control was what she hung onto. *As the storm whirls around you, taking out some things you may have grown accustomed to, things you may have trusted, be sure of this: God is not going anywhere; find him and hold on tight.*

Storms do not last forever, even though it may seem like they do. Let me assure you that someday you will look up and realize the storm has passed almost as suddenly as it arrived. The world around you may look very different. You, more than likely, will be stronger from the experience, but the storm itself will be gone. At that moment, do what Barbara did; go to the one waiting on you, the one who loves you. For Barbara, it was her husband a few miles away who missed the storm. For us, it is a loving God who was there in the midst of the storm the whole time.

When it comes to holding on for dear life, make sure the arms you find yourself in are God's; He is not going anywhere.

Scripture: Psalm 9:9-10: "The LORD is a refuge for the oppressed, a stronghold in times of trouble. Those who know your name will trust in you, for you, LORD, have never forsaken those who seek you."

Prayer: Dear Lord, we are thankful indeed that we have a God that loves us, that walks through the storms with us and keeps us in safe care. We praise your name that you will never leave us or forsake us. Today we simply say thanks, in the name of Christ, Amen.

Field of Dreams

When I first saw the movie *Field of Dreams* in 1989, it made little sense to me. I just could not figure it out. Over the last 20 years, it has not only become a movie with a clear message, it has become one that inspires me and reminds me of my own dreams and how to respond to them.

In this movie, Ray lives in rural Iowa with his wife, Annie, and daughter, Karin. One day as he walks through his cornfield, he hears a voice whisper "If you build it, they will come" and sees a vision of a baseball field. Ray, who fears of becoming like his father who lacked any spontaneity and with whom he stopped playing catch with at the age of 14, convinces Annie to allow him to plow under a section of corn and build a baseball field in the middle of nowhere.

After a year of nothing happening, Ray and Annie had to consider replacing the field with corn to stay afloat financially, but things change at the last moment when Annie sees someone on the field. A player from the past appears, Shoeless Joe Jackson, and asks if he can bring others. Ray agrees and in and out of the corn in the outfield comes players from the past to play the game they love. Only Annie, Ray, and Karin can see these players, at least at first.

Now through all this time, Ray is not making a lot of money—enter the brother-in-law who is insisting that he sell the farm to him and some investors so he will have a place to live. Mark, the brother-in-law, cannot see the players until one moment during a scuffle, and from that moment on, he changes his mind and insists Ray not sell the farm.

Let me move quickly without turning this into a review of movies from the 80s. Throughout the movie he hears whispers: one is "ease his pain," which leads him to a recluse writer who eventually ends up disappearing into the corn field behind the outfield with the players. Another voice comes to him that says "go the distance" while at a Boston Red Sox game with the writer.

Indeed, Ray goes the distance, builds the field, has a chance to play catch with his dad again, and ends up restoring more than a few lives along the way, including his own. During the movie, he believes that the voice he keeps hearing is that of Joe Jackson's, but at the end of the movie Jackson tells Ray the voice he has heard is his own.

I believe that in each of us God has placed a dream, that in His still, small voice He encourages us to follow that dream. That dream is what will give us purpose and add flavor to our lives. For some, it is to build homes or practice law. For others, it is to buy stocks, feed the homeless, or raise children. **The list of dreams is endless and the point of this life God gives us is not that we have a dream (we all do)—but that we follow it.**

As we chase the dream God has set in our heart, we need to remember a few things. First is that our dream is not everyone else's, and they may not buy into what your dream is. Don't be discouraged by that. Continue to chase what God has purposed in your heart.

Keep in mind also that in each life he will send an Annie that believes in you, that gives you the freedom to chase your dream, and encourages you along the way, even if it makes little sense to them. The "Annies" (Ray's wife) are invaluable in chasing your God-given desires. Be sure and thank them along the journey.

Just as there are encouragers, there are those who have lost sight of their own dream and will discourage you around every corner. They do not believe in you or your dream, and their desire is for you to fail. **Listen to their legitimate concerns, then move on, keeping in mind that success or failure does not come from reaching a destination in life but in following the will of God for your life. It is all about the journey.**

No matter how old you are today, there is still a dream in your heart. Chase it. Perhaps times have gotten hard or things are not working out quite as you planned. Don't stop. More than anything, listen for that still, small voice of God which gives direction, encouragement and hope to those who follow their dreams. Do what the voice encouraged Ray to do: "go the distance."

Scripture: Ephesians 2:10: "God has made us what we are. In Christ Jesus, God made us to do good works, which God planned in advance for us to live our lives doing." *New Century Version*

Prayer: Dear Lord, give us the courage, the strength, and the power to follow the dreams you have placed in our hearts. Have us learn to listen to you and find joy in the journey you have prepared for us. We ask these things in the name of He who loves, Jesus Christ, Amen.

Lifeguard on Duty

If you go swimming at a hotel, you will more than likely see this very visible sign near the pool, "No Lifeguard on Duty." This sign is very self-explanatory; it means you are on your own while swimming. If something happens, then there will be no professional lifeguard there to help you out. Basically, and I have seen this sign as well, "swim at your own risk."

I am sure that in the lawsuit-happy world in which we live, this sign is a must. It gives you the warning that if you are using the pool, you might need to take some precautions, like making sure you do not swim alone. If you're a parent, it lets you know that you need to keep a better than normal eye on the kids, because if something does go wrong, you will have to take charge of the scene.

Of course for the hotel, the best thing about the sign is that it takes them totally off the hook in regard to something happening at the pool. They don't have to pay anyone to watch the pool, and you are forewarned as a customer that, if you swim, you do so at your own risk.

I remember when I was a child swimming at the hotel my grandfather managed that there were lifeguards on duty. My parents could take it easy because there was someone watching us kids. When the lifeguards where there, we could swim. When they were not, the pool was closed. It was as simple as that. It was a good system, but that was another time and day.

Not having a lifeguard on duty to watch people and take care of them in order just to save some money seems kind of cold to me. Thankfully, our God does not operate that way. As far as He is concerned, your life is always important, and the good news is that He is always on guard.

We operate in a risky world filled with danger. Many times we do not even know what risks might be out there. Isn't it good to know that you have a God that cares for you and does not simply say, "Hey, you're born. Now live the rest of your life at your own risk!"

For an unfortunate number of people, they choose to live a life that denies God and His care. They think they are better off on their own and can take care of themselves just fine without any help from God. They look around the pool of life and for some reason don't even see the "lifeguard" on duty. When accidents happen, they simply try to handle them on their own and choose to keep the lifeguard on the stand. Or worse than that, go to people who have no spiritual clue how to handle life.

That would be like you swimming at the beach and finding yourself in over your head, and instead of calling on the lifeguard on duty to help you out, you allow me to swim out to you. I can barely swim and have no skills in how to save your life. More than likely, we would both end up in jeopardy, making the trouble worse instead of better.

It may not seem like it all the time, but God is always on duty. He knows your every move before you make it. You—yes, you—are very important to God. He always has your best interest at heart. You are His priority. God has all the power of the universe at his disposal to help you in your time of need. You need only call His name, and he will throw out the life preserver because isn't that what He is all about anyway, preserving the life He created?

The very name Lifeguard implies that someone is guarding your life. That is good to know while you are swimming, but it is even better to know that in a life filled with risk, danger, and heartache there is always a Lifeguard on duty—God!

Scriptures: Psalm 91:1-2: "He who dwells in the shelter of the Most High will rest in the shadow of the Almighty. I will say of the Lord, "He is my refuge and my fortress, my God, in whom I trust."

Psalm 23:4: "Even though I walk through the valley of the shadow of death, I will fear no evil for you are with me; your rod and your staff they comfort me."

Prayer: Dear Lord, with nothing but thanksgiving, we praise your name that you care for us enough to walk with us each day and to lead us to green pastures, to rescue us from harm and danger, and to love us even though we fail you often. Thank you, Lord, for being such a loving God. In Christ's name, Amen.

Disaster Recovery

I have come across a new phrase over the last several years. It is "disaster recovery." Up until the last several weeks, this phrase meant little to me. It was something others had to worry about, but not now.

Disaster recovery—what does that mean? One example would be if your computer shuts down. How are you going to recover the information that was in that computer? The disaster is your computer going down; the recovery is the plan you have if it goes down, such as having a backup of your information. You see, it is a disaster if you lose your computer at work. Trust me on this one. I am living it.

I believe disaster recovery plans have been around for a while, they just had a different name. People these days like to give new buzzwords for old phrases. Perhaps a disaster recovery plan would have been a contingency plan 30 years ago.

For more examples of disaster recovery, think of what you would do if your lights went out. How would you take care of your family? Do you have batteries in your flashlights or candles with matches close by? What if you lost your job? Would you have anything to hold you over until you found employment? In a way, you can think of a savings account as a disaster recovery plan.

A lot of people use God as their disaster recovery plan. They run their lives as they please, doing what they want, when and how they want to do it. They rarely pay any attention to the things of God. While things are going well—good health, nice kids under control, consistent job—no God until disaster strikes.

The kids get in trouble, the doctor delivers a bad report, or the boss hands out a pink slip. Then people head to church, they turn to prayer, they call their Christian friends, and they turn to God as their disaster recovery plan.

There is good and bad in this. Let's talk about it. First, let's deal with the good news. God is more than willing to be your disaster recovery plan. He is always there, willing to forgive past sins when confessed, and more than ready to give comfort and leadership for you in your time of need. God is not like a fair-weather friend. He is always there for you even if you have not always paid Him much attention. If you find yourself in trouble, do not hesitate to turn to God.

The negative is that many times we could have avoided disaster had we been spending the proper time with God in the first place. Spending the proper time with God may not keep you from losing your job, but it certainly will help you avoid the pain created when you turn to sin. Not paying the proper attention to God opens us up for all kinds of different disasters. The best way to avoid disaster is to get into God's word, worship, service and prayer, and stay there. It's best to be pro-active when it comes to disaster.

Ask yourself this question: if disaster comes to my family or me what will we do? Will we be strong in the Lord, surrounded by a loving church that will pray and love us? Will we be able to go to the scriptures and find not only comfort but also wisdom that will help us make our decisions? Will we have Christian friends willing to listen without judging while being able to shoot straight with us even when it hurts?

Let me assure you that disaster will come your way. My question is what will your plan be? Let me suggest there is only one—God!

Scripture: Psalm 27:5: "For in the day of trouble he will keep me safe in his dwelling; he will hide me in the shelter of his tabernacle and set me high upon a rock."

Prayer: Dear Father, help us to always lean on you through good times and bad. We are thankful that you are always having our concern at heart, and that you are a refuge, a very present help in danger. We love you and ask all these things in the name of Jesus. Amen.

To Really Die

Dietrich Bonhoeffer was one of the great theologians of the last century. What draws me to Bonhoeffer and his story is his unrelenting love of God, his courage, and his love for his homeland of Germany. His story is one of inner struggle, intrigue, and bravery.

He was born in Germany in the early 1900s and was an outspoken critic of Adolf Hitler during the 30s and 40s as Hitler came to power. He taught young students to resist the Nazis until 1939 when he moved to New York. He could stay only a month before he returned to Germany, stating "I shall have no right to take part in the restoration of Christian life in Germany after the war unless I share in the trials of this time with my people." The decision to return would eventually decide the fate of his life.

He became a double agent upon his return and was imprisoned for being a part of a plot to kill Hitler in the summer of 1944. He was hung on April 9, 1945, just 11 days before the Allies would liberate the prison camp he was detained in at Flossenburg. He died at the age of 39 with these final words, "This is the end for me, the beginning of life."

Bonhoeffer's most famous quote is this, "When Christ calls a man, he bids him come and die." Bonhoeffer not only gave his life physically, but also spiritually. God may never call you to put your life on the line for your country, your neighborhood, or your family, but He still is in the business of calling us to die to the selfish former life and to be transformed. Romans 12:2 says, "Do not conform any longer to the pattern of this world, but be transformed by the renewing of your mind."

God is "bidding you to die" to the things of this world that stand in the way of your relationship with Him. In the society of the West, with our affluence, there are many things that we need to learn to die to—our possessions, pride, status, looks, and reputation are only a few on the list. God calls for nothing less than an all-out commitment to Him and His ways. There is no partial transformation for Him. He is, as the saying goes, "Lord of all or not Lord at all."

Jesus himself said in Mark 8:34-35, "Then he called the crowd to him along with his disciples and said, 'If anyone would come after me, he must deny himself and take up his cross and follow me. For whoever wants to save his life will lose it, but whoever loses his life for me and for the gospel will save it.'" What are we hanging on to?

Jesus is saying if you really want to live, the only way to do it is to passionately give your life to Him, no strings attached. Lose yourself in God and then, only then, will you really be living.

I ask the question again—what are we hanging on to? We become possessive of this life when in reality it is never our own in the first place. As we seek to hang on to things, they in turn hold us captive, never quite allowing us to fully live for Christ.

Has Christ called you? Have you heard his voice calling you to give up the things of the past to come and join Him and His family? As you reach for the hand of God, there is more than likely something you need to let go of before you can fully take His hand. Bonhoeffer released his life into the hands of a life-giving God and really lived. What about you? Are you willing to really live? First, you must really die.

Exercise:

Pray to the Lord and ask Him if there is something you are hanging on to that is keeping you from fully serving Him, then write it down.

_____

_____

_____

Then pray to God for the strength to release it.

Scripture: Ephesians 4:22-24: "You were taught with regard to your former way of life, to put off your old self, which is being corrupted by its deceitful desires; to be made new in the attitude of your minds; and to put on the new self, created to be like God in true righteousness and holiness."

Prayer: Dear Lord, lead us to shed our old desires of the flesh, to die to self, and to live for you with all of our hearts. Forgive us where we fail you, lead us to righteousness. Our old habits are hard to break. Help us to lean on you for the strength to truly overcome. In Christ's name, Amen.

Jaci V.

Funny how God works. When we are in shut-down mode, we are reminded that God never is. As Kim and I were walking out of a conference last night, heading for a late dinner, we stumbled onto the equivalent of a church service. God still wanted to speak; dinner had to wait.

As we walked through a giant hall, I heard a familiar voice. I looked to the stage, and thought I recognized the one singing. I said to Kim that sounds like Jaci Velasquez, so I picked up a bulletin and sure enough, I was right. Jaci has a beautiful voice and is one of my favorites of all time, so we stayed for the next song.

Jaci shared her feelings for just a moment before she sang "On My Knees" (one of her best, by the way), and she made this statement: "I was fifteen when I first started recording and did not understand totally the depth of what I was singing." As she sang, I thought about how her life had transpired over the last decade.

She is now thirty, with two very young children and a marriage of some three years to a fellow musician. Life seems to be going well now, but the last decade has not always held the best of times. She suffered through the pain of divorce and moved to London, far from her support system of family and friends. For many, she dropped off the map at that time. Then, on top of that, her parents divorced, and this caused a strained relationship with her father. Through it all, there she was in Dallas lifting her voice with the same words as a decade earlier, but with a greater understanding of what the words meant.

I can relate. My guess is you can, too.

On our way to knowing all the answers, life happens; we make wrong choices, people important to us let us down, and at times, we let ourselves down. We fight through life trying to make sense of it all.

We have two choices in life once we have discovered we do not have all the answers: we can quit and give up or we can struggle through it with the care, nurture, and instruction of God. Many have given up on God, on themselves, and on life in general. That is why

I was happy to see Jaci V. on stage, still singing the same song she did so many years earlier. Through all of life's challenges, she still was true to the message. She hadn't quit, and for me, this made her message stronger than ever before.

I have read the words of scripture consistently for the last 30 years of my life, and though the words have not changed, experience has added a great deal to the meaning of those words. Through my failure, I have grasped the real meaning of God's forgiveness and unconditional love. Through personal loss, I have found that defeat is never final. In victory, I have learned what real praise is: not the superficial showy kind the world has to offer.

The message for the day is: never give up; God always has something for you. Never stop singing, and you will find His words and love will be deeper and more meaningful as the years go by.

Instead of scripture here are some of the words to "On My Knees": "There are days when I feel the best of me is ready to begin. Then there are days when I feel I'm letting go and soaring on the wind. **'Cause I've learned in laughter or in pain how to survive! (My guess is those words mean much more today than 13 years ago.)** ....I get on my knees! There I am before the love that changes me. See, I don't know how, but there's power when I'm on my knees."

Prayer: Dear Lord, give us the strength and courage to carry on, to overcome our past failures, and to look squarely into your current love for us. Help us to examine scriptures clearly and consistently. Help us to grow deeper and less superficial in our walk with you. We ask these things in the name of Christ, Amen.

If I Could Write a Letter to Me

I love all music, and country artist Brad Paisley is one of my favorites. Most of his songs, not all grant you, are good fun or speak to your heart. Last year he wrote a song that made me think about a lot of things in life.

In the song, he is writing a letter back to himself when he was 17. How interesting would that be, to be able to look back and give yourself advice based on the experiences you have had? Of course, that is impossible, but it helps to put some things in proper perspective and forces us to examine how we have lived our lives up to this point. So here, for a second, I will share with you a letter to me.

"Dear Richard,

At 17, I would learn now to give a full effort in all that I did, including school. You will learn this later, but it would be helpful if you would do it now. As you grow up, pay closer attention to family and friends. Make sure you attend the special moments like weddings and graduations with those you love. Richard, that is part of being a better friend and person. Learn it now; perfect it later.

Richard, don't listen to the naysayers in life. You don't have to ignore their efforts to help you, but do not be so affected that you lose sight of your dreams. Don't be so afraid to fail that you never try. Failing is part of life.

Be true to your word, especially when it comes to your wife and children. Treat Kim like the special gift she is; don't ignore or take that gift for granted. You're lucky, by the way, that you found her at such a young age! By the way, take her to the prom—don't just sit at the same table as her!

Some darn good years are in front of you, and you will see some wonderful and special things. You won't believe how many kids you will have and how neat they are. Treasure each minute with them.

Lastly, but most importantly, jump in full force with God now. Don't wait another minute. Learn all you can about Him. Learn to love God and love people now and carry that on for the rest of your life. Be sure and share that way of living with your children. God is amazingly good to you and very forgiving of your errors, be sure and thank him daily for that.

Richard, life is good, but it is short. It goes by fast. Make the best of it. By the way, when you're at the foul line against Garland High School, go just a little softer on the follow through.

Yourself 30 years later, Richard"

That might have bored you, but that is okay—that was from me to me. Age, time, and experience change a lot about what you think and how you respond to certain things in life. Unfortunately, we do not have the option of having someone come back from the future to give us advice. We have to live life out one day at a time.

What is the point? God gives us one life to live. There are no do-overs no matter how much we wish there were. Let us all learn from our past, share our experiences in a loving and caring way when asked to, and most of all, point to the future with the knowledge that we have a loving God that both forgives us and has a plan for us.

- Exercise of the weekend: write a letter to yourself in the past and then reflect on what it tells you about your values and priorities today. Take a moment after that and ask God to lead and guide your future. Share your thoughts with someone who loves you.

Scripture: Psalms 25:4-6: "Show me your ways, O Lord, teach me your paths; guide me in your truth and teach me, for you are God my Savior, and my hope is in you all day long. Remember, O LORD, your great mercy and love, for they are from of old."

Prayer: Dear Lord, guide us to share wisely with those when given the chance, and most of all, let us learn at your feet. Help us to learn from the past but not dwell in it. Lead us to accept forgiveness for our past sins and your guidance for future blessings. We ask these things in the name of Christ, Amen.

Golfers: Need Perfect Conditions

I love all sports and have played golf off and on ever since I was in elementary school. Of all the sports I have played and of all the players I have been around, golfers seem to have the greatest needs.

For example, they need the sun to be shining and for it to be over 50 degrees and under 90. They don't want it too hot or too cold. In Texas, that allows for about six days to play golf all year long.

Golfers like it best when there is almost no wind. Wind, of course, pushes the ball one way or another—so a good day is when there is little wind to deal with. On my side of Texas, there is little to stop the wind from blowing, especially out on a wide-open golf course.

The golfer expects the grass on the fairway to be at the perfect height, perfectly green, and not too tall in the rough. Then, the green should have no bumps and should be perfectly manicured to just the right height. The grounds crew at a golf course has the impossible task of pleasing everyone.

The need of the golfer that makes me smile the most is the need for total silence while they play. In every other sport, the crowd is encouraged to yell and scream at the top of their lungs. In golf, you don't dare sneeze at the wrong time or the golfer will turn and scowl at you and have you escorted from the gallery.

I have yet to figure out how a basketball player can shoot free throws with a thousand people standing behind the goal waving all matter of things in his face and a golfer has trouble concentrating if someone clears their throat 70 feet away.

The reason is simple: golfers think they deserve perfect conditions. Thus, they are a frustrated group. Some of us have the same golfer mentality: we expect perfect conditions in life and it leads us to be frustrated people as well.

You ask how? Here are some examples:

1) We expect our spouse to look like George Clooney or Carrie Underwood while we look like Jay Leno or Rosie O'Donnell.

We have unrealistic expectations of others while we do not hold ourselves to the same standards.

2) While we are on marriage, let's keep at it. We expect our wives or husbands to be passionate and on fire for sexual activity like we see in even the most tame movie or television show we witness. All the time we forget that our wives just worked 9 hours, cooked a meal, cleaned the house, and got the kids ready for bed. Wives expect the husband to be a hopeless romantic, caring only for her every need while forgetting what happened at work, the bills, or how the kids are doing. These perfect conditions exist about as often as it is 70 degrees with no wind in Texas. (Side note here: be careful what you watch!)

3) We expect everyone at work, church, or the local clubs to think our ideas are the greatest and never disagree with us. As brilliant as we are, how could anyone dare think our plans are not the best ever? We forget we are all individuals created in the image of God with different gifts and personalities. Expecting everyone to agree with even your good ideas is a sure way of leading a frustrated life.

4) We think our kids should make straight A's just like we did. (Ha!) We think they should have a passion for whatever it is we put them in and for them to say all the right things to the people we come across so that it will reflect well on us. Talk about unreasonable expectations and something that causes great frustration on our kids and us.

In an imperfect world with imperfect people, the worst thing we can have is a golfer's mentality. In real life, the wind blows, the weeds grow, and the guy next to you will cough at just the right moment.

The best way to overcome this mentality is to remember your imperfections and the grace God has bestowed upon you and then be liberal in passing that grace on to others.

Scripture: 1 Peter 4:7-11: "Everything in the world is about to be wrapped up, so take nothing for granted. Stay wide-awake in prayer.

Most of all, love each other as if your life depended on it. Love makes up for practically anything. Be quick to give a meal to the hungry, a bed to the homeless—cheerfully. Be generous with the different things God gave you, passing them around so all get in on it: if words, let it be God's words; if help, let it be God's hearty help. That way, God's bright presence will be evident in every-thing through Jesus, and he'll get all the credit as the One mighty in everything—encores to the end of time. Oh, yes!" *The Message* by Eugene Peterson

Prayer: Dear Lord, guide us in our expectations of others and our-selves. Lead us away from the trap of expecting too much from others and not enough from ourselves. Have us to give out your grace and love to all we come across. Help us most of all to do this in our closest of relationships. We ask all these things in the name of Christ, Amen.

Follow the Bouncing Ball

Let's go back—way back—to when I was a young child watching cartoons. From time to time they would show a really old cartoon, one that probably dated back to the early 60s. These were far simpler cartoons than today, and there is one type I want you to focus on.

There would be cartoons that would come on, and they would ask you to sing along with the music. It would give you the words on the screen and then the speaker would tell you to follow the bouncing ball. A ball would appear, and it would bounce from word to word letting you know when and how to sing along with the song. Always there was a great choir singing with you. Now for this too-cool generation, that might be kind of hokey, but I loved it.

Well this morning I woke up in the middle of the night, and a toy, for one reason or another, was going a little crazy. It kept playing the song "If You're Happy and You Know It." This is the kind of song that they would play on the old cartoons. Now this is a great song, one of my all time favorites, and it has a great message for today's devotional. So please follow the bouncing ball. Okay I don't have a bouncing ball but play along with me anyway.

Now don't be bashful, sing right along, and if you happen to be in a cube at work, make sure the person next to you either sings with you or can't hear you!

"If you're happy and you know it,
Clap your hands
If you're happy and you know it,
Clap your hands,
If you're happy and you know it,
Then your face will surely show it
If you're happy and you know it,
Clap your hands."

Now, that is just the first verse. After that, it asks you to tap your toes, then the next verse asks you to nod your head. Go ahead—throw caution to the wind and finish the song.

Here is today's very simple truth: if you're happy and you know it, then your body language should show it. Put a smile on your face, tell someone hello who needs to hear it, laugh a little—no—laugh a lot! Hug the right someone, shake someone's hand, or give them a high five (my kids love that).

Sure, life is serious, but really now, can we not every once in a while let our face and those around us know how happy we are to be alive, to be blessed, to have special children and grandchildren. Is life so serious you can't put a smile on your face? I think not.

If you're happy and you know it, do what we do at church—say AMEN!

Scripture: Proverbs 15:13: "A happy heart makes the face cheerful, but heartache crushes the spirit."

Ecclesiastes 5:19: "Moreover, when God gives any man wealth and possessions, and enables him to enjoy them, to accept his lot and be happy in his work—this is a gift of God."

Prayer: Dear Lord, let our lives reflect the joy we have in our hearts from first knowing you and then knowing your blessings. We ask this in the name of Him who puts joy in our lives, Christ, Amen

Did I Really Say That?

Some of the smartest people can say some of the most absurd things. Things I know that when they said it, they thought to themselves, "Did I really say that?" Need some examples? No problem. Enjoy.

- "Smoking kills. If you're killed, you've lost a very important part of your life." Brooke Shields *You can't argue with that, can you?*
- "Outside of the killings, Washington has one of the lowest crime rates in the country." Mayor Marion Barry, Washington, D.C.
- "It isn't pollution that's harming the environment. It's the impurities in our air and water that are doing it." Al Gore *what's in a name?*
- "It is wonderful to be here in the great state of Chicago." Dan Quayle
- "I haven't committed a crime. What I did was fail to comply with the law." Mayor David Dinkins of New York City *He must be a lawyer!*
- "Pitching is 80 percent of the game, and the other half is hitting and fielding." Mickey Rivers *one of my all time favorite quote guys!*
- "If your parents never had children, chances are you won't either." Dick Cavett

When you put a microphone in front of some people, you never know what is going to come out. Are you as thankful as I am that no one is recording every word you say? As a father, businessman, husband, and pastor I have heard some pretty bizarre things. Unfortunately, many of those things have come from my own mouth.

I am sure that these folks would love to have those statements back, but here is the fact of the matter: they can't get words spoken back, and neither can we. With that in mind, we need to be very careful about what we say. We all know we should watch our tongue for the hurtful things we might say, so we will not dwell on that today.

Instead, let's dwell on a couple of other thoughts. First: please learn to laugh at yourself. People in my house love to laugh at the silly things I say and do, and I enjoy the laugh right along with them. Goodness! Don't take yourself so seriously. When you do something laughable, then laugh for crying out loud! Lastly: use words to lift people up. Think about all the positive things people have said to and about you and emulate them. When you think of your language, think two l's: **Laughter and Lifting!**

Scripture: Proverbs 16:24: "Pleasant words are a honeycomb, sweet to the soul and healing to the bones."

Prayer: Dear Lord, we praise you because with the knowledge of your love, we can be people of joy. Help us to spread your love by using our words with the right spirit. We thank you for the life you give. We ask these things in the name of Christ, Amen.

Going to the Wrong Home

I lived in the same house for 23 years. The address was on 5th street. For 23 years, I drove to and from the same house. Everywhere I went; the final destination was 5th street. The car knew how to get there—I was just a passenger.

A year and half ago, I moved six miles from 5th street. Home is a different place now, and everywhere I go ends up at the new home, no longer on 5th street.

The other day my family and I ate at a restaurant we had been eating at for years. We finished our meal and headed for home. I jumped on a familiar highway, made a familiar turn, and headed for home—the wrong home! I was heading for 5th street.

What I did in my car, many of us do in life; we change our life, but are tempted to return to the old way of living, the old house if you will. Let me give you some reasons why that is a bad idea.

- First and foremost, it is not your house any longer! Remember, you moved for a reason. You changed. The past is behind you. If you have committed your life to the Lord, then you do not belong there (II Corinthians 5:17). The old house is not home; don't go there.
- Secondly, it will only bring you down. My new house is a considerable upgrade from my former house. There is no way I would consider moving back. Yet in life we choose to return to the same old addictions and destructive lifestyle of our past and forget about the better position we find ourselves in. Examples: we return to drugs though we know they destroy us and our families; those who commit adultery find them-selves back in an illicit relationship though they have loving families; those who steal get a rush from the excitement and though they know better, they keep returning for another high; and we gossip though we know it hurts others. Those are just a few. Once you have been delivered, don't go back because with it comes the former pain that led you to seek change. **Thought: Move out; Stay out!**

- Never forget you take others back with you. I looked up and noticed where I was going, but a whole family was just sitting in the car going wherever I took them. Innocent people headed in the wrong direction—think about that the next time you are tempted to head to the old house. The same pain we caused them in the past will come back to them. You never go anywhere alone; go to the right house and stay there: that is best for everyone.

It is tempting to go back to a former way of living, to return to old habits and destructive behavior. Just as with me in the car, we can go back at times without even thinking about it. The longer the habit, the harder to stay away. That is why you need God in your life. Without him, the temptation is just too great.

Remember: don't go to your 5th street in life. You have a new and better home waiting for you. Go there.

Scripture: 2 Peter 1:5-9: "So don't lose a minute in building on what you've been given, complementing your basic faith with good character, spiritual understanding, alert discipline, passionate patience, reverent wonder, warm friendliness, and generous love, each dimension fitting into and developing the others. With these qualities active and growing in your lives, no grass will grow under your feet; no day will pass without its reward as you mature in your experience of our Master Jesus. Without these qualities you can't see what's right before you, oblivious that your old sinful life has been wiped off the books." *The Message* by Eugene Peterson

Prayer: Dear Lord, lead us to avoid the temptation to return to an old destructive way of living. For those who have never been there, we pray they never will, and we give thanks that you care enough to lead us all away from destruction. As we lean on you for power and strength, we ask these things in your name, the name of Christ, Amen.

Finding that Elusive Balance

Over the last several months, and especially over the last week, I have investigated the beliefs of both the Amish and Quaker people. Something about their spirituality has drawn me to them. Understand that both of these religions have vastly different beliefs from each other and are especially different from mainstream religion in America as a whole. Though I do not agree with all of their theology, there is one aspect I have found not only interesting, but also missing in most of mainstream American religion.

That aspect can best be described as an inner peace, the peace that only comes from spending many hours in quiet peace away from the busy world we live in. Most Americans are doers. We are busy achieving things, and we carry this attitude over to our religion. I believe this has created a very surface spirituality in America that really leaves us not spiritual at all.

This week as the Amish people have had to deal with an unspeakable tragedy, I have found they handle it quite differently than many in our society. Most Americans cry for justice and change and look to blame authorities when wrong is done. The Amish instead have drawn upon their deep religious beliefs and faith in God. In reality, they have gone to the only place for real peace, and fortunately, they are in familiar territory.

Have they suffered hurt? Of course they have. Hurt has no boundaries. All you need do is look in the face of the Amish people, and you know their pain is real. Their outward response has revealed their inner peace.

Gertrude Huntington, an expert in Amish society, had this very telling quote, "The hurt is very great. But they don't balance the hurt with hate." How you respond to the most difficult circumstances will tell you everything about your inner peace.

Balance that can handle hurt without having hate does not come easily. It only comes from spending quiet moments alone with the Savior. Finding the place in your heart to avoid becoming bitter, hateful, and resentful only comes from allowing the Prince of Peace to reign in your heart.

We do not have to live our lives out as if we are in the 17th century to have peace, do we? The point is not what you do for a living, or what you wear, or if you live on a farm or in a townhouse in the city. The question is, do you spend time with the Savior? Let's close by asking some questions about ourselves:

- Do you attempt to overcome evil with evil?
- Are you bitter about something or with someone for a deed done years ago?
- Have you spent 15 minutes of peace and quiet in the last 24 hours?
- Have you spent any time with the Lord through study of His scriptures or prayer over the last 24 hours? Week?
- Are you addicted to cell phones, cable television, CD players, radios, and noise in general? A good way to find out the answer to that question is to just turn it all off and see how long you last.

What a different society we would live in if we could somehow find the inner peace that comes from a saving faith and peaceful time spent with Him. What a different world it would be if we could balance the hate in this world with the peace that passes all understanding.

My prayer is that in our churches and all of America we will have a revival, not of activities, but of peace. That type of revival is an inside job, and it will start first in quiet moments for all of us alone with the Lord.

Scriptures: 1 Timothy 2:2: "Pray this way for kings and all who are in authority so that we can live peaceful and quite lives marked by godliness and dignity." *New Living Translation*

1 Thessalonians 4:11 & 12: "Make it your goal to live a quite life minding your own business and working with your hands, just as we instructed you before. Then people who are not Christians will respect the way you live and you will not need to depend on others." *New Living Translation*

Prayer: Dear Lord, help us to make you a priority. Help us to slow down, be quiet, and feel your presence in a very real way. Lord, we ask these things in the name of Jesus Christ, our Savior. Amen.

Dental Hi-Jinks

I took one of my older children to the dentist the other day and got a little education in the process. We went in for a simple cleaning and some x-rays to see just how much more that gold mine is going to cost me. With several kids, I am a dentist's best buddy.

I was sitting out in the waiting room reading a good magazine when a friendly young lady came to the door and asked for Mr. Harris. Being that I don't go to the dentist real often with the kids, I was not sure what was coming. She took me to the back by my son and began to talk to me about his condition.

She said all was good except for one thing. He needs to give up the sodas. In the first split second, I had to figure out what a soda is. Being from Texas, everything is a "Coke," not a "soda," but that story is for another day. She went on to tell me that he had good teeth, but the sodas were doing a number on them.

This nice, friendly young lady then went on to tell me the whole family needs to give up sodas. At this point I laughed out loud; loud enough I am sure for the dentist next to me and his patient to hear. When I figured out she was not kidding, I tried to put my serious face on for a quick recovery. I would not want the word to get back to my wife that I was not adult enough at the dentist's office.

I listened to her good points on dental hygiene and paid close attention. I did not crack a smile. I was afraid she would look at my teeth. I even listened to the dentist chime in with an affirmative as one last time I heard the plea for the family to drop the sodas.

This all came at a really bad time for me because it was lunch-time, and I was about 200 feet away from a Biggie Coke at Wendy's. I have a slight addiction to Biggie Cokes, and guilt was starting to set in. How could I be doing this to my family, destroying their teeth with my careless drinking habits?

As I was waiting to check out at the dentist's office I decided to make a vow, one more Biggie for lunch, and then no more sodas, Cokes, or whatever you want to call them. A funny thing happened to me while I was standing in line. I looked to my left, and there, to my shock, was a Coke machine!!! I know it was a Coke machine because it had Cokes all around it. How could this be?

I just received a lecture on drinking sodas, and before I can get out of the office, they would have been glad to sell me as many as I want. What a double standard! I guess what goes on in the chair does not match what goes on at the front desk while you're checking out. I laughed out loud again.

You might say that perhaps the Coke machine is for employees. Does that make it any better? Of course not. If the nice lady is going to lecture patients about soda consumption, then she should pass her knowledge on to the folks who work with her as well. Don't they deserve the same warning I received in order to protect their family's teeth?

While I may find humor in a double standard at the dentist's office, the world surely does not find a double standard in the way we Christians live our lives quite so funny. They hear us talk about loving one another but hear us gossip and speak hatefully—especially towards others within the church. They hear us talk about sacrifice and servant-hood, but they see little service toward others. It's a mess, and it really is not funny.

Let's take one more step in the world of double standards. Parents, let's take aim at ourselves. Do we tell our children about the evils of drinking but have a few cool ones in the fridge? Do we bemoan the evils of pornography but keep a few good Sports Illustrated swimsuit editions hanging around the house? Or worse, do we cruise the net looking for illicit sites thinking no one will know?

Let's keep going. Do we encourage our children to abstain from sex before marriage but have no problem living with someone? Here is my favorite: do we try our hardest to get our children into a youth group or children's activities when we have little to do with the church ourselves? What do we expect?

I am not saying that if you have ever committed a sin you have no right to attempt to lead someone away from it. As a matter of fact, that is what I expect. If you have ever been duped by drugs, alcohol, pornography or any of the other evils of life, then you should stand up and tell those who come behind you what a pit from hell those additions are. As you do, your testimony should stand strong telling about a Christ that saved you from those evils. There is no double standard there, just transparent living, the kind Christ calls us to.

A double standard at a dentist's office? Oh, it makes me smile. Pass the soda. A double standard in my walk with Christ? Oh, it breaks His heart. There is nothing funny about that.

Scripture: Matthew 7:3-5: "Why do you look at the speck of saw dust in your brother's eye and pay no attention to the plank in your own eye? How can you say to your brother, "Let me take the speck out of your eye," when all the time there is a plank in your own eye? You hypocrite, first take the plank out of our own eye, and then you will see clearly to remove the speck from your brother's eye."

Prayer: Dear Lord, we thank you that you save us from our sin. Help us to share your redemption from sin with others who are suffering from the schemes of the evil one. Rescue us from the temptation to lead a double life. We ask these things in Christ's name, Amen.

What IF......

The other day I was talking to a friend and, in a nutshell, they made this statement, "I tend to make life harder than I should." My first thought was "who doesn't." All of our lives are filled with the "what ifs" that make life harder than it should be.

Let's look at that for a moment. What if we never lied and were completely honest with all around us? What if we never lusted—or worse yet, acted upon our lust? What if we never filled our eyes or ears with unholy things? What if we never got angry? What if we never said things we shouldn't have? What if we never hurt another person's feelings with our words or actions? What if we always thought of others and never had a selfish action or thought?

Let's stop and answer the question, what if we never did anything wrong? Life would be so much easier. We would have a truly wonderful life here on earth and just cruise into heaven. What a deal!

The odds of taking care of all the "what ifs" with a positive answer are about as good as the odds that the sun will not come up tomorrow. Nil. Nada. No way! I would love to tell you otherwise. I have yet to meet anyone, including myself, who has made it safely through life without falling into the pit at least once, most of us much more often than once.

Let's pretend that you do make it for just a moment. What then? Will your life not be wonderful? Once again, I have bad news. Though you may be doing the right things, those around you are just as prone to mess up as you are, and their mess-ups will make your life harder than it should be. The bottom line is there is no way to avoid the "what ifs." Life is going to be harder than we think it should be, and that is all there is to it.

Now, of course we need to be smart here and live our life in a pattern that follows Christ's as much as we can. We can only do this through the working of the Holy Spirit in our life. When we attempt to live without the working of God in our lives, we most assuredly will make it much harder than it should be, and we are doomed to fail and fail often.

The good news of the great "what ifs" of life is that we have a God that can overcome our "what ifs." He knows us well. He created us, you know. He knows we are prone to get off the beaten path. There is no question that He is the God of the second chance. He offers forgiveness of our sins. He assures us He will always be there for us. Best yet, He offers a life after this one in which we will not have to worry about any "what ifs." I am surely looking forward to that day.

Yes, indeed, life is harder than it should be in our eyes, and we tend to make things worse by our actions. Let me close this time with a few more "what ifs."

What if we didn't have a God that loved us? What if we didn't have a God that gives us second chances and allows us to overcome our "what ifs?" The answer is that life would not only be harder than it should be, it would be impossible. Praise God that He is the God that can indeed overcome the great "what ifs."

*Do you know the great God that overcomes the "what ifs" of life? Answer that one correctly and the other "what ifs" don't seem to hurt as much.

Scripture: 1 John 1:8-10: "If we claim that we're free of sin, we're only fooling ourselves. A claim like that is errant nonsense. On the other hand, if we admit our sins—make a clean breast of them—he won't let us down; he'll be true to himself. He'll forgive our sins and purge us of all wrongdoing. If we claim that we've never sinned, we out and out contradict God—make a liar out of him. A claim like that only shows off our ignorance of God." *The Message*

Prayer: Dear Lord, we thank you greatly for your love, that though we make a mess of things, you are always there for us, ready and willing to forgive. We thank you for heaven and that some day we will be free from these humanly bodies with their bent toward evil. We look forward to *forever* with you. We ask these things in Christ's name, Amen.

Tattooed

Let me place a disclaimer before we get too far into this devotional. I am not a big fan of the tattoo—never have been, never will be. That is my personal preference, and I hold nothing against those who have them, as long as they're not my kids.

Now down to business. The other day I am eating lunch and snooping like I always do. You know how it works when you eat lunch alone; you listen to other people's conversations and watch those who come in, just to pass the time. While looking around, I see a guy with this real mean-looking tattoo of a skull on his arm. If you looked at it, you would think this was some kind of gang member, or just a real tough guy.

Seeing this, my curiosity is aroused. I take a look at who is with him and expect to see some other tough guys all coming in for lunch together. Not quite. He has a little boy in tow and a wife to boot. He is helping with the little boy, and you can tell he really cares for him and his wife. Then I look at his shirt and find, to my surprise, that it is a Christian T-shirt telling of the grace of God and Jesus' death on the cross for us.

At that moment, I had to deal with the contradiction. What was tattooed on his arm did not match his actions or the shirt he wore on his back. In asking myself which one I believed, I immediately voted for the actions over what was etched into his arm.

Why? It works like this for me; the actions were what was happening then, and who knows when that tattoo was put on his arm. Maybe there was a time when he was a mean dude, but it did not appear to be now. Perhaps his past was shady (or maybe he just likes tattoos), but that did not appear to bother the little boy being taken care of by him or the wife with whom he was having sweet conversation.

Letting our imaginations run wild for a second, maybe there was a day when he carried a gun or belonged to a gang. Maybe there was a day when he used foul language as commonly as we use *if*, *and*, or *but*. Maybe there was a day when he cared little for God and laughed at people wearing Christian T-shirts.

Maybe that was all true, or maybe none of it was, but the deal is this—I can only make a call as to what that person is like right now. I do not know his past and, really, if I did, what would it change? It is the now that really matters—not just for him, but for all of us.

Maybe, just maybe, he wishes he could replace that tattoo of his former life or at least replace it with one of his now life. He knows that can't be done and so he moves on. Think about it for a moment. We are all in some way branded with our past. Though it may not be physical, people put a label on us, some rightfully so, and it sticks. No matter what we try, we cannot remove it.

Just some reminders as we think of the thought of being branded. First, be very careful what you do. In this life, what you do sticks. People seem to remember, especially the negative. Don't do anything you don't want to live with the rest of your life.

Secondly, it is a huge waste of time to worry about the past when there is plenty of today to take care of. What people think of you is their business; you cannot change it. You can only take care of your life today. Keep straining forward.

Lastly, though a tattoo is very difficult to get rid of in this life, God is the great eraser. God is in the business of making new creations when people truly make Him Lord of their lives.

Just a question to walk away with: "If people saw you today, what would they see engraved in your life?"

Scripture: Isaiah 49: 15-16: "Can a mother forget the baby at her breast and have no compassion on the child she has borne? Though she may forget, I will not forget you! See, I have engraved you on the palms of my hands; your walls are ever before me."

Prayer: Dear Lord, we are so very thankful that we are ever before you. Help us to live in such a way as to be a transmitter of your love to others. Be with us as we deal with the past, put it behind us, and move forward, experiencing your love and forgiveness fresh and new each day. We ask these things in Christ's name, Amen.

Labels

Labels are critical in our society. When you buy any product, you can count on a label that will tell you certain things about the product you are buying. The government even regulates what goes on certain labels.

Let's look at the common label for just a second and what it provides in the way of information. It tells you what the name of the product is. We can generally know what is inside the container simply by reading the name on the label. But if you can't, that is not a problem, because the label itself tells you what is inside, probably the most important part of the label.

The label also gives you instructions on how to use the product—how much to take if it is medicine, or cooking instructions if it is a food product. In our health-conscious world, another important part of the food label is that it tells us its nutritional value. Does it have sugar, or is it high in calories, etc.

Then, it tells us who made it; for some this is very important. Some people won't do anything but buy Craftsman tools or drink anything but Coke products. They believe in the quality work of who made the actual product.

We live in a world of labels. Unfortunately we have gotten in the habit of labeling people just as we label products. You're a cracker if you are white, a wet back if you are Mexican, retard if you have any learning disability, poor if you don't make as much as the next guy. Need more? No problem. If you are a Muslim, you are a terrorist; if you're from the south, you're a redneck, and if you're from the north, you're a liberal. The list is endless, and might I add, foolish. It insults the maker of the product.

Labels are sticky. They are almost impossible to remove. Once you get one, the world around us is very slow to remove it, if they wish to at all. Today, let me encourage you with some proper labels.

- Maker: You are a creation of God! Genesis 1:27: "So God created man in his own image, in the image of God he created him; male and female he created them."
- Craftsmanship: Fearfully and wonderfully made! Psalm 139: 14: "I praise you because I am fearfully and wonderfully made; your works are wonderful, I know that full well."
- Price: Paid in full! 1 John 4:10: "This is love: not that we loved God, but that he loved us and sent his Son as an atoning sacrifice for our sins."

Labels of this world got you down? Forget them—they're man-made. Remember your creator is unsurpassed in craftsmanship, and no one knows the product like He does.

Scripture: Psalm 139:13: "For you created my inmost being; you knit me together in my mother's womb."

Prayer: Dear Lord, help us to shake off the labels the world assigns to us and focus on the fact that we are your creation. Help us to build our self-esteem on your love for us, we ask these things in the name of Christ, Amen.

A Freefall

My guess is that two months ago, 90% of you could not have told me who Lisa Nowak is, though she had one of the most prestigious jobs in America as a Space Shuttle astronaut. My guess is most of you know her name now. Not because she was one of the brightest and well-respected astronauts. Or not because she garnered much praise and respect for her work on the shuttle last summer. Most of us know her now because she has been arrested in Florida under an attempted murder charge.

We watch in disbelief as a life freefalls into disaster, and we wonder how it could have ever happened. We hear statements like this in *People* magazine from Doug Peterson: "Everything I've ever seen gave evidence to me that Lisa was one of our good astronauts, she had all the right background credentials, skills and abilities." In the same article, her brother-in-law makes these statements: "She is a very loving mother and a caring person." Then he adds that she was someone who played by the rules. Hear his last statement: "To say this is out of character would be a gross understatement."

She is described as a loving mother of three and someone who played by the rules. She was a part of one of America's pride and joys, the space program. She was married for 19 years and lived in a wealthy suburb of Houston. In our minds, she had it all, and we ask ourselves how this could be. Here is how I see it.

1) Nothing is always as it seems on the surface.
2) No one has it all.
3) And this is my main point: **we are all just one slip from a complete freefall.** We need to be careful.

Evidently her marriage of many years was faltering, and she had fallen in love with a co-worker. Her sister said in the *People* magazine article that Nowak never quite recovered from losing three former colleagues in the 2003 Columbia shuttle explosion. Stress and heartache at home, stress and disaster at work, and who knows what else, and in just a few months all she has worked for is gone, for now anyway.

People seem shocked that someone so smart and gifted could fall. I laugh at that, because what that is saying is that only uneducated, average folks make mistakes or lose control. Nothing in the world could be further from the truth.

Would you like some examples? No problem:

Moses: Brought up with the best education of his day. Looks around one day and sees no one watching, commits murder, and before he knows it, he has lost his standing in the court, his room in the palace, and is wandering around in the desert.

David: A strong king, well loved by the people, known as a great warrior and fierce leader, a man known as one after God's own heart. He, too, looks around, but he sees a beautiful young lady, commits adultery, then tries to cover it up, and commits murder. He finds himself broken in spirit and out of fellowship with God. Though he finds mercy, things are never quite the same.

Solomon: David's son, and well known as the wisest man ever. He knows the consequences of sin, but he, too, lets his guard down and brings in many foreign wives with many different gods. This wise man finds himself far from the instruction and will of God. Oh, how the mighty have fallen.

These are just a few examples from the Bible, but you need only look around your neighborhood or office to find someone who, in a moment, lost their way and lost it all. They seemed to have everything, or so you thought, and then, *boom*, the bottom falls out.

My heart breaks for all concerned in this story. As in all cases, there are far more than just one or two victims here. I can only pray for healing for all involved and for the grace of God to cover each person.

I pray we can learn from these circumstances and stay on our guard so as to avoid a freefall that will lead to heartache in our lives. There is much to learn. Let's ponder a few of the lessons.

- Education, wealth, and success do not guarantee a happy life. Real and lasting joy comes from God.
- We have never arrived completely until the Lord takes us home. We must never drop our guard against the evils and temptations of this world.
- When the cracks begin to form, we need as many godly friends as we can find to help put things back together again. We need friends we can be real with and who will tell us what we need to hear, not what we want to hear. The devil's plan is to isolate us. We need to avoid that at all cost.
- Grace is always available; if someone has God, they have never lost it all.

That last point is where I want to begin closing. It may indeed seem as if this freefall has left an astronaut totally lost. She may end up in jail, she will likely never fly again, and she almost certainly will end up divorced. Honor, praise, and public acclaim will never be hers again. They are replaced with shame, depression, heartache, and disappointment to name a few. I am sure those things crush Ms. Nowak's heart, but I have good news for her and for all of us who have fallen, and that is, God is still there.

We have a loving God that is in the recovery business. He loves all His children, even those who have made a mess of things. Sometimes it is only after everything has been taken away that we can see God more clearly. When the dust settles, He is there. He always is.

Are your freefalling? Look up before you crash. God is there. Have you hit rock bottom? Look around. Others may have left you, but He never will.

Scripture: Galatians 6:3-5: "If anyone thinks he is something when he is nothing, he deceives himself. Each one should test his own actions. Then he can take pride in himself, without comparing himself to somebody else, for each one should carry his own load."

Prayer: Dear Lord, help us to keep ourselves from falling or from comparing ourselves to others. Assist us in staying away from the evils of this world and the temptations that are all around us. Lord, we thank You that You love us even when we make a mess of things. We are thankful that though we are weak, You are strong. We ask all these things in the precious name of Jesus Christ, our Savior. Amen.

Knowing No Boundaries

If you have never witnessed a preschool soccer match, you are missing a real treat. These guys and gals are a lot of fun to watch as they move in a swarm around the ball.

Here are some things you will see at a game of preschool soccer. They all hang out around the ball, one big blob of preschoolers around one defenseless ball. They love to kick the ball, and it really does not matter which way; they just kick it. They also know no boundaries. They just keep kicking the ball, and if the referee does not pick up the ball, they will keep right on into the next county!

Preschoolers playing soccer are a lot like us; without someone to stop us we will probably overstep our boundaries! Though most don't like it, we need boundaries in life. Show me someone who has no boundaries, and I will show you someone whose life is chaotic and completely out of control. God gives us boundaries not because He is some kind of egomaniac God who wants to boss us around, but because he knows without limits in life, we will find ourselves in deep trouble.

Let me give you some thoughts using preschool soccer to get my point across:

1) **Don't follow the crowd.** In preschool soccer, the crowd just keeps on going; the crowd knows no limits. Such is the crowd in life. Don't get caught up in the world's games and short-term pleasures. The majority is not always right, and when it comes to morals, normally is not. Be careful of hanging with the crowd.

2) **Listen to the whistle of the referee.** Most of the time, the referee blows the whistle but preschool soccer players just keep on going until he has to take drastic measures. We need to listen to God. When he blows the whistle on what we are doing, we best pay attention. If God puts an uncomfortable feeling in your spirit, that is a queue to listen up. You are probably too close to the out-of-bounds line. STOP before it is too late.

3) The game is best played within the confines of the rules. If preschoolers were left to just run all over the county, there would never be a focus on the goal, only on the ball. The big picture is the goal; you cannot score if you are out-of-bounds. This is very much the same in life. God created life to be enjoyed. He knows what is best. Do not get caught looking at the short-term pleasure and miss out on the long-term goal.

Providing limits to Americans who love to do their own thing is not always a popular thing. God is not looking for popular. He is looking for what is best for His children.

Let me close with one last thought about boundaries that all of us can appreciate: We have a God whose love knows no boundaries. His love is limitless, and though we step out of bounds often, He never stops loving us. *Now there is an ignoring of limits we can all appreciate!*

Exercise: At some point in time today, take a few minutes to do two things:

1) Ask God to reveal to you where you might be creeping up on the out-of-bounds line.
2) Thank Him for his abounding and unconditional love.

Scriptures: Psalm 36: 5-7: "Your love, O LORD, reaches to the heavens, your faithfulness to the skies. Your righteousness is like the mighty mountains, your justice like the great deep. O LORD, you preserve both man and beast. How priceless is your unfailing love! Both high and low among men find refuge in the shadow of your wings."

Prayer: Dear Lord, we thank you for your unfailing love. We praise your name that you reveal to us your limits. Help us to rest within the confines of what is best so that we can enjoy our days on this earth. We ask these things in the name of Christ, Amen.

Happy Hour

On my oldest son Andrew's 18th birthday, we held a special celebration. We invited a round table of influential men within his life to come and share a meal with us. At that meal, we went around the table and each man had a chance to share some words of wisdom with Andrew.

It was a wonderful night, one I will never forget. As we went around the table, we came to my father. He stood up and gave his words of advice, words I will not forget, and words we would all do well to heed.

He told my son to make sure every day he had a "Happy Hour." Now be careful where you go with this. When most of us think of a happy hour, we think of a couple of guys sitting in a bar drinking alcohol for half price. This waste of time was not what my father had in mind.

He went on to elaborate: each day, my father went on to say, find one hour to do what you want to do. Find time each day to enjoy at least one hour a day. Those were his words, nothing earth shattering, nothing super-deep, but good words—and they have stuck with me to this day. Sad to say that I have not always taken his advice, but I do give it a shot. You should too.

We only get 24 hours a day. We only get a certain amount of time on this earth. Life is a gift. We should treat it as such. Let's face it—most Americans pride ourselves on how busy we can be, on what we can accomplish. I am positive when we are all older, we are going to find that being so busy was foolish and having a Happy Hour every day would have been far more productive.

Do you love music? Then find an hour to listen to it, to play it if you can, to sing if that is your deal. Maybe you have a young family, and they are your passion; take them to the park, play with them, sit and watch them play. Just enjoy them. Maybe you love to read. Take a moment at the beginning of the day or a quiet moment at night and read.

Do you love to serve? Well, get to work! Find a place to serve: a soup kitchen, a retirement center. My father reads to children and listens to them share their thoughts in the public school. Schools, libraries, nursing homes, and churches all need people who are willing to serve. If you love to serve, then serve.

The lists of things to do during your Happy Hour are as endless as the people who read this devotional. God gives each of us different loves and desires. The only cautions I can throw at you are: make sure your Happy Hour is not a sinful thing; make sure it does not consume you (we tend to go to extremes); and make sure it does not lead you to neglect of the things of God. Other than that, go for it.

Is your life boring? Do you just wander through each day waiting to get through it? Is your life filled with endless activity, but little fulfillment? Friends, what you need is a Happy Hour. I think both my earthly father and my heavenly Father would agree.

Scripture: Ecclesiastes 3:1-6: "There is a time for everything, and a season for every activity under heaven: a time to be born and a time to die, a time to plant and a time to uproot, a time to kill and a time to heal, a time to tear down and a time to build, *a time to weep and a time to laugh, a time to mourn and a time to dance,* a time to scatter stones and a time to gather them, a time to embrace and a time to refrain, a time to search and a time to give up, a time to keep and a time to throw away, a time to tear and a time to mend, a time to be silent and a time to speak, a time to love and a time to hate, a time for war and a time for peace."

Prayer: Dear Lord, lead us to love and enjoy all of life, to not take ourselves too seriously and to honor you in all of our days. We ask these things in the name of Christ, Amen.

Perrier — Or Is It?

I was visiting with a co-worker the other day, and I looked down on the desk and noticed she had a bottle of Perrier sitting there. Perrier is the high-dollar bottled water from France for those of you who do not know such things.

I proceeded to give her a hard time about being a big-timer and drinking high-dollar water. She, on the other hand, told me how she came across it and then offered me a bottle. Now, when I was younger, much younger (like about 20 years ago), I used to drink Perrier. This was before everyone walked around with bottled water, so I thought I was something back then to be drinking Perrier. Of course, I was wrong, but that is another story. Bottom line is I accepted, and I took off with my Perrier.

Of course, this generated a lot of conversation with people who know me as I proudly walked around with my bottle of Perrier. The same things I had said to my co-worker, people were saying to me. They were kidding me about drinking high-dollar water, but the deal was they were only half-right. You see, I drank the original water in the bottle quickly, and then after that, I filled it up with water from the water fountain.

The bottle said France but the inside said City of Dallas. To everyone it looked as though I was spending the extra dollars to partake of some exotic water from Europe, but if they had opened up the bottle and drank it, they would have found a very familiar taste. You see, the inside did not match the outside.

There is the point of the day. When we call ourselves Christians, many times we put on happy faces, pretend as though everything is okay, say "God bless you" and "Praise God" at just the right times and generally put on our Christian look. On the outside, we look as if we have it all together, but on the inside, well, that is a different story.

Anyone can look Christian on the outside. It really is not that hard to do. Just a few hours at your local church and you can pick up on the lingo and actions of what people think a Christian should say and act like. But when it really counts is when God opens up the bottle and looks at the inside at your heart.

I dare say there are a great many Perrier-looking Christians out there with tap-water hearts on the inside.

Sooner or later, the bottle will be opened. We will let our guard down and what is in our hearts will be revealed to those listening or watching. Then people will know who or what we really are. Are we counterfeit or are we the real thing?

Test for the day:

1) Do you harbor hate and envy of other people in your heart?
2) Do you attend church or Christian functions to be seen or to really worship? Do you care if you are seen at all?
3) Do you act one way at church and another way at the office, or, more importantly, at home?
4) If God were to open up your heart today, what would He find there: a love for Him or a love for self?

Perrier or tap water? Follower of Christ or counterfeit? He who will eventually open the bottle already knows. Why pretend to everyone else? Get real. Start today.

Scriptures: 1 Samuel 16:7: "But the Lord said to Samuel, 'Do not consider his appearance or his height, for I have rejected him. The Lord does not look at the things man looks at. Man looks at the outward appearance, but the Lord looks at the heart.'"

Matthew 15:17-19: "Don't you see that whatever enters the mouth goes into the stomach and then out of the body? But the things that come out of the mouth come from the heart, and these make a man 'unclean.' For out of the heart come evil thoughts, murder, adultery, sexual immorality, theft false testimony, slander."

Prayer: Dear Heavenly Father, help us to lean on you so that our outside matches our inside. Deliver us from a lifestyle of hypocrisy and help us to be real, and help that realness be a reflection of your love coming from our hearts. We ask these things in Christ's name, Amen.

Best Idea—Read the Instructions First!

I was sitting around a table the other day with some friends, and they began to tell me of their experience at a local gas station. A man was doing some yard work, and he evidently hit something that sparked a fire. Then things got interesting.

Of course, like all good men, they decided they could put it out themselves. And, of course, like many good men in this situation, they were wrong. They were hitting this fire with everything they could find, but it continued to spread. My friend was calling "911" and watching all this go on.

Then someone from the inside made the wise decision to get a fire extinguisher. He came running out of the building, extinguisher in hand, ready to be the hero who put out the fire. He came to the fire, aimed, and nothing happened. He looked down and realized he had not taken out the pin that allows the extinguisher to work. He had to step back and figure out how to operate the machinery.

One of my friends made this statement concerning the gentleman with the fire extinguisher: "He should have read the directions before he used it." I told her, yes, it would be best to read the instructions before the fire starts. This got me to thinking.

How many of us read the instructions before the fire starts? We would be wise to do so. As a matter of fact, we could avoid a lot of fires in life if we would simply read the instructions and heed them.

Many of the fires in our life are self-inflicted because we ignore the instructions in the Bible, and we think we can get by on our own. We stand too close to the fire and eventually get burned. Why this should surprise us, I will never know.

Many turn to God only when the spark of sin has turned into a raging fire. We look to His word and His comfort only after we have exhausted our human efforts. When we work it that way, we waste a lot of time catching up. While the fire is burning hotter and hotter, we are scrambling back to God.

As a person who has stood in the fire, let me assure you that it is much easier to put out a little one than a big one. Will there be fires in our life? Yes. Can we be ready for them? No doubt.

Imagine this: the yardman starts a fire, the man working the counter sees it, walks outside with his extinguisher, and puts it out. They turn around, walk in. End of story. No "911." No working themselves to death trying to put it out. No fire department called. Quick and easy.

Imagine this, you step too close to the fire of sin, you notice things are out of control. You call on God, you read His word, you call on Godly friends, and before you know it things have cooled off. No long-term consequences, no charred life to deal with, no length of time out of fellowship with God. Quick and easy. That is how it was meant to be.

One side note here is that normally when we find ourselves in a fire, it is because we have put the instructions on the shelf and decided we can handle things on our own. As a matter of fact, that attitude is normally what leads to the spark in the first place.

One last illustration I want you to think about. Everywhere you go, there are fire extinguishers all around. Many see them, but in reality, few know how to use them. Same with Bibles. They are all around, always best sellers. Many have them, few use them.

Next time you find yourself in a fire, make sure you have read the instructions for your safe return first.

Friendly Helps to Stay Out of or Avoid the Fire:

- Read the Word daily. Make a habit of it.
- Never play with fire (sin). It burns. Prevention is the best medicine.
- Don't wait! At the first sight of trouble, get help.
- Remember, you cannot put it out yourself. Use prayer, scriptures, and worship.
- Pride will never extinguish a fire. It only keeps you in it longer. Humble yourself before the Lord, and He will lift you up. (James 4:10)

Scripture: Romans 8:5-6: "Those who live according to the sinful nature have their minds set on what that nature desires; but those who live in accordance with the Spirit have their minds set on what the Spirit desires. The mind of sinful man is death, but the mind controlled by the Spirit is life and peace."

Prayer: Dear Father, help us to use your word and your Holy Spirit to live lives that are pleasing to you. Help us to avoid sin, but when we find ourselves in it, convict us so that we might flee from it as soon as possible. We thank you for your forgiveness of sin and how you love us. In Christ's name, Amen.

Guilty or Not Guilty

Recently I read an article about a young lady whose two-year-old had apparently been abducted. To make a long story short, she had become a suspect, or I believe the wording was *a person of interest*, due to some of her answers not matching up. She went on Nancy Grace's program on CNN and was grilled by the host. She did not answer the questions to the host's satisfaction or anyone else's for that matter. Maybe she was guilty or maybe she was just confused or did not handle being on television very well. No one really knows with certainty.

Just before the show came on the air, this young lady took her own life. Her father was quoted as saying his daughter was not handling the pressure of all the reporters very well. I just thought to myself, what a very sad story for all concerned.

If indeed this young lady had something to do with the disappearance of her child, then we may never really know what happened. If she was innocent, then what a horrible tragedy for each family member involved. Also in the back of my mind, I keep wondering how the host of the program is doing. The only word I saw from her was a note from someone in her camp that did not sound real sympathetic.

Guilty or not, one thing is for sure—now we never know all the facts. There are a dozen different directions we could go with this story, but let's focus on the zealous news reporter that hounded the young lady. Part of the quote I read said she was concerned with the little boy, as indeed we all should be. But there was indeed another life at stake here, a young lady missing a little boy and being suspected of his disappearance. Imagine for one second what that would feel like, especially if you were not guilty. We should be very careful in how and what makes us judge people.

We should be zealous for what is right. For that, there should be no question. But we should be very careful of how we judge, because 90% of the time, we do not know the whole story. I have learned this lesson the hard way on several different occasions over the last 30 years of my life.

This all reminds me of a somewhat less serious incident that occurred about 25 years ago that has effected how I judge situations. My best friend and I were big baseball fans, and my friend loved the Dodgers and hated the Astros. It just so happened that the Astros had a pitcher named J.R. Richard. He was very good, young, and had a great future.

But throughout one season he kept complaining to the team that he just was not feeling right. The team ran some tests and found a blood clot that they did not seem to think was too serious at first. Even the team doctor suggested that Richard might have mental problems. With that knowledge under their belt, many reporters and fans alike were accusing Richard of faking it. I remember my friend rode him hard and often called him a dog for not pitching.

During July of 1980, both of us went to an Astros game, and while there, I could see that the fans and press were really on Richard. I will never forget watching him walk around the Astrodome going through his workout and wondering what was really wrong with him while many, including my buddy, were riding him hard.

Just a few weeks after we went to the game came the disturbing report that Richard had suffered a serious stroke while playing pitch on the sidelines. He, in some way, had been feeling the onset of this stroke and no one had been able to detect it. While everyone was giving him a hard time and questioning his heart for the game, he was dealing with the knowledge that something wasn't right, and no one understood or had compassion.

The stroke affected Richard for the rest of his life and effectively ended his career; he was never the same after that. Honestly, I have not been either. Even though I was not one of the people riding him hard, it taught me that you just never really know, and that to pretend otherwise is foolish. I am now quite sure and believe it is always better to give someone the benefit of the doubt and be wrong than to pass judgment too quickly on not enough facts.

No matter if we admit it or not, we all, in some way, pass judgment about other people's lives quite often. The fact is that we are in no position to judge in the first place. That job is better left to God who knows all the facts and hearts of those involved. Why should we concern ourselves with something God is far better at than us?

Guilty or Not? God knows, and He will eventually make the call. Let's leave it up to him.

Scripture: Romans 14:10-12: "So where does that leave you when you criticize a brother? And where does that leave you when you condescend to a sister? I'd say it leaves you looking pretty silly—or worse. Eventually, we're all going to end up kneeling side by side in the place of judgment, facing God. Your critical and condescending ways aren't going to improve your position there one bit. Read it for yourselves in scripture: 'As I live and breathe,' God says, 'every knee will bow before me; Every tongue will tell the honest truth that I and only I am God.' So tend to your knitting. You've got your hands full just taking care of your own life before God." *The Message*

Prayer: Dear Lord, we thank you for your grace, that you are a fair and forgiving judge that sees those who love you through the blood of Christ. Simply, we say thanks for not giving us what we deserve. We ask these things in Christ's name, Amen.

Daddy Can Do It

I coach a little league baseball team, and it is always a wonderful experience to hear what the children have to say. There is so much to learn from their simple and honest words.

I always like to give words of encouragement to them, especially to those who are not the best players on the team. I always have a soft spot in my heart for the not-so-athletic.

The other day at practice, I walked by third base and there just happened to be Anna. Now Anna has never played baseball before, but she has a willing smile and a good spirit. So I stopped by and told her how much I appreciated her being on my team, and I let her know that I thought that by the end of the season she would improve a great deal. Her answer made me smile.

Anna quickly agreed with me that she would indeed improve, and she gave me one quick reason—her father. She said, "I will, with my father helping me." (I wish he played on my team.) Anna knows she is going to get better because she knows her father is going to help, and she knows he has a history of being good at what he does. I just loved her confidence in her father.

When I think of Anna's confidence in her father, I cannot help but think of my relationship with my heavenly Father. You see, I know I can do better in life. Like Anna in baseball, I have plenty of room for improvement, and like Anna, I know that if my life is to become more Godly, it will not be because of anything I do, but because of what God can do. You see, I have confidence in God because he has a long history of being good at what He does.

The good thing about Anna is that she knows that on her own it (getting better) is just not going to happen. But she can smile with confidence at her prospects because she trusts that her father will help her, and she has released her improvement into his hands. You see, it is a trust and release issue. When we trust God, we can release our lives into His hands. It is no longer about us making our lives more Godly. We are trusting in God that He can do it, and that takes all the pressure off. When we learn to do that, we too can smile with confidence at our future prospects.

Scripture: Philippians 1:6: "Being confident of this, that he who began a good work in you will carry it to completion until the day of Christ Jesus."

Philippians 4:13: "I can do everything through him who gives me strength."

Prayer: Father, help us to find a corner of our spiritual lives that needs improvement and release it to you. Help us to have the courage that when you speak to us about change that we will be willing to take the steps you ask. Thank You, Father, that you give us the strength to make it through each day. In Christ's name, Amen.

The Road I Would Least Like to Travel

I hesitate to continue to refer to my experiences over the last seven weeks because I understand that they are my experiences, not yours, and that I may feel them deeply, but that you probably don't. With that risk in mind, I need to share another devotional thought with you. This time, it's about going where you don't really want to go.

Whoever says, "I want to lose my job just as my kids enter college?" Or who says, "I am so glad I lost my wife at such a young age?" Who says, "I am so glad my kids have been rebellious?" Or, "My parents are in great need of care, and I have no room to care for them or money to pay for it?" While I spent my days in the NICU, I noticed a group of great people, but I never noticed anyone really rejoicing that they were there.

I must admit that people who have it all together during difficult moments make me nervous and extremely skeptical. Some, of course, do have it all together, but the majority, just like you and me, are trying to cope the best they know how and are taking it one day at a time.

If we had our way, of course, we would never experience difficulties in life. We would sail right along, and the sun would always shine. Good health would be our constant friend. Our kids would always mind, not to mention they would always do well in school. Our boss would give us the money we deserve. Our family would be the picture of harmony. And we would never argue with our spouse.

Here is the deal. We don't have it our way, and so many times in life all of us will have to travel roads that we would just as soon avoid. Seven weeks ago, I was expecting the normal—good pregnancy for my wife, healthy baby born, the family celebrating, the insurance paying, the baby coming home in three days, and life being great. That, unfortunately, was not in the plans and, thus, I have begun to travel an unfamiliar road of hospitals, insurance issues and government programs, not to mention disappointment at first. Fear of the

255

unknown has become a constant companion. I have learned new meaning to the words "taking it one day at a time."

If I had been given the choice, of course, I would not have traveled this road, but no one asked me, and here I am. I am sure of this—God has something in it for me, something to draw me closer to Him. He has already used it to draw me closer to Him and to reveal Himself in ways I never knew existed. So what if I had traveled my road? What would I have missed? Good question—and here are some answers to that.

- I would have missed the chance to be a real father to my family, helping them through difficult times. I had become lazy in that area and had a sudden wake-up call.
- I would have missed the chance to be a better husband. I would have missed meaningful conversations, holding hands, helping with chores, protecting her from business aspects as she cared for our child, and crying together. I feel closer to my wife than I have in a long time.
- I would have missed my older children stepping up to the plate in a big way. I would have missed seeing them act as adults, which, of course, they are, but it is hard to admit. I would have missed watching them love and care for Gracie. I would have missed them crying and holding her with compassion.
- I would have missed meeting a whole set of people whose very lives are to care for sick babies and their families.
- I would have missed a hundred conversations about God that would have never happened otherwise.
- I would have missed sitting with people and really for once understanding at least a little how they feel.
- I would have missed some great phone calls with close friends and some family members I had not talked to for months or years.
- I would have missed seeing how really wonderful my church family is. I had watched with admiration as they cared for people in the past, and now I was able to receive it. What a family!

- I would have missed knowing what it really means to "feel the prayers" of friends, family, and people I do not even know.
- The biggest loss would have been this: I would have missed holding Gracie and looking in her eyes and loving her so much, wanting to whisk her up in my arms, and make sure life is good to her.

I could have gone on for another three pages, but I believe you get the point. Would I have chosen to travel this road? No. But look what I would have missed. I know I have just begun a new journey in life, but I am certain God is there with me because he proved to be there for me as we took the first steps.

It is hard to see at times, but God has a plan for our lives, and I am thankful He reveals it to us slowly; otherwise, of course, we could not handle it. Maybe God has started you on an unwanted road. Know this—He goes there with you. Know this—He cares for you. And know this—He does not waste any experience in life on you. Each one comes with a purpose. Sometimes the lessons learned are hard, but with God they come with a purpose.

I am no expert on difficult roads. Many of you have been on them for years and have far more experience than I. But this I know— God's light shines brightest on the roads we least want to travel.

Scripture: 2 Corinthians 1:3 and 4: "Praise be to the God and Father of our Lord Jesus Christ, the Father of compassion and the God of all comfort, who comforts us in all our troubles, so that we can comfort those in any trouble with the comfort we ourselves have received from God."

Prayer: Dear Lord, we honestly do not understand your ways. We struggle with tough roads and circumstances; we ask not that you show us the reason why but that we simply feel your presence while on the journey. You are a good God, and we praise your name that you care for us and walk with us! We ask these things in the precious name of Jesus our Savior.

On your Knees?

Over the last month or two, I have had the privilege on several occasions to take my 14-month-old daughter, Gracie, to her speech and occupational therapy sessions. Gracie is doing quite well, and we love the people that work with her.

Speech seems to be a piece of cake for her, not too much stress, and Gracie does what she is asked when she can keep her attention on the task at hand. She has a habit of checking out all the people around her (a bit nosy like her dad).

On the other hand, there is occupational therapy. Gracie is not quite so fond of the activity that goes on during these thirty minutes. For a while she will play and all is good. But then the hard work begins, and she is not too enthusiastic about one specific part of this therapy.

Gracie is getting around very well, and she does it in a way I have never seen before. She scoots on her bottom wherever she wants to go. I can look at her one minute, and then, *zoom*, she is across the floor the next. It really is very impressive how she pulls this off.

This works just fine for Gracie, but Cheri, her physical therapist, knows she needs to crawl. Gracie does not think this is such a grand idea. Thus, there is a conflict between the two, one trying not to crawl and the other trying to get her to.

Cheri is good at what she does, and she will use her skills to entice Gracie to move forward for something. As she does, she will then take Gracie's legs and put them into the crawling position, which of course means putting her on her knees. Gracie fights this with all she has and will only stay in the position for just a moment before she finds herself back on her bottom.

They go around and around with this, the one who knows best working to get the other to do what is best by getting her on her knees. It is the same with us and God.

God wants us on our knees; we think there are better ways.

We, like Gracie, find ways to get around what is best. We think our way is the easiest, and so we try that first. Our way still gets us around, and so we can't imagine why God would want us to do anything different. "Hey, it works," we think, and onward we go scooting along on our own path.

The Lord may be working on you and putting you in some very difficult positions all in order to bring you to your knees where you need to be. Crawling does not seem to be exciting to Gracie, and it does not seem to be that exciting to us as well. We want to fly into what we want without ever taking it our knees. Unfortunately when we do that, it leaves out a necessary step and disaster occurs.

Then where do we go? You got it. On our knees, asking God for help. God wants you to reverse the process because He knows best how to help you walk for the long haul. A little trust goes a long way.

Gracie one day will walk, I am sure of it. But only after those who love her and know what is best for her do their utmost to put her in the proper position. Trust me—God is doing the same with you. Though you may be fighting Him, He is working in your best interest.

Do you want to walk or scoot? Stop resisting; go to your knees. You will be walking before you know it.

Scripture: Psalm 95:5-6: "The sea is his, for he made it, and his hands formed the dry land. Come, let us bow down in worship, let us kneel before the Lord our maker."

Prayer: Dear Heavenly Father, help us to not resist the urge to pray but to be persistent in praying. Help us when our faith is weak; give us resolve and the knowledge that your way is best. Lead us to be people of prayer. We ask these things in the name of Jesus Christ, Amen.

Keeping the Windows Rolled Up

I am a great guy, really I am. Okay, maybe not that great, but goodness, I was a good guy yesterday for a few minutes anyway. While I was talking to a group of folks I work with, we received the news that it was raining hard outside. You know how it works. Everyone gets that look on their face, they grab their keys, and they start for the door because they left their windows down. One of the ladies started for the door, and I said, "I will go out and roll up your window for you." For a moment, she had a stunned look on her face. I guess she did not realize what a great guy I am. After the initial shock that I was willing to do it for her, she gave me her keys and showed me where her car was. She stood at the door, and I took off in the pouring rain and fierce lightening.

I took off for the car and when I got there, I unlocked it, jumped in, and found, much to my surprise, that every window was rolled up to the top. Nothing needed to be done. I had risked my life for nothing. Well, okay maybe it was not that serious. I headed back to the office. Instead of giving her a hard time about this, I was determined to keep being a great guy. I just told her all was okay and handed her back her keys. She apologized.

As we turned around, another co-worker was standing at the door with her keys in hand. Of course, being the great guy that I am, and having no other choice since I had already gone out in the rain for the other lady, I grabbed her keys and headed out again. This car was even further out, and by the time I reached it, I was soaked. Once again, I got to the car, opened the door, looked around at all the windows, and just as with the first car, all her windows were already up. I double checked the situation and headed back to the office, handed her keys back to her, and she apologized as well.

One rainstorm, two runs in the rain, and two nervous folks who were worried about something that they never should have been. Isn't that so us? We are fine when the sun is shining, but let a storm blow in, and we lose focus, get nervous, and start sending Jesus to take care of windows that are already shut.

We have a bad habit of worrying about things that are already taken care of by God. That unexpected pregnancy a little later in life? God is the Creator. That window is rolled up. We lose our job? God knows our need. No water getting in here. That window is airtight. You hear disturbing news at the doctor's office? God is the Great Physician. No need getting wet. Rest assured, He is in control.

Perhaps it is not worry I am talking about so much here, but fear. It was fear that sent me out in the rain. They were afraid the rain would ruin the inside of their cars. It is fear that has us running in circles in life when things happen that we cannot control. One of the hardest aspects of faith is to trust a God we cannot see with our lives. Yet it is the growth of this trust in God that drives out fear and leads us to a better understanding of His power and love.

Here are a couple of closing thoughts in an attempt to tie this all together. One thought is that though Jesus may have shut the window, He left us with words of assurance. He is such a loving God that in times of need, when you really just need another bit of assurance, He will do a double-check for you. That's because He is the God of peace and compassion. My second thought is that my friends parked their cars, rolled up their windows, and came into the office only a few hours before the rain hit. How soon we forget once the rains come! Next time the storm comes, slow down, don't panic, and remember—He rolled that window up for you not too long ago.

Scripture: Psalms 56:3-4: "When I am afraid, I will trust in you. In God whose word I praise, in God I trust; I will not be afraid. What can mortal man do to me?"

Prayer: Loving father in heaven, have us to learn to trust you more and more each day. Help us to stand strong in the storms of life knowing you will never leave us or forsake us, that you are indeed an ever-present help in danger. Thank you for being such a peace-giving God. We ask these things in Christ's name, Amen.

Little is Much...

We live in a world that recognizes success by numbers: how much and how many. At work, the boss gets the biggest office; in sports, the best get the largest salaries; and don't forget your friends who judge their efforts by having the biggest toys.

I would love to tell you people who work at ministry for a living are not tempted by this "big equals success" mentality, but many of us fall into that trap just like everyone else. We judge our success by things like how many people we have in church, or how large and shiny our buildings are, or how many people we are able to serve.

Before I move too far, I want you to know that big is not bad—just the lust for it and the objectivity we lose by chasing it. People who are passionate about what they do are most likely to fall into this trap. Anyone who loves what they do has a natural tendency to be passionate. People who minister love what they do; at times, this passion can blur our vision and affect our priorities.

Before you tune this one out and say, "this devotional is meant for the pastors and church workers of America, not me," let me reel you back in. In reality, this devotional is for the people who are just the opposites; the unpaid and underappreciated.

When we make a decision to follow Christ, we have made a decision to join in His ministry. That might mean you feed the hungry at a shelter or spend time watching your neighbor's kids for free because you know they could not afford to pay for day care. It might mean you teach Sunday school at church, or it could be that you make the people in the cubes around you feel special on their birthday at work.

It could be that you spend your time in prayer at the house because you physically can't get out, or you care for the elderly at a local senior center. The list of ministries is endless. Chances are, you will never get paid. Chances are even better you don't care to get paid. People who are truly passionate have the proper perspective, and money and recognition are low on their list.

The world has a way of giving the people who minister in seemingly small places what I call "ministry self-esteem" issues. Not today, not in this devotional. I say let it go. If you do it for God, then your ministry is as big as the God you serve. Today we tip our hat to the little guy doing great things for God in small and unappreciated places.

A friend of mine showed me a hymn written to encourage those who minister in seemingly small ways in out-of-way places. Let this song bring you encouragement. You ones faithful to the task deserve it.

"Little Is Much When God Is In It"
By Kittie J. Suffield

In the harvest field now ripened,
There's a work for all to do.
Hark, the voice of God is calling,
To the harvest calling you.

Little is much when God is in it.
Labor not for wealth or fame.
There's a crown and you can win it,
If you go in Jesus' name.

Does the place you're called to labor
Seem so small and little known?
It is great if God is in it,
And He'll not forget His own.

Little is much when God is in it.
Labor not for wealth or fame.
There's a crown and you can win it,
If you go in Jesus' name.

When the conflict here is ended
And our race on earth is run,
He will say, if we are faithful,
"Welcome home, my child, well done."

Little is much when God is in it.
Labor not for wealth or fame.
There's a crown and you can win it,
If you go in Jesus' name.

Prayer: Dear Lord, Remind us of our personal ministries that you have given us, the importance they play in the lives of others, and the blessings we receive by following your call. We ask these things in Christ name, Amen.

How is Your Favorable Rating?

Needless to say, Tiger Woods has been in the news lately. But if you pause and give it thought, he is always in the news, only this time it is not in a good light.

When it comes to golf, only Jack Nicklaus stands with him in greatness. When it comes to mental toughness in any sport, I have never witnessed anyone close to as tough. He intimidates all who play against him.

There is one other area that Tiger is the absolute best at: marketing. No one, and that even includes Michael Jordan, has been as good at it as Tiger. He cultivated an image and turned that image into a business that has made over one billion dollars. He is the first athlete to ever turn that kind of money.

In front of the camera, on the course, and in the magazines you could see Tiger selling you everything from clothing to cars. He made much more money outside of golf than he did in front of it. Why? Because Tiger was just as great at his public image as he is in golf.

Before Tiger became a regular on TMZ and The National Enquirer instead of the golf channel, his favorable rating was a stunning 84 percent. Being seen in a favorable light by the world meant money, and Tiger had done very well at that. He is not the first person to cultivate a favorable rating; he was just the best at it.

After the last few weeks where his personal life and sins have been exposed for the world to see, his favorable rating has taken a plunge. The last report I saw was that now only 42 percent of the people see him in a favorable light. That is a stunning free fall and who knows where it will end.

If we are all honest with ourselves, we all have a little Tiger in ourselves. We all like to be seen in a positive light. We all like to have a high approval rating. We also, like Tiger, do a little cultivating of our image.

In public, we talk one way, and many times, in the privacy of our home, it does not match. We know what to say and who to say it to. If that means being a little hypocritical, that's okay, because it keeps the favorable rating up. I will be the first to say I am guilty, guilty, and guilty! Everyone likes to be liked, and I see nothing wrong with that. The real problem here is who we are trying to please.

We, like Tiger, get into trouble when we attempt to please man instead of God. Our first priority should be not to create a great public image, but a private one that recreates us in the image of God. Our lives should be lived out in a way that finds favor in God's sight, not man's.

No amount of money or popularity in the world can replace the peace that comes from knowing you are "right" with God. This does not mean perfect; that was Tiger's problem. He had a perfect image to uphold. No one could ever do that. God knows you're not perfect. Stop wasting your time on your perfect image. Instead of seeking perfection, seek God. Seek His forgiveness for your sin, repent of it, and spend time with Him in quiet moments. Being right with God takes living for Him daily.

It is time all of us stopped worrying about what our favorable rating is with man and asked ourselves one simple question. What is my favorable rating with God?

Scripture: Proverbs 3:3-4: "Let love and faithfulness never leave you; bind them around your neck, write them on the tablet of your heart. Then you will win favor and a good name in the sight of God and man."

Prayer: Dear Lord, convict us of our double lives. Help us to make our priority to be to please you. We ask these things in the name of Christ, Amen.

Getting a Belly Full

The other day I was walking past an old friend. I had been ignoring this friend because it had the audacity to tell the truth about me. In days gone by, this friend encouraged me to great heights and assisted in confirming that I was on the right track. Lately, though, this friend had been brutally honest.

My old friend: the bathroom scales. They are always available to speak the truth to me no matter if I like it or not. Earlier this week, I decided to just take a look. It was neither pretty nor encouraging. As a matter of fact, as I stood on those scales looking over my belly to see the numbers, I just became angry—not mad at the scales (they told the truth). I was mad at myself for letting things get to where they are. Finally, I had gotten a belly full of it all (literally).

Nothing ever changes for any of us until we do. I am not talking about just weight; I am talking about any positive change we need to make in life, especially spiritual. Nothing ever gets better until we have finally had enough.

Today let's look at the scales in our life for a minute. Don't worry—no one else is watching. Let's be honest with ourselves and ask the hard question: what are you tired of about the way you're living your life?

Are the scales tipping away from relationships? Having some trouble at the house? Things not going the way they need to, but you really haven't done anything about it? What about those kids—do they share your lack of discipline or cynical speech? It might bother you, but how much? Have you gotten a belly full of it yet?

Since this is a devotional, what about your spiritual life? How many times have we committed to change in this area, yet fallen short? Until we look up at our relationship with God and realize it is not all it should or could be, we will continue on the same path.

As we continue down the path of honesty, we have to realize that public enemy number one for change is laziness. Public enemy number one to laziness is getting a belly full of it.

Are there areas of your life that are tipping the scales in the wrong direction? Areas that you are not proud of and you know you need all the help God can give to move forward? He is willing and waiting on us.

Keep in mind when we allow God to lead, love, and assist us, the weight of the world is lifted off of our shoulders. Get a belly full. Sure, that is where it starts, but don't attempt change on your own—call on God.

Follow these steps for change:

1) Be honest with yourself. You won't get a belly full until you are.
2) Take little steps, but take steps. Remember, Rome wasn't built in a day, and you aren't either.
3) Don't let one moment of failure stop you. Dust yourself off and keep going.
4) When you're tempted to quit, remind yourself often of the day you got a belly full of it.
5) Pray about it often—just short little prayers, just asking God for help.
6) Rejoice as you look at what God is doing in your life; give Him the credit.

Scripture: Colossians 3:9-10: "Don't lie to one another. You're done with that old life. It's like a filthy set of ill-fitting clothes you've stripped off and put in the fire. Now you're dressed in a new wardrobe. Every item of your new way of life is customer-made by the Creator, with his label on it." *The Message* by Eugene Peterson

Prayer: Dear Lord, help us to see things we need to change from your point of view and to take the steps with your help to change them so they will give honor to you. We ask these things in the name of Christ, Amen.

The Outside Looks Good

Hospitals, like people, come in all different shapes and sizes. Having spent a lot of time at hospitals over the last 20 years, I have seen a lot of different kinds. The good thing about going to so many voluntarily is that when you do have to go, you know where the good ones are.

This week I made a visit at one that had gone through a complete reconstruction over the last several years. It sits by a lake in a very nice part of the city, and to say the least, the place is nice. It looks more like an upscale hotel than the hospital that it is.

It has nice wooden chests for people to keep their valuables in. You could eat off the nice tile floors. In the waiting rooms are beautiful couches with televisions that I would love to watch my favorite sporting events on. The emergency room looks like someone's living room as opposed to a place where hurting people come to get care. Beautiful pictures adorn all the hallways. The place looks first class all the way.

Now let me ask you a question. With all of those nice-looking walls, halls, and rooms, does that mean the care you get there is first class? Many would say "yes" simply because things look so good on the outside. Really, though, there are times the outside can fool you.

What if the nurses there do not care for you? What if the hospital spent all its money on making the place look nice, yet hired the cheapest doctors available and worst nurses in the area? Now tell me, which would you rather have? Something that looks nice on the outside but is crummy on the inside? Or would you rather have something that looks okay on the outside but first class on the inside?

For most of us, the answer is an easy yes to the second question. For God, the answer is an easy yes as well when it comes to our spiritual lives. However, many of us worry about our exterior, how we look to the world around us. We spend money on the best clothes, on making ourselves look younger. We worry about our reputation at the expense of God's. We buy the biggest and best

Bibles, all the latest Christian CDs, the best-selling books, and we know all the words to say.

Often, we have spent a lot of time and energy on the outside only to let the inside suffer from serious neglect. God mentions this type of attitude several times in His word. Of course, the Lord wants us to take care of our bodies, but He is much more concerned with our hearts.

The hospital I mentioned earlier took several years to restore its outer beauty. It had a plan and stayed with it, and now it looks beautiful. We need to learn a lesson from the hospital. If our inside life (spiritual) needs to be restored, we need to follow this plan of action:

a. Set your course; determine to work on your spiritual life.
b. Get a plan: find a daily Bible reading, set a time to pray, make sure you worship.
c. Find someone to make you stay at it. Nothing would look worse than a half-finished hospital, and there is nothing good about a half-finished spiritual life either.
d. Overcome the obstacles. When it rained, construction came to a halt that day. They did not quit; they picked it back up the next day. Same should be true with your spiritual journey. If you miss a day, don't quit. Pick it back up the next day and stay focused on the finish line.

We as Christians are always under construction. The completion day is known only by God, but when He does the final inspection, it will not be the outside He is worried about. It will be the inside spiritual life He takes a look at.

• I think God sees a lot of beautiful projects in progress, stay at it.

Scripture: 1 Samuel 15:7: "But the Lord said to Samuel, 'Do not consider his appearance of his height, for I have rejected him. The Lord does not look at the things man looks at. Man looks at the outward appearance, but the Lord looks at the heart.'"

Prayer: Dear Lord, help us to show as much concern for our inner beauty and Godliness as we do for our outer beauty and how we look to the world. Help us to construct a life that is pleasing to you, overcoming all obstacles to be more like Christ. We ask these things in His name, Amen.

The Community of Chili's

Our favorite family restaurant is our local Chili's. We love the food, the atmosphere, and the fact that it is close to the house. Over the past years, we have eaten there a great deal and have gotten to know several of the waiters and waitresses. They know us when we come in, and though some do not know our names, they know several things about us just as we do about them.

Not too long ago, I told Kim that if I were going to start a church, the word "community" would be in the name. I feel that for a church to really make an impact, the feeling of old-style community must exist with all the members. By that I mean we need to not only know one another on a surface level—name, age, and marital status—but also to really know each other. What makes us tick? What brought us to Christ? What do we love to do? What are our hurts and fears? Where are we weak? What makes us smile?

Community brings people together and helps to serve the purpose of the local church. Let me give some examples of our community at Chili's. During recent visits, we have gotten to know one of the waitresses who just finished school and is planning to become a medical assistant. She sat down and told us all about her plans and school. Now when we see her, we have a great point of reference.

On another occasion, we have gotten to know a young lady, to know where she goes to church, and to know that she loves to sing. That has even led to her singing at our church on more than one occasion. But not only that, my wife has also been invited to her baby shower, and we have been able to keep up with her even after her work at Chili's.

Recently, I went in for a take-out order, and as I stood at the counter, the man waiting on me began to talk to me about my boys playing baseball, and as we were speaking, a waitress came by to say hello. As I looked around the corner, I saw a waitress who always comes by to speak to us even when we are not at her table. At that moment, I thought to myself, this is what I meant by "community."

I enjoy eating at a place where I know the people, where we have served one another, where they know me, and where we have shared some of our joys and concerns. How much better is worship when I have done the same things?

Sure, I could go to a great place of worship and hear beautiful music and a wonderful sermon. But what if I don't know why the person next to me is crying or why the people up front are celebrating? What if I don't know the struggles of the guy three rows over? How meaningful is that kind of worship?

One of my greatest concerns for the church today is that we may grow in great numbers without growing in proper community, that perhaps we have shied away from really knowing each other out a spirit of mistrust, or we have just disconnected.

We must all do our part to build community. Here are some suggestions for us all as we seek to build a church that meets all of our spiritual needs.

- ❖ **Find a place to serve.** You will build great relationships with those you serve with.
- ❖ **Allow yourself to be served.** This is difficult, especially for servants, but being vulnerable helps you see the other side and allows others to serve.
- ❖ **Be around.** If I never went to Chili's, how would I know anyone there? If you simply walk into church and run out, how can you know anything about anyone? Community takes time.
- ❖ **Be trustworthy.** If someone is real and vulnerable with you, do not abuse that by being a gossip. Nothing kills community like gossip.

Scripture: Ephesians 4:14-16: "Then we will no longer be infants, tossed back and forth by the waves, and blown here and there by every wind or teaching and by the cunning and craftiness of men in their deceitful scheming. Instead, speaking the truth in love, we will in all things grow up into him who is the head, that is, Christ. From him the whole body, joined and held together by every supporting ligament, grows and builds itself up in love, as each part does its work."

Prayer: Dear Lord, work within our hearts to shape us into the kind of person you desire for us to be. Teach us to listen, serve, and love others in your name. We ask these things in His name, Amen.

Unfathomable Forgiveness

I have been brought up spiritually in a faith known, unfortunately, for its great battles. These battles come from those inside the local church and the denomination as a whole. We love grace; we just don't give it out as much as we should, especially to each other. Thus, when I witness true forgiveness, it makes an impact on me.

It is hard to believe it has been almost exactly three years since the horrific murders of five school-age girls and the wounding of five others that took place in a peace-loving Amish community in Pennsylvania. This event touched my heart as a father, and their response of forgiveness has left an everlasting impact on me spiritually.

I would be insensitive and foolish to say that I can even begin to understand the feelings of those who lost those girls that day or of those who had to attempt to repair the psyche of those who were present. I pray very few will ever have to attempt such a thing. But in the midst of such darkness, the Amish shined the light of true forgiveness.

Before I deal with their response, I will share with you that their witness led me to seriously investigate their religion. What could make such a people respond this way? What is it they draw upon that helps them capable of such an uncharacteristic response? Then, finally, why do the rest of us who call upon God respond to even minor crisis so differently? I looked inside my own spiritual life and did not like what I saw; if you choose to do something about it, that is not always a bad thing.

Real forgiveness was their response. Within hours, they were at the house of the man who had committed the murders comforting his now widow and family. Mrs. Roberts (the killer's wife) was one of the few outside people invited to the funerals of one of the girls. The day after the shootings, Mrs. Roberts's aunt was invited into one of the victim's homes, and indeed, Mrs. Roberts's uncle did attend one funeral.

It did not stop there. In a show of worldwide compassion, the Amish received 4 million dollars. With whom did they share some of this money? Indeed, with Mrs. Roberts. I am only touching the highlights of their response.

How does such forgiveness affect people? See some notes from Mrs. Roberts letter below:

"Your love for our family has helped to provide the healing we so desperately need. Gifts you've given have touched our hearts in a way no words can describe. Your compassion has reached beyond our family, beyond our community, and is changing our world, and for this we sincerely thank you." She went on to say that her family had been "overwhelmed by the forgiveness, grace, and mercy shown to them by the Amish."

Just from her letter, I can find exactly what real forgiveness does. It helps to provide healing especially to the innocent. True mercy is indeed indescribable; there is no feeling like it. True mercy, when witnessed, does reach beyond the original target and tells a world, people like me and you, that it can be done, even in the most excruciating and painful circumstances. It does change the world, and if it were practiced more than preached, the world would be very different.

I recently heard a person who wrote a book about the Amish and their response to the event that struck me. He said, "Forgiveness is in the fabric of the DNA of the Amish." I have thought of that statement and what it says, and I believe it says that this is all they know. It is natural to them. The only way it can be that way is if it is taught and practiced from day one. What a different world it would be if we could all say the same.

In the midst of the most unimaginable hurt, they showed unfathomable mercy. Shortly after the event occurred, the school house was torn down in an effort to move on. The building is gone, the girls rest in the Savior's arms, and Mrs. Roberts's wrestles with raising a family, but instead of being a side note of violent history in our country, the Amish instead became a witness and left a legacy of what real forgiveness is. That legacy is one all of us who call on the name of Christ should wish to leave.

Scripture: 1 John 1:9-11: "Anyone who claims to be in the light but hates his brother is still in the darkness. Whoever loves his brother live in the light, and there is nothing in him to make him stumble. But whoever hates his brother is in the darkness and walks around in the darkness; he does not know where he is going, because the darkness has blinded him."

Prayer: Dear Lord, help us to love and not hate, help us to seek and give forgiveness. Guide us to be people of mercy not justice. Lord, drive us past our human response of revenge and hate to a Christ-centered response. We ask these things in the name of He who paid the price for our forgiveness, Jesus Christ. Amen.

Free, Really?

What would you do for something free? I am the kind of guy that can get into things without really knowing what is going on. Such was my Thursday night. A friend of my sister-in-law had given us free tickets to see the premier of a new children's movie, *Everyone's Hero*. Being that I have a great many children, the word *free* normally strikes a chord with me. So I took her up on it.

There were only enough tickets for my three younger boys, ages 9, 7, and 2, and me, so my wife stayed behind with the newborn, and I ventured off to the movies. Due to our car situation and the fact we had to be there early to ensure us getting our tickets, we arrived 2 and 1/2 hours early. Being the great dad I am, I think I can work this all out with little trouble.

First on the agenda is a trip to Sonic before getting in line for the movie. Being the wise father I am, I forget that my 7-year-old, John, inherited his father's excitable stomach. Let's just say that when he gets excited, he is prone to lose his lunch. Sure enough, just after eating and before getting in line for the movie, right on the beautiful spotless floor of this new portion of the mall, he begins to lose his Sonic kid's meal. Now cleaning this up is normally Kim's job, because I have a very weak stomach. But there is no Kim, and so I do the best I can. Fortunately for me, I have picked up several napkins at Sonic and the cleaning lady came by to help out. I may have been embarrassed, but I was glad to see her.

After that, it is off to the line for some popcorn and coke at the bargain price of $10. We grab our goodies and go jump in line. We take a seat on the floor because the wait in line is going to be a while. After a few minutes, dad comes up with the great idea to let the kids play with the cars we received from Sonic. This works out great until we knock over our $5 box of popcorn on the brand new carpet of the theater. Matt, my 9-year-old, and I get it picked up and in the trash while the waiting continues.

While in line, the folks from the movie decide to give out some very good ball cards to all the kids. I think this will be great and will kill some time. I am all about killing time right about now. Once again, there's a kink in the system. My 2-year-old, Caleb, takes his cards and, for some reason, really wants to throw them in the trash. I cannot let him for several reasons, but looking back, none of those reasons were good enough to put up with the trauma of the next few minutes.

He cries and tries to get around me, forcing me to pick him up. This did not stop the crying, and from my vantage point, I can see all the mothers around me starting to stare at this father making his 2-year-old cry. And of course, I was at the front of the line, so everyone could see what was going on. I stopped him for a minute, and then he got it back in his head to do it again, and the cycle continued. Here I am standing in line with a 2-year-old crying and all these mothers staring at me. Now there is sweat pouring off of my head. The pressure is starting to get to me when, to my great relief, they opened the doors to the movie. I think that finally, at last, we will be okay.

Of course as we get going, with Caleb still very upset because he cannot throw his cards in the trash, we spill more of our $5 popcorn on the nice new floor. The stares were still coming, but I do not care. I know we will be okay when we make it to the movie.

Being the smart guy that I am, I sit near the bottom and close to the door in case Caleb has any other wild thoughts or gets upset again. I am looking for a quick exit. As we sit down, once again Caleb gets something in his head, and he is not going to let it go. He wants to throw away his cards (by now I am wanting to throw his cards away, too!) and decides to let loose right at the not-so-understanding lady in front of us. After apologizing, I have Matt go and grab the cards for me as I sit holding Caleb and praying for the movie to start.

Then, out of nowhere, things start to change. This is a premiere. That means nothing to me. I have no idea there is anything going on here but a movie. Up comes a morning news personality to speak to us, and before I know it, she is giving away T-shirts, and John wins. Then out comes Lone Star, a country music group with lots of hits. So all of a sudden, we are sitting here surrounded by celebrities with a new T-shirt for one of the kids. Things are looking up, and best of all, this has gotten Caleb's attention.

Then, since I am sitting down so low, I happen to be in the right spot, and they give me a free autographed poster of the group and a new CD to boot. After a little while, they give us free posters to go with our cards, CD, and picture—not to mention the fact that we are watching a movie with all these big-time entertainers for no cost.

Just before Caleb falls asleep, the movie starts. I wake him up because, hey, he has made it this far—I sure do not want him to miss the movie! We watch a pretty good family movie, grab us a popcorn refill on the way out the door with all of our goods in tow, and call it a night to remember, and all of it (except the coke and popcorn) for free!!

The message today is short, though the devotional is long. The grace we receive from God is free, no charge whatsoever; Jesus paid the price. That does not mean there will not be any turmoil in our life, or that our life will be pain free. No, not at all. But it does mean the admission into heaven has already been paid for us by someone else—Jesus.

Will there be trouble? Yes. Will there be pain? Yes, but let me tell you when you get through the line, the payoff and gifts will be great! Too many people give up while still waiting in line. Don't let the troubles of your life keep you from looking forward to the great gifts of eternity with God in heaven. Just think—it is all for *free!!!*

Scriptures: Ephesians 2:8 & 9: "For it is by grace you have been saved, through faith—and this not from yourselves, it is the gift of God—not by works, so that no one can boast."

Prayer: Dear Lord, we thank you for your free gift given to us by your one and only Son, Christ, on the cross. Help us live our lives looking forward to the day we will meet you face to face. We ask these things in Christ's name. Amen.

"Why Don't We Just Dance"

Are the money woes getting the best of you? Those annoying phone calls from bill collectors making your heart skip a beat when the phone rings? How about those kids? Making you a little nervous? Those guys keeping you up late at night worrying about what direction they are going in? How about those clothes they wear? It is all enough to send you straight for a nervous breakdown.

The future, what about it? Will you have a job in the future? Will it be the one you want in the place you like? Money for retirement? Is it going to be there? How about health? Age starting to creep up on you? Don't move as fast as you once did? Starting to get those little aches and pains as you move around?

Life's tough. I am not kidding. At a time like this, a little country music can really hit the spot.

I have to admit, I am somewhat hooked on the folksy genre and its timely lyrics. I love the stories. Recently, I ran across a new one called "Why Don't We Just Dance" by Josh Turner. This song is right on time for the theme of our day. I want to assure you that not every song has to have some deep meaning, and not every second of our life has to be spent worrying about our problems or pondering lives bigger questions. There is a place for those things. Let's just say not today.

Let's start with the opening lyrics: "Baby why don't we just turn that TV off? Three hundred fifteen channels of nothing but bad news on. Well it might be me but the way I see it, the whole world has gone crazy, so baby, why don't we just dance."

There we go. Hey, the world is going to pieces, sure, but what the heck—today, let's just forget it—and dance, or read, or laugh, or play a game with the kids, eat a greasy hamburger, or whatever you like.

More lyrics: "Guess the little bitty living room aint gonna look like much. When the lights go down, and we move the couch, it's gonna be more than enough. For my two left feet and our two hearts beatin' nobody see us go crazy." Hey, shut the door, get with the one you love, cut a rug, and have a good time. Who really cares what the world thinks? We spend way too much time worrying about that meaningless stuff.

Turner himself said this about the lyrics, "...forget about all of the bad stuff going on the world and just concentrate on each other." Yea, why don't we?

Seriously, some people were turned off when I wrote that I liked country music, you know I am right. Others expect me to sit around the house with my legs crossed, looking to the east, pondering the second return of Christ or the theological implications of the trinity. Hey, there is a place for all of that, but come on guys and gals, let's have some good, clean fun every once in a while!

In so many ways, we have let the world set the tone; we have let them steal our fun. Let's stop it! Or we have found the "spiritual boogie man" in everything from Easter to Christmas. Stop it already!

Let's put a smile on our face. Turn up the music, move the couch, grab your partner, and dance until we can't dance anymore! The bills will wait, the kids, well, hey, catch them later. Grab some fattening ice cream or eat a slice of pizza. Live a little.

Me, I hear the music playing and my feet are starting to tap! Hopefully you're smiling already. It's about time.

Scripture: Psalm 37:3-4: "Trust in the LORD and do good; dwell in the land and enjoy safe pasture. Delight yourself in the LORD and he will give you the desire of your heart."

Prayer: Dear Lord, let us rejoice in the good things of life. Enjoy them as you would have us to enjoy them—things like close friends and loved ones, blessings of family, and good health. The list is as endless as your love, and we thank you for them all. We ask these things in the name of Christ, Amen.

P.S. Love the video of this song.

The Triumph of the Broken

As I mentioned in an earlier devotional, I coach a YMCA base-ball team. Now, I need to let you know that Y baseball is a little different than the city leagues. The Y baseball is not quite as good as city baseball. The kids that play at the Y could not always get to play in the city. Oh, some are pretty good, but many have never played before and are not the greatest. That's okay, and really it is one of the things I like about it. With that knowledge in hand, that brings us up to last Saturday.

On my team is a little boy who has very little hearing, Blaine. His condition is hereditary. His father has the same hearing problem. As a matter of fact, with the help of modern medicine, they were both able to hear sounds for the first time at the same time. That must have been a special moment. Blaine tries hard and really is a pretty good hitter, but he cannot hear a thing I say most of the time. Before each at-bat, I have to stand in front of him to give him instructions. It is the only way I can know for sure that he hears what I say.

On my team is also a young boy who has just the slightest of palsy. His name is Tyler. You can only tell it when he tries to run real hard. If you didn't know, you would think he was not trying to run his hardest. Instead, he is running as fast as his legs will allow him to. The effort is there; the body won't always cooperate. He is a great young boy with a sweet heart and a joy to be around. But in athletics, he will have to work harder than anyone else to be able to keep up.

On the opposing team last week, there was a young boy of great courage. He stood at the plate with crippled legs and crutches under each arm. He would swing and do his best to make contact. When it was time to run, off he would go on his crutches. Out in the field, he maneuvered himself in an amazing way attempting to field the ball. I spoke to his dad, and he said he tells his boy every day how impressed he is with his courage and drive. In watching his son just for the afternoon, I had to agree with him.

In the city league, these guys wouldn't have a chance, but at the Y, well, great things can happen to the broken. It was a great game; we got behind early, but hung in there and made a charge at the end. With the game on the line, Tyler gets a hit and keeps the game going.

Then, with the pressure on, Blaine gets the game-winning hit (his second hit of the day!) and drives in the winning run, which happens to be Tyler. I had to tell Tyler he was the game winning run, and I am not sure Blaine ever heard the cheers of the crowd. At the end of the game, we awarded Blaine the game ball for his clutch hitting. I said some words of encouragement, but I doubt seriously that Blaine heard a word of it. By the proud look on his parents' faces, they surely did.

Saturday was the day for the broken to win, for the unlikely hero to have his day. I floated off into the rest of my day; it could not get any better than this. That is what I love about Y ball, and that, by the way, is what I love about God. With God, the broken have a chance. In fact, with God the broken can't lose. As a matter of fact, God specializes in using the broken to do great things. God used Moses, a murderer and really not that good a speaker, to deliver his people. Paul, a former persecutor of the church and with his "thorn in the flesh" in tow, becomes the greatest missionary the world is to know. Jacob, the trickster, wrestles with God, ends up with a limp, gets a name change, and becomes the father of a nation. The list could go on and on.

If you know God, then the list includes you. At one time, at one moment, you were broken. Perhaps that day is today. Maybe you've gotten behind in life, and a comeback seems unlikely. Oh, but remember, you serve a God of the unlikely that specializes in the triumph of the broken. Remember, the game's not over until the last broken soul reaches home base. There, the God of the broken will be waiting for you, loving arms reaching out to welcome you home.

Scripture: Mark 10:27, "Jesus looked at them and said, 'With man this is impossible, but not with God; all things are possible with God.'"

Prayer: Lord, we thank you that you love us in spite of our brokenness, that you use us in spite of our imperfections. Help us to lean on you and to acknowledge that with you all things are possible. In the sweet name of Christ, Amen.

Getting Directions

I have always prided myself on knowing my way around Dallas pretty well. I grew up in the city and spent fifteen years working on a moving truck on the weekends covering every area of town. On top of that, my father was always taking us different places that would expand my horizons.

But it seems lately I have been running into places that either I had never been to or had not been to in a long time. This has caused a bit of a dilemma because I am not real used to asking for directions. I also do not own a map or one of those very handy Mapsco books that tells you every street in the city. My family counts on me to know where I am going.

What is a guy to do? Simple. Call the father. My dad has lived in Dallas for all of his 68 years. He has worked in every section of the city, and he was working with me on that moving truck much of the time. This guy knows everywhere. So when I have needed directions lately, I have simply picked up the phone, called my dad, and said, "Where is it?" He has never let me down.

Perhaps as you read this, you are totally lost. You just feel like there is no direction for your life. Maybe you feel as though you are being asked to go somewhere you have never been before and you are unsure how to get it done. Maybe your family, like mine, is counting on you to know the direction and to get them safely to the destination.

Does all of this make you a little nervous? I have the answer: call the Father. Works every time.

We often seek to run our own lives. We seek to go in the direction we want to go in, and then we ask God to bless it. We get married without asking God, and then when it starts to turn sour, what do we do? Perhaps we buy a house without seeking the Lord's will, and it turns out to be the wrong house at the wrong time, then what do we do? I could go on and on, with decisions like where to go to school, where to go to church, where to work, or how will we run our family.

We're lost, because no matter how good we think we know the territory, we don't know the way. The bad news is that we are not as smart as we think we are; the good news is God has a plan for our life.

There is nothing worse in life than being unsure of what you are doing or where you are headed. Though there are days you might be unsure, there is still a sense of peace that comes from knowing that you are heading in the direction God would have you.

One last thought about my father is this. He has been around, he knows the area, and he has walked the roads. I can trust him; I know he loves me and would not send me in the wrong direction. He is always home when I call, too. I never get his answering machine. The same is true of the Heavenly Father, even more so. He has walked the same roads of life we have, He loves you and would never send you in the wrong direction. We can trust Him. It should give us all comfort to know the Father has a plan and a direction for our lives.

Lost? Uncertain where you're headed? Call the Father. He is always at home.

Scripture: Matthew 7: 7 & 8: "Ask and it will given to you; seek and you will find; knock and the door will be opened to you. For everyone who asks receives; he who seeks find; and to him who knocks, the door will be opened."

Prayer: Dear Father, may we seek your will and direction for our life. Help us to take the steps to hear your voice; lead us to worship, prayer, study and service. Help us to trust your direction even when it seems like a difficult road. We praise you for your love, and we ask these things in name of Jesus Christ our Savior. Amen.

Where's Your Hideout?

Every thief needs to have a get-a-way plan. So when a young man in Wyoming decided to steal a bottle of booze and some cough drops, he had to devise an escape route. He had a plan. It just wasn't a very good one.

I am assuming this thief was low on money, had a drinking problem, and a bad cough. In the rush of the moment, he picked up his stolen goods and headed to a nearby building in order to hide out. My guess is he thought he would hang out in the building until the police gave up the chase.

His plan might have worked perfectly, except for one minor detail. The building he decided to hang out in: it was the local police station. He made a run for it, only to be caught just outside of the building.

His plan: do the deed, find a safe place to hide, then get away from authorities—it didn't work, and our attempts to hide don't work much better.

We all make mistakes in our life. It's where we choose to run after those mistakes that makes the difference. Will we live life to its fullest or will we be a fugitive from a loving God?

We, like our wrong-way thief, often run to places we think are safe, only to find we could not be more wrong. We hide in our work or accomplishments. We hide behind bottles and pills. We run to religion or good works. Anything, anywhere—just somewhere that keeps our mind occupied and feeling good for ourselves.

The only problem with all of these and a hundred others just like them is that they are shallow, and eventually the pills run out or the high of accomplishment runs its course. Sooner or later, doing good works is not good enough, and religion always has a way of leaving us empty.

At that moment, we make a run for it, and that is when we are caught. It's the best thing that can happen to us. Not a face to face with a policeman or news reporter, but a head-on collision with the one we have truly wronged: God.

Maybe the thief in this story will get help for his issues. Maybe he can get a job, stop drinking, and do something about that nasty cough. But the truth is, he never was likely to get help as long as he had a safe place to hide; the truth is, we won't either.

God knows that about us as well, He knows that as long as we have a place to get away that we will never face the issue, that we will never get right, and that we will always feel guilt and pain. He does not wish for us to live that way. He has a remedy: complete surrender.

Today, if you're hiding from God, I have news you need to hear: he knows where you are at. With that, I have good news: He is in the business of granting nothing but pardons. Best advice, give yourself up, plead for mercy at the judge's feet. I assure you, He will give it. When he does, you will find yourself freer than you ever have before. Stop hiding. Rehabilitation is just around the corner.

Scripture: 1 John 1:9: "If we claim that we're free of sin, we're only fooling ourselves. A claim like that is errant nonsense. On the other hand, if we admit our sins—make a clean breast of them—he won't let us down; he'll be true to himself. He'll forgive our sins and purge us of all wrongdoing. If we claim that we've never sinned, we out-and-out contradict God—make a liar out of him. A claim like that only shows off our ignorance of God." *The Message* by Eugene Peterson

Prayer: Dear Lord, help us to come to you when we have wronged you, help us to seek forgiveness and not hide behind the things of this world. Help us to hide behind you and find refuge in your love and forgiveness. We ask these things in the name of Christ, Amen.

The Center Ring

The loud music, the smiling kids, the clowns, the juggling, the amazing gymnastics moves, and, no, I am not talking about my house on a rainy Saturday afternoon. I am talking about the circus. Three rings of constant entertainment.

A couple of weeks ago the younger folks in the family and I were gifted with some free tickets to the local circus. It had been a while since I had been to the circus and some of my younger children never had, so going was a must.

When all three rings were working, I found it impossible to keep up with them all. I just found one to focus on and kept my eyes on it. What I really enjoyed was when one act was working in the center ring and nothing was going on in the other two. This way I did not have to decide which act I was going to watch, I just focused on the center ring and enjoyed the action.

After a while, my eyes would see something moving around in the other two rings, and I would have to take a look. What I would see was the circus workers busy getting the alternate rings ready for the next act. Quietly, they went about their business without anyone seeing them; all eyes were focused on the ring with all the lights shining on it. Though there is action in all three rings, only one is getting any attention from the spectators in the stands.

These behind-the-scene workers do their task without anyone knowing their names or giving them any attention, yet without them, the circus would grind to a halt. The fans would sit and have to wait for the next act to be prepared. They may be behind the scenes, but they are very important players in the action of a circus.

I see our lives in God within the activity at the circus. We are busy with our lives; all the lights of our attention are focused on one thing. We keep juggling the same balls or walking the same tight rope (raising kids, performing our jobs, getting married, etc.). What is happening today is in the center ring; it is the main attraction.

Though we may be very busy with today, God is busy preparing the next act in our lives. He is using what is happening in the main ring, no doubt, as a part of that preparation. All the while, there is something happening that we have no idea about. Your life is going on, but God is using events all around you to prepare for the next plan in your life. Quietly, without being seen, but like the workers at the circus, He is working behind the scenes to keep His plan for your life from grinding to a halt.

You may wonder why you have been in the same ring so long, why nothing has changed. It is simple: God (the ultimate Ringmaster) is not through preparing the next ring for you. He is not ready to close down the ring you're in, or better yet, He knows that we are not ready to close down the ring we are in. He has not finished preparing us and lining up the next event. Of course, we do not know this because we are focused on the here and now, but God sees the overall plan.

Nothing happens before its time. Nothing happens without God's hand in it. We must be patient to wait for the plan to take shape. Though we do not see God, we must trust that He is always at work.

While your life may seem like a circus, be sure of this—the Ringmaster is in control, and nothing happens without His direction. Somewhere in the dark outside the sight of others, He is working the next plan for your life.

With that in mind, keep on juggling until the lights come on and the band begins to play, thus making another ring of activity the main focus of your life. Then, move in that direction with the confidence that the behind-the-scenes work has been completed and it is time to go.

Scripture: Proverbs 16:9: "In his heart a man plans his course, but the Lord determines his steps."

Proverbs: 19:21: "Many are the plans in a man's heart, but it is the Lord's purpose that prevails."

Prayer: Dear Lord, help us to keep the proper focus on today while trusting you with the future. We ask this in the precious name of our Savior, Jesus Christ.

That's a good question

I must admit that I am not the best at listening to my children while they are talking to me in a car. That is nothing I am proud of, because that is a great time to listen to what they have to say.

Yesterday, coming home from basketball practice, I was attempting to do better. That is when my ten-year-old, John, started pounding me with questions. They came fast and furious.

Questions like this: how long would it take to get over this bridge if you were walking? Is that water tower close to the house? This is a good question since we live in the water tower capital of the world. What is the speed limit? I was asked that one several times. Maybe his mother had him ask that question.

Keep in mind my John is somewhat like his dad in the imagination department, meaning he is a little "out there" at times. Thus, the next question went something like, "If you were invisible, could you see the things on the other side of the car?" I didn't have an answer for that one.

Then he asked this question: "How do you know there is an air bag behind where it says there is one?" I had no answer for that one except we had to have faith that the people who said they put it there really did. Many people ask similar questions of God, questions that can only be answered with faith.

While I have your attention, let me ask you some questions, and let's see how you are doing with the answers. I think you will recognize many of these:

Kids breaking your heart?
Money issues keep you awake at night?
Marriage on the rocks?
Job not going so well? Rumors of more layoffs?
School a little harder than you thought it would be?
What about those tests from the doctor's office; results not so good?

It is times like the above that we need to trust that God will be true to His word:

Psalm 118:6: "The Lord is with me; I will not be afraid. What can man do to me?"
Hebrews 13:5: "Keep your lives free from the love of money and be content with what you have, because God has said, 'Never will I leave you; never will I forsake you.'"
1 Peter 5:7: "Cast all your anxiety on him because he cares for you."
Psalm 9:9: "The LORD is a refuge for the oppressed, a stronghold in times of trouble."

When it comes to times of stress in our lives, we are a lot like John. We ask a lot of questions. Trust me, God is listening, and He already has all the answers.

Scripture: Isaiah 49:16: "See, I have engraved you on the palms of my hands; your walls are ever before me." One of my all time favorites!

Prayer: Dear Lord, lead us to you daily so we can find the right answers to life's hard questions. We indeed thank you that you will never leave us or forsake us. Help remind us of that daily. We ask these things in the name of Christ, Amen.

Old Haunts

This week I walked to the ICU waiting room on the 12th floor of Children's Hospital. I stood there a year earlier while my daughter, Gracie, unknown to me, fought for her life, and while a gifted doctor took care of an emergency situation during surgery. While I stood there, I had a funny feeling, and I didn't really like it.

I was 100 yards from the room where I had handed my 6-month-old girl to a nurse I did not know, and they headed for surgery. I will never forget those big, blue eyes staring back at me, not knowing what was about to take place. This week as I walked by that room, I had an uncomfortable feeling. I didn't really like it.

I stood in an ICU not far from where I visited my daughter after surgery. There, she had tubes and wires all over and around her, and though they were needed, it was a sight I really can't forget and never really wanted to see. As I stood there this week, my mind drifted back to a year earlier. I had a funny feeling in my gut. I didn't really like it.

Even the parking lot where I parked was a reminder of the time spent in the hospital. A reminder of walking back and forth with little ones, taking care of business outside the hospital while Gracie recovered, and, yes, even the parking lot gave me a funny feeling, and I didn't really like it.

Though the memory is still fresh and the experience overall was great with Gracie's quick recovery and wonderful care, the uncomfortable memories are still there. I guess they always will be. Old haunts are that way; they never seem to totally go away.

My guess is you have some old haunts of your own. Perhaps the final days of divorce: maybe you can remember exactly where you were when it was final. Maybe it was a house where you received verbal abuse on a daily basis: you drive by, or see it, and the old haunt just reappears.

Perhaps yours is a hospital, but with a different experience and ending than what I had. Maybe it was there that you received the news of the death or critical illness of someone you love. Each trip by the hospital, and your mind drifts back.

Maybe yours is a school where you experienced failure often or where you were left as one of the unpopular people. Your heart still aches from the rejection. You see the yearbook or someone from that time, and the old haunt reappears. Perhaps there is a place in your mind where sin took place. You did things you now believe are horrible. You wish to forget and move on, but you can't. Each time you pass that place, it is a constant reminder of a tragic time in your life.

When I think of the word "haunt," I think of dark, scary places like a dark hall to a young child. Old haunts, what are we to do with them? How are we to get past them?

On our own, old haunts will do just what the word says—they will haunt us forever, never letting us have total peace. In most cases, the evil one lives for old haunts. He desires for you to have a long memory of times and places when things were not good. He desires to control your thoughts so that you never forgive yourself for the past or never put the old haunts out of your mind. By doing this, he controls the mind and wins the battle.

What are we to do with old haunts? Give them to the Prince of Peace. Christ came that you might have life and have it to the fullest (John 10:10). That is in direct contrast to the evil one who came to kill, steal, and destroy (John 10:10).

God does not desire for old haunts to control your life. He desires to give you rest and peace from those scary times. He desires to shed light in the dark hallways of your life. Perhaps you never will forget it, but He can help fade it and replace it with places of light and goodness. I believe replacement is God's greatest gift to those who have been in dark places. And who among us has not been to old haunts at least once?

Though the evil one wishes to use old haunts for bad, God can use them for good. He can even use your old haunts to motivate you to help others that might be living with some of your same haunts. (A word of caution: Be careful about quick returns to old haunts.)

For example, why do I go back to a hospital with such a rush of memories? Because people I love are there, and there I can help with prayer and signs of love. There I can gather a fresh sense of perspective as I see others in far worse situations than me. There I can stop for a moment and thank God that I am only visiting. What an unbelievable God that He can even use "old haunts."

The only way to beat an old haunt is to call on the Power that is greater than the "haunt." Call on God. The good news about God is that he is like an old haunt in this respect: He never goes away!

Scriptures: John 10:10: "The thief comes only to steal and kill and destroy; I have come that they may have life, and have it to the full."

Philippians 4:7: "And the peace of God, which transcends all understanding, will guard your hearts and your minds in Christ Jesus."

Prayer: Dear Lord, help each of us as we deal with the past hurts of our lives. Help us to forgive ourselves as you do and to forgive others as you do. Guard our hearts and our minds, help them to stay in the right place and give us peace. Help to keep a focus on godly things, letting go of things we can do nothing about. Help us to leave justice and mercy in your hands. We ask these things in the name of Christ, Amen.

Everyone Should Have an Extra Chromosome

I have seven children and each has changed me in one way or another. I have a great love for them. They have made me laugh, smile, cry, and really given me more purpose to live than I could have ever had without them.

Number seven was born with Down syndrome, and she just turned one year old last weekend. Her birth has changed a lot of things about how I see life, about my priorities, and about God. I am most grateful for her and for the changes she has made in me. If they are not seen on the outside, they are certainly there on the inside.

Children born with Down syndrome are born with an extra chromosome. This causes a variety of issues for whatever reason. There are mental handicaps as well as some physical ones. Often Kim and I will look at each other and say, "Do these kids get a break at all?"

Here is what I have found out about children like Gracie. They are sweet beyond measure. Gracie, for certain, has a smile that melts everyone's heart. She has a spirit unmatched by anyone around her. Without exception, everyone I have talked to who has a child with Down Syndrome has shared with me what fun they are to be around and how good-spirited they are.

Over the last year, the word "normal" has become one that bugs the devil out of me. For instance, many believe we have six "normal" children and one, well, I guess who is abnormal. I beg to differ. I am not sure there are not eight abnormal people in my family and one normal one.

We normal people hate, get angry, cheat, lie, are rarely as happy as we should be. We have to work at putting a smile on our face. Is that what God thought of when he was thinking of normal? We do unspeakable harm to one another, are capable of holding a grudge for years, and when it comes to forgiveness, we fall well short of what the Bible expects. Is that what God thought of when He was thinking of normal?

Here is a thought—maybe that extra chromosome is normal, and those of us without the extra chromosome are abnormal. Maybe God created us to have joy, to show love, and to have smiles that break across our face in an instant. Maybe He meant for us to be innocent and to love all things and all people no matter what they look like or what they have done in the past.

Perhaps that was normal before the fall, and after Adam and Eve sinned, He took that chromosome away. Maybe every once in awhile, instead of creating people with a disability, what God is really doing is creating people in His perfection, and the rest of us can't understand it because we are missing something.

Is what I am saying absolute truth? Probably not. But I know this—there is something missing in our lives that only God can replace. There are things Gracie already appears to have—contentment, happiness, and unconditional love.

We are sinful people with a sinful nature, living in a broken world, and only God can fix it. He chose to do that on the cross and through the power of His Holy Spirit. Many are looking for happiness, joy, peace, and contentment. You can be sure that God holds the key.

When we get to heaven, I assure you we will be a lot more like Gracie than she will be like us, and that will be a good day.

Disabled?.........I wish we all were.

Scriptures: Psalm 139:13-14: "For you created my inmost being; you knit me together in my mother's womb. I praise you because I am fearfully and wonderfully made; your works are wonderful, I know that full well."

John 3:16: "For God so loved the world that he gave his one and only Son, that whoever believes in him shall no perish but have eternal life. For God did not send his Son into the world to condemn the world, but to save the world through Him."

John 10:10: "The thief comes only to steal and kill and destroy; I have come that they may have life, and have it to the full."

Prayer: Dear Lord, we are thankful that you sent your Son to die for our sins. That you love us, and that some day we will be able to spend eternity with you in heaven. We thank you for those you send into our lives that teach us how to love and how good your love really is. We ask these things in Christ's name, Amen.

It's Your Serve

This week was the final week of the U.S. Open tennis tournament. The final match happened to be at a time that I could watch, and so I sat down for a while to enjoy the event.

I enjoy playing a little tennis from time to time, and lately the kids and I have started playing a little bit at nights. I thought by watching it might help me be a better player. So I sat and watched these two guys go at it. Their returns were 100 mph, while mine are somewhere around 20. Their serves go super fast with all kinds of spin on them, while my serve gently floats over the net. There is little comparison between my game and theirs, and the thought that just watching them was going to help was, well, let's say it: foolish.

The only way for me to get better is to participate in the game! The same theory applies to the Christian life. This reminds me of a quote by John H. Holcomb, *"You must get involved to have an impact. No one is impressed by the won-lost record of the referee."*

Life is filled with those who love to talk about the game and tell you about how the game should be played. They love to call foul when we make a mistake and blow the whistle on us when we get out of line. They are observers in life and in their faith. They, like me, will never improve until they get on the court and take a few swings.

If we are going to be more like Christ, learning to serve and love as He does, then we must get into the game. Getting your hands dirty changes everything.

One last tennis reference for the day: I sent two of my children to tennis camp for a week one time. They learned the rules, they learned how to hold the racket, and they learned how to serve as well as learned the boundaries. Then we proceeded to get super busy, and they did not play again for weeks. They had lost their momentum and had to be reminded of what they had learned. There stand a lot of believers: many have lost their momentum. We know the book, we know the boundaries, we know the music, we love to worship, but when it comes to putting what we know in practice, well, not so much.

One thing I learned by watching these two champions play this week is that the serve is the most important aspect of the game. It's the same in our Christian life. Let me close with one more quote, this one from Bill Hybels: *"I would never want to reach out someday with a soft, uncalloused hand—a hand never dirtied by serving—and shake the nail-pierced hand of Jesus."*

Scripture: Mark 10:43-45: "Not so with you. Instead, whoever wants to become great among you must be your servant, and whoever wants to be first must be slave of all. For even the Son of Man did not come to be served, but to serve, and give his life as a ransom for many."

Prayer: Dear Lord, lead us from the sidelines of life to the middle of the need around us. Help us to not merely be hearers of the word, but doers of it also. We ask these things in the name of Christ, Amen.

The Storm; What Storm?

Hurricane Jimena passed close by the Mexican resort Los Cabos this week, which means little to most of you unless you had a Labor Day fishing trip planned for the area. Since I am a bit of a hurricane buff, I always pay close attention to any news reports on such things. This week, the reports got my attention in a way that had little to do with a hurricane.

The news, as they love to do, had a man on site reporting on the weather from Los Cabos. They love to stand these guys outside while the wind is blowing a hundred miles an hour, I guess to show everyone how hard the wind is blowing. I am fine with taking their word for it. Anyway, the report then discussed what people were doing all over the city. This is where the report got interesting.

First, the report showed a couple in a very nice resort hotel sipping wine and talking about how they were going to stay for the hurricane. They did not seem the least bit worried, and they actually showed them lifting a toast together.

The next site of the report was another hotel where they showed some guys standing on a balcony. They had big smiles on their faces, and when asked about the hurricane, they said they were staying. It was "just a part of the vacation." There seemed to be a bit of excitement in their voice as the storm approached. The paper reported a gentleman as saying he "was going to get some more liquor and go back to the hotel and just watch it."

By these reports, you would think the storm was a planned outdoor event for people on vacation. No one was worried, no one upset; they were just going to drink wine and liquor and enjoy the wind, surf, and storm.

Let me move you to the second half of the report that took place just a few miles from the hotel. There, people were living in shacks that barely stood up. They showed the Mexican army pleading with people to leave for safer shelters. They were having trouble with this because most of the people were concerned someone would steal their only valuables if they left.

What these valuables would be, I am not sure of. Electricity ran off extension cords, and the only valuable that anyone could see was a refrigerator, and let me assure you that it did not look like anything you or I bought at the local Sears.

Instead of a cavalier attitude, you saw desperation—desperation on the faces of the people trying to help them and desperation on the faces of the people who were stuck in the poverty that made them an easy target for the oncoming onslaught of wind and rain.

Wealth and lack of concern just a few miles from poverty and desperation—there is the perfect picture of our world.

While we sit in our nice homes, watch our 45-inch television sets, filled with unknown channels and all the food we can eat, there are those struggling for the basic of needs all around us. It is not that God condemns our wealth. He is most concerned that we use it responsibly and with real compassion.

Wealth, and you are more wealthy than you think, leads to a disconnect with the real world—a world that is drowning in poverty or can't get a clean drink of running water. It can also lead us to ignore a hurting and hungry world right under our nose, probably just a few miles away. We count on others to take care of "those folks."

The devotional thought today is not to make you feel guilty for having things but to make us all consider how blessed we are to have those things and also to help us take a good look at what we are doing with the resources we have in the world in which we live.

There is a storm of poverty and pain all around us. *The question of the day is not necessarily "what would Jesus do," but "what would Jesus think of what we are doing with what He has given us?"*

Scripture: Colossians 3:12: "Therefore, as God's chosen people, holy and dearly loved, clothe yourselves with compassion, kindness, humility, gentleness and patience."

Matthew 9:35-38, "Then Jesus made a circuit of all the towns and villages. He taught in their meeting places, reported kingdom news, and healed their diseased bodies, healed their bruised and hurt lives. When he looked out over the crowds, his heart broke. So confused and aimless they were, like sheep with no shepherd. 'What a huge harvest!' he said to his disciples. 'How few workers! On your knees and pray for harvest hands!'" *The Message* by Eugene Peterson

Prayer: Dear Lord, we who have much bring our offering of thanks to you this day thanking you for taking care of every need in abundance. We ask that you would help us to not to become cold and callous to the world around us that has need. Lead us in the proper direction to use our gifts and resources. We ask these things in the name of Christ, Amen.

Cleaning Out the Closets

Over the past few weeks, we have been working hard to take care of a few duties around the house. Part of that task has been for some in the family to clean out their respective closets. So, it was no surprise when my wife suggested that I do the same.

I thought to myself, this will be a piece of cake. I never thought of myself as being the kind of person who had a great deal of clothes even though I had noticed that my closet was getting a bit full. I figured it would take just a few minutes, I would have a nice clean closet, and I'd be back sitting on my couch. I was wrong. Oh boy was I wrong.

I just kept pulling clothes off the rack. It seemed as though they were growing in there. I thought maybe someone was slipping behind me and putting clothes in my closet while I wasn't looking. Needless to say, this was not a short-term project.

After a good bit of work, the job was done. There was more room in my closet, and I found clothes I'd forgotten I had. I filled two boxes of clothes for our church's clothes ministry that I was not able to wear. As I looked at the closet, I thought to myself, "I should do this more often."

Cleaning out your closet is a good thing, both at your home and in your spiritual life. Many of us have closets full of things in our life. We need to get in the closet and clean out. It would do us well, and it would send us on the road to a good, healthy relationship with God. Let me give you some comparisons of the two.

1) When I checked in my closet, I found many good things I had not worn in months. They were buried in the back where I could not see them, and they were going unused. When we take a look in the closets of our life, we will find many good things God had intended for us to use, but we have either forgotten about them or put them on the shelf. Take a peek back there and see if there is something God can use that you have ignored lately.

2) Be liberal in what you get rid of. As I looked at these clothes, some of them were still in good shape, but in order to really clean out the closet, I had to let even some pretty good things go. This will allow someone to have some nice clothes who really needs them, and it will clean out my closet to make room for some new things. Same with your spiritual closet. There are some aspects of your life you need to let go of so that God can send some new experiences into your life.

3) The further back you go in my closet, the darker it gets. I just had to reach back there and pull things into the light. Same with our spiritual life. There are things we have pushed back into the darkness of our life, hoping they will go away. They will not on their own, and they do nothing but bog down your spiritual life. Pull them out into the light, expose them to God, seek His help in dealing with them, put it in a box, and send them on their way. Certainly do not keep putting it in the closet as so many do. For many, the dark places of the closet are the fullest. Those dark places are the places God needs to get to the worst. Let Him have them.

4) As I cleaned my closet, it left me with some room, but I guarantee you that in a matter of just a few months, it will be full again. Closets need to be cleaned often, and that goes for your spiritual one. Check in their daily; make sure you're not loading it down with unneeded worry, guilt, or heartache. You already know this, but let me remind you: the more often you check your closet, the easier it is to keep clean and uncluttered. The same goes with your spiritual life, the more often you check it, the easier it is to keep your life clean and uncluttered of the burdens of life.

Closets were made to hold things so they could be found and used when needed. Your spiritual life lessons are to be used the same way. Make sure your closet of spiritual experiences is clean, positive, and ready for use when needed. To do that takes work. Well, what are you waiting for? Get in there; it's not going to clean itself, you know!

Scripture: Isaiah 43:18-19: "Forget the former things; do not dwell on the past. See, I am doing a new thing! Now it springs up; do you not perceive it? I am making a way in the desert and streams in the wasteland."

Prayer: Dear patient Lord, we thank you that we can give you the things of the past and that you forgive us for our sins. Help us to be bold not to hold anything back from you, but to give you all of our lives. We thank you for new experiences that help us grow, and we look forward to the day we shall see you face to face. In Christ's name, Amen.

No Way He's 70!

I remember him as the man standing on the sidelines cheering me on when I played peewee football. He sat in the heat and rarely missed a baseball game, one of my biggest fans. I can never forget the hottest summer of my life, spent in the back of a moving van with this man, working harder than I had ever worked and ever would work again. Looking back on it, I am amazed we both made it through that summer.

Fishing is not my favorite thing to do, but some of my favorite nights were spent sitting on a bridge listening to a baseball game on the radio with this man and waiting for the fish to bite. I will never forget the day this guy and I saw a snake while fishing at night, and we both broke the world's land speed record running back to camp.

Memories. More memories. Memories of going to work with him, and getting to stay up all night when he worked the night shift, of picking up political signs together on the night of the election, Saturday afternoons at the State Fair, and sitting in the end zone at SMU football games. He introduced me to music of all kinds, Shakespeare in the park, nachos, and Fletcher's corny dogs. To say the least, he is a champion of gathering as many different experiences as one can.

He is more emotional now, and really it has been a joy to watch him age. My kids love to be around him, and they laugh when he says something is "neat." Whenever life threw my family a curve, no one jumped in with more of a willing heart and helping hand.

This man shaped the course of my life more than anyone else did. He set my life in the proper direction and gave me every chance possible to succeed. Today my father turns 70, and I can hardly believe it.

Dad taught me to love everyone and that each and every person was special. He taught me to be colorblind and was a champion of the underdog. The helpless, the hopeless, the underprivileged, the oppressed: he taught me not to just pull for them but to find a way to help them. My father taught me not to be an activist, but to be active.

His life was not easy, nor is it a picture of perfection. Looking back on my childhood as an adult, I can see those imperfections, but I can easily look past them as I see the effort and love afforded me by this man I call dad. Love was shown in actions and encouragement more than shared in words.

Married young, lots of kids, and not the highest of educations, yet some 50+ years later, he and my mother have beaten the odds. He taught me to laugh and have fun in life. He taught me the value of having good friends. Though our house was not the largest, it was made into a home, one where love, joy, discipline, and direction could be given freely. I love that house. Not the brick and mortar, but the care and purpose delivered there.

My father, well, it is his last several years that have really been the most impressive. On New Year's Eve of 2000, he suffered a stroke. I remember driving home on snowy Texas roads, wondering how it would affect this very important man in my life.

I should have known it would be inspiring and impressive. Though the stroke affected the speed in which he gets things done, it has not effected what he gets done. Meals on Wheels, mentoring children in school, spending time just listening to children who have suffered horrible tragedies in life, helping immigrants become citizens, being politically active, rarely missing a grandchild's event, and there are many more. All of these activities really just scratch the surface of what he does with his time. While others are retiring, he's catching his second wind, always, and I mean always, looking for the good to do.

Knowing my father the way I do, he never set out to be a great inspiration. He was just doing what he was supposed to do. Taking care of his family and the children God blessed him with. Nothing fancy or flashy, just getting things done.

If this devotional sounds like a tribute to my father, well, in part it is, but we can all use a reminder of how important our lives are to our children and grandchildren. My father's influence is profound in my life, and for me, it is a daily reminder of how critical being the best parent we can be is.

Know this—no one, and I mean no one, will influence your kids more than you. Not rock stars or super star athletes; no, it is you.

How you treat your wife, what your priorities are in life, how you love and serve your God, how you work, and how you play — it is all being watched and will someday, more than likely, be mirrored. It is our task, no, our honor to shape the course of the future. What a great opportunity we have to lead our children to God, to shape a course of loving and caring for others, of being givers not takers.

It does not take a high education or someone who has read every child-rearing book by all the best authors. No, it takes someone willing to be honest, real, loving, and shaped by God.

Somewhere out there, parents, grandparents, I assure you some very important people are in need of shaping. I pray we are up to it. Let us mirror the effort of those who went before us while learning from their mistakes and growing from their wisdom.

The most important man in my life turns 70 today, and I cannot imagine in what direction my life would have sailed without him. Thanks, Dad. Godspeed, and keep finishing strong.

Scriptures: Proverbs 23:22: "Listen to your father, who gave you life, and do not despise your mother when she is old."

Proverbs 14:26: "He who fears the Lord has a secure fortress, and for his children it will be a refuge."

Proverbs 17:6: "Children's children are a crown to the aged, and parents are the pride of their children."

Prayer: Dear Heavenly Father, we thank you for the people you place in our lives that influence us greatly; we praise your name for the faith and love of those who came before us. Help us to live our lives as you would have us to, catch us before we fall, and guide us in your wisdom in all we do. We humbly acknowledge that we cannot do it without you, and so we seek your help. We ask these things in the name of Christ, Amen.

Note: I acknowledge that as some of you read this, maybe you have few good memories, or perhaps even little knowledge, of your parents; there is little positive example for you to go by. I pray that God will bless your heart, and as you lean on Him, you will understand more than ever that the best Father of all is the Heavenly Father who is perfect in all ways and loving to all He created. May God bless you and send you comfort on this day.

On the Outside Looking In

Our church sits around a few houses. If you lived in one of these houses and were outside very often, you would recognize my family easily. Over the last few years, we have gotten to know a couple of the neighbors on a conversational level.

Last night we were at the church well before the normal time, preparing for an outdoor event for the kids of the neighborhood. As was the norm, we saw the neighbor across the street that always sits on his front porch. We exchanged waves as we often do and went about our business.

Kim had spoken to our friend recently and had shared with me that his face had been disfigured by surgeries to his lower lip and chin, and that he also had to speak through a tracheotomy. She told me only to warn me since she knows I struggle with such things a bit. Until last night, I had not met him face to face—until last night.

As we were working outside, our neighbor started to walk over and straight for me. Note that he is not a member of our church, just an observer. He came over to offer up a game for the evening that he had for his grandchildren. He had a really sweet spirit; we talked for a few moments, and I took him up on his offer.

His rough exterior told only the outside part of his story. His obvious good heart told the other side, the more important side. Kim always says the words I wish I had said. Last night was no different. She told our neighbor that he did not have to watch from the porch but could come over and be a part of the activity. She invited him to be an insider instead of an outsider.

He shared with us that he did not go out in public much or any. Then he pointed out the obvious to us: his surgically repaired lip and chin, as well as the fact that he drooled all the time due to those surgeries. With a smile, he said he had two more surgeries coming up and thought after those, he might be able to get in public again. We talked a bit more, thanked him again, and he turned and walked away.

We were the last ones out of church, and as we were leaving, I looked over to the porch where he always sits, and there he was.

I stopped, yelled thanks, he returned the greeting, and we drove away.

I thought of him much of the night; how his public appearance was keeping him from real fellowship. I understood his position. He did not want to call attention to himself. He probably feels self-conscious, and it is easier to watch from the front porch as opposed to taking the risky steps across the street.

There are a lot more people like our neighbor than we all think. Their public appearance or past is keeping them just a few steps from making real relationships with the body of Christ. There is the fear of being misunderstood, the anxiety of being talked about and pointed out, and the very real chance of being judged.

We can't push anyone to be in a place where they do not wish to be, but we can make the trip across the street a lot easier by doing just a few things:

1) We can remember our "personal disfigurement." Face it, we have all failed in our past and unfortunately have failure in our future. When we remember the grace God has given to us, we can better hand it out to a nervous world.

2) I focused on his eyes and listened to his voice. We need to take our focus off the handicap or failure and focus on where the heart is at that moment.

3) If the church wants to be Jesus, this is where it should start. Read the gospels (first four books of the New Testament) and you will find a Savior that never dodged anyone with "issues" and actually sought them out.

I think our friend really wants to cross the street, but just can't. I understand. I think there is a whole other world that could, but still will not because they don't feel safe. That breaks my heart, convicts me of my own prejudice and missteps, and makes me determined to be different.

Scripture: Matthew 9:35-37: "Then Jesus made a circuit of all the towns and villages. He taught in their meeting places, reported kingdom news, and healed their diseased bodies, healed their bruised and hurt lives. When he looked out over the crowds, his heart broke. So confused and aimless they were, like sheep with no shepherd. 'What a huge harvest!' he said to his disciples. 'How few workers! On your knees and pray for harvest hands!'" *The Message* by Eugene Peterson. I love this scripture. I use it often.

Prayer: Dear Lord, help us to be like you, to look to the heart of the matter instead of the surface. Help us to see things as you do and to avoid the temptation to judge and be prejudiced. Help us to guide others to the same saving light you have shown us! We ask these things in the name of Christ, Amen.

Richard + 2 Preschoolers + Super Target = A Hard Day's Work

Since I have been off work for a while, I have tried to be helpful around the house. One of those ways is to do some of the shopping for Kim. I pride myself in being able to handle some preschoolers and shop at the same time. Not to mention, Gracie and I have become very popular at the local Super Target! Believe me, they know us well.

Last Friday I really stepped it up another notch. We had some guests coming over, and I told Kim early on that I would do my part by doing the shopping. I had no idea how much of another notch I was taking.

First off, my normal list is about half a page and never anything too hard. This time, Kim stacked the list to the max. Unmercifully, she had me picking up stuff all over the store. The list was very intimidating, but I took it like a man and acted like this would be no problem. The outside looked good, but the inside was scared to death!

The normal crowd going to the store is Gracie and myself, but this day, my five-year-old, Caleb, was thrown into the mix. I have been around long enough to know this addition was going to make things a little trickier.

So off we go. First, we get one of those 18-wheel buggies with two seats up front. Then, it is over to the food court for a number one: popcorn and a coke! Gracie has the coke, Caleb has the popcorn, and I have the list.

For anyone interested, you have to understand that in these situations, you are under a time limit. You know something is going to go wrong, so what you have to do is minimize this risk by moving quickly and getting out as fast as possible before you have a preschool blow up. I didn't make it.

We were doing great until about half way when Gracie decided she was done with the buggy. I let her walk for a second, but she does not like sticking by the rules, so I had to corral her back in. She has a way of going totally limp (it is very impressive) when she gets upset. This limp-dish-rag-move makes it very hard to put her back in the buggy. So there I am in the middle of Super Target, an aging father of a crying preschooler attempting to buckle her back into the buggy, while Caleb eats his popcorn and watches the scene like a good Disney movie.

Remember, speed is important, and I did well with the stuff I knew, but Kim sent me for Hershey miniature bars. What is that? I am speeding up and down aisles looking for this candy with a full 18-wheel basket. Finally, I give up and ask someone who does not know either. Mercifully, I remember I did the right thing when I left and took the cell phone with me. One call to Kim, and I had Hershey miniature bars in the basket!

Oh yes—did I tell you I forgot a pen, so I have this super long list, but can't mark off anything on it. Just about the time I notice how difficult this is going to make things for me, I look over and this "together-looking woman" has a pencil in her hand, calmly marking off items on her list while her kids sit stoically in the buggy. I must admit, for a split second, pushing her down and grabbing her pencil did cross my mind. Fortunately a cooler head prevailed.

Then, just as I looked to finish, the unexpected happened; Caleb needed to use the restroom. I tried my best to put this off with bribery, but I know better. When that train starts rolling, it is best to just take care of business. So off we go to the front of the store for the bathroom: loaded buggy, me, Gracie, and Caleb.

Finally, we make it to the checkout line where God is exceptionally good to me. I must have had a funny look on my face because the friendly older clerk checked me out and treated me with extra care. They never put your bags in the basket anymore, but she did. And they never ever ask to get someone to help you to your car, but she did more than once. I assured her I had it all together. I lied.

Holding Gracie, I signed for the goods, put her back in the basket, wiped the sweat from my brow, stopped by for a refill of my coke, and made it to the car. Mission accomplished! Of course, when I arrived at home, I told Kim, "no problem." I lied, again! So what can we learn about God from all of this? Here we go:

1) Kim gave me a long list. I was good with it because I had been working on smaller list. **God does not give you more than you can handle, though it may be scary.** Also, each experience with Him builds on the next. This leads you to more faith and the ability to serve Him better. If you have stopped serving him, you have stopped growing and are not ready for a next step.

2) **Sometimes, your service does not look that good to the crowd. Don't worry about the crowd, do what God has called you to do to the best of your ability.** Great service is not always a slick production; things do not always go as planned. God wastes no experience on you. Don't worry about the crowd; concern yourself with pleasing God.

3) **Take any good, Godly help you can get.** Do not stumble around looking for directions when there are plenty of people standing around with the answers. It is silly to learn from your own mistakes when you can easily learn from the experience of others. Also, if someone knows more than you and is in your area, God has placed them there for a reason. That reason is to help you and to have His will completed in the best possible way. Drop the pride and USE THE HELP HE PROVIDES!

4) **Service is not always easy. Stop looking for the easy way out.** To really help someone out, you may have to inconvenience yourself. Do it anyway. Service can be a hassle. It can be difficult with difficult people. So what? If God calls you to do it, then do it. Do you think He did not know that stuff before hand? It may not always be easy, but it is always satisfying to serve the Living God.

Last words of wisdom: always take a pen with you when you have a long list; preschoolers are optional.

Scripture: Matthew 20:27-28: "and whoever wants to be first must be your slave—*just as the Son of Man did not come to be served, but to serve, and to give his life as a ransom for many.*"

Prayer: Dear Lord, take us by the hand and lead us to where you would want us to serve. Help us to stand strong when things are difficult. Lead us to focus on your love and to share it with others. We ask these things in the name of Christ, Amen.

Heard any good Hymns lately?

From my experience, it seems as though not as many churches are singing hymns anymore. In the so-called "music wars" in the church over the last two decades, it seems as though hymns have largely lost out to the newer praise and worship songs.

In my book, both have value, both have a place in worship, and they can bless all. The subject today is not to get in the middle of a debate about which style is best. I find debates like that totally worthless. The thought I want to send your direction is the theology that comes from the hymns and how valuable it is.

With that thought in mind, let me share some words from hymns that will preach to you as well as or better than any preacher can:

"Come and He will give you rest; Trust Him, for His word is plain; He will take the sinfulest; Christ receiveth sinful men." Good news for all of us from "Christ Receiveth Sinful Men."

"Once earthly joy I craved, Sought peace and rest; Now Thee alone I seek, Give what is best; this all my prayer shall be; more love, O Christ, to Thee, More love to Thee, More love to Thee!" What a great prayer from "More Love to Thee," written by W. H. Doane.

"Shun evil companions, Bad language disdain; God's name hold in reverence, nor take it in vain; Be thoughtful and earnest, kind hearted and true; Look ever to Jesus, He'll carry you through." It is good to know He will carry you through. Good words from "Yield Not to Temptation," written by Dr. H.R. Palmer.

Talk about a praise song, here is one from "O Happy Day," written by E.F. Rimbault. "Happy day, happy day, When Jesus washed my sins away! He taught me how to watch and pray, and live rejoicing every day. Happy day, happy day, When Jesus washed my sins away!"

I find this chorus to be a very good prayer from "Open My Eyes, That I May See," written by Chas. H. Scott. "Silently now I wait for Thee, Ready, my God, Thy will to see; Open my eyes, illumine me, Spirit divine!"

Hear the message and face the question from the hymn "What Will You Do with Jesus?" written by B.B. McKinney. "Jesus is standing at your heart's door, Standing and knocking, He's knocked before; this is the question you face once more: What will you do with Jesus? What will you do with Jesus? Neutral you cannot be: Someday your heart will be asking: 'What will He do with me?'"

The messages are clear, the praise sincere; "Heard any good hymns lately?"

Scripture: Psalm100:1-3: "Shout for joy to the LORD, all the earth. Worship the LORD with gladness; come before him with joyful songs. Know that the LORD is God. It is he who made us, and we are his; we are his people, the sheep of his pasture."

Prayer: Dear Lord, help us to heed the messages we sing and to not merely go through the motions of worship. Guide us to bring sincere and worshipful hearts to you, we ask these things in the name of Christ, Amen.

Mrs. O'Leary's Cow: Not Guilty

On October 8, 1871, a great fire spread across the city of Chicago. After the fire had died down, it was discovered that it had cut across 3 and 1/3rd square miles of Chicago. It is estimated that property valued at $192,000,000 was destroyed and 100,000 people were left homeless. 300 people lost their lives in this "great fire."

As with everything, rumors of where and what started this great fire spread like, well, wildfire. Also, as is the norm, a commission was formed to discover the cause of this tragic fire.

All historians agree that the fire started in the barn of Mr. and Mrs. O'Leary. From there, the facts get a little foggy. You, like I, may have heard that the fire started when Mrs. O'Leary's cow kicked over a lantern onto some hay in the barn. For me, this is the only reason I had ever heard. It must have been fact to be so widely reported. Not so, or at least not 100 percent known for sure.

As is with every story you will ever hear or tell, there is more to the story than meets the eye. The Board of Police and Fire Commissioners held an inquiry with the purpose of seeing what or who started the fire.

They interviewed 50 people, including Mr. and Mrs. O'Leary, and created 1,100 pages of handwritten testimony. With all of that testimony and time, here is what their report said: "whether it originated from a spark blown from a chimney on that windy night, or was set on fire by human agency, we are unable to determine." I see no mention of a cow here.

The first thing I think of when I see that report is someone owes that cow an apology! Or at least someone needs to clean up those nasty rumors. The cow was assigned blame, but never proven guilty. I have bad news for the cow and for you: it happens all the time.

People, and unfortunately Christian people, are much too quick to assess blame, to point fingers, and to find people guilty before getting all the facts. Unfortunately, we are not prone to change or correct rumors, even after differing facts are presented, not that it would change anyone's mind about a person or action. Once a word goes out, people access it as the truth, and that settles it. This is a particularly dangerous habit in light of the communication-over-loaded society that we live in today.

Here are some lessons we can learn from Mrs. O'Leary's cow, and more importantly, the Bible.

- Rumors, like fires, destroy lives; don't start them, don't spread them. Gossip is a sin as much as any other sin.
- Even if you think you have the facts, ask yourself what good will come of me telling this story. If that question were asked, a lot less people would be hurt. We live in a "tell all" society; Christians need to get away from being a part of it.
- Pride, arrogance, and revenge are some of the reasons many people tell rumors or even unnecessary factual stories. They think it makes them look better if they can bring the other person down. Remember, God hates all three: pride, arrogance, and revenge. Be careful. Remember this, the town burned down all around the barn, but did not burn up the O'Leary's house. The rumor may bring you down with it.
- What you say can't be taken back; after you say words they can't be returned to your mouth. Talk less, pray more!

Rumors, falsehood, and unnecessary gossip are like a great fire still spreading across our land. As believers in Christ we are to put out these flames and not spread them. Are you extinguishing fires or spreading them?

Scripture: Psalm 141:3 "Set a guard over my mouth, O Lord; keep watch over the door of my lips."

Prayer: Dear Lord, help us with the use of our words, help them to be words of healing and encouragement instead of rumors and gossip. Forgive us where we fail you and help us to walk in your ways. We ask these things in the name of Christ, Amen.

You Will Play Like You Practice

I don't watch a lot of Monday night football, but the other night I happened to come across a game played by the New Orleans Saints. They happen, at this time, to be one of the best teams going, if not the best.

I watched for just a few minutes, but while I was watching, they were doing very well. They showed the coach, and then the announcer went on for the next few minutes about what a detail freak the coach is, how they go over certain situations several times in practice. They rarely make the same mistake twice and look very prepared. This announcer, who also is a coach himself, said he had never seen anything like it.

This got me to thinking about my team, the Cowboys. They are one of the more average teams, and they seem to make the same mistakes all the time. It is hard to watch. When they are asked about their constant mistakes, they seem to act like it is no big deal. Their coach seems to be a really nice guy, but not much of a detail freak.

The difference is obvious: detail-freak teams make few mistakes and win; nice guys who are not detail-freak teams make lots of mistakes and win every once in a while. Question: Who do you want coaching your favorite team?

Yes, that is what I thought—me too. For a moment, let's think of our spiritual disciplines. Most of us are not exactly detail freaks. Guess what—because of that, we tend to make the same mistakes over and over again, only winning battles against sin and temptation on rare occasions.

Having been around a lot of coaches in my life, I can just hear the detail freak yelling at his players, "Get it right!" "We are not leaving here until we do it right!!" I can see the players grudgingly getting in line to do the same play over again. Why? Why is he this way? Because he knows what we should know, and that is without the right practice, we will not perform well in the game.

Perhaps the last thing we want to hear is someone getting on us about how much time we spend in prayer, worship, service, or Bible study. Maybe, though, it is just what we need—someone to get in our face and remind us that without good practice, we are destined for failure.

One of my favorite sayings at any practice of any sport is "you will play like you practice." I believe it, because I know it to be true—in sport and in spiritual issues.

Question: How is your practice? If you are looking for the answer, check on how you're playing out your life. It will tell the tale. Are you the Saints or the Cowboys? You ultimately will make that decision.

- If you need a little direction, give this acrostic a try.

Adoration—Tell God how much you love him
Confession—Take time to confess your sins before God
Thanksgiving—Take time to give God the thanks he deserves
Supplication—Take time to pray for others before you close

Scripture: 1 Timothy 6:11-12: "But you, man of God, flee from all this, and *pursue* righteousness, godliness, faith, love, endurance and gentleness." *Pursue is the key word.*

Prayer: Dear Lord, lead us to take seriously the things that will lead us to a closer walk with you and life's richest blessings. Motivate us for this, not so we can say we are better people but so we can know you better. We ask these things in the precious name of Christ, Amen.

Saving Millions

The *Dallas Morning News* had an editorial on Norman Borlaug the other day that had a wonderful first paragraph. First, let's look at the paragraph, and then we will examine who Norman Borlaug is.

Here is the *Morning News'* statement, "There are men who see human suffering and say, 'That's the way of the world.' There are also men who see human suffering and say, 'The world doesn't have to be this way,' but do nothing. Then there are the much rarer men who work to improve the world…"

Never a truer statement has been written. Now, who is Norman Borlaug?

Norman Borlaug died last week at the age of 95. He grew up during the Great Depression and was affected by the pain and suffering that he witnessed during that time. He became a plant pathologist and dedicated his life to fighting world hunger, thus attempting to do something about the hunger that he witnessed.

Keeping this part as short as I can, he is credited with being the founder of the Green Revolution and won a Nobel Peace Prize in 1970. He is credited with saving millions, some even say billions, of people who otherwise would have died of starvation. It was said of him in 1970, "More than any other single person of this age, he had helped provide bread for a hungry world."

I could load up this devotional with quotes from and about Borlaug, but that is not the point. His life should lead us to ask questions about ourselves, and the most important question we can ask ourselves is "what are we doing with the life God has given us?" Perhaps even more importantly is, "what are we doing with the desires and burdens he has laid upon our hearts?"

Borlaug saw a world in need, took the gifts God gave him, and used them to change an entire world. Most of us will of course never win a Nobel Peace Prize or feed an entire continent. Prizes were not his goal, nor should they be ours. What we need to ask ourselves is, "what are we doing about the world around us?" Do we have the "that is just the way it is" attitude? Or do we see opportunity and choose to do little or nothing about it?

We have a way of making excuses by saying things like "I am just a customer service rep" or "I just work at the local grocery store." Maybe we are those things, but there is a whole world that swirls around us that calls for our attention, no matter how we make our living. The most important impact we may be called to make could be in the cube next to us.

For example, maybe God has laid children on your heart, and you can mentor them after school. Perhaps God has blessed you with a family, and your calling then is to raise them up in the love of the Lord—there is no greater calling. Maybe God has laid senior adults on your heart and called you to love and care for some of the forgotten of society. Maybe you can counsel the hurting or hold a baby at a hospital. Need is everywhere and has a thousand different faces.

I am certain that there is something inside each of us that calls us to God, and a part of that calling comes with a desire to serve and love others in His name. I have met very few people who have not been burdened about some need in the world around them. Unfortunately, I have met great numbers both inside and outside of the church who choose to ignore that calling.

Borlaug said, "I think there are a lot of potential leaders who never become leaders because they don't put out that extra effort to move into unexplored territory. It's pretty boggy ground out there on the front lots of times. But the difference is courage. I think there is a lot of innate talent that's not utilized to anything approaching its real potential." Pay close attention to the last two sentences.

Are you important to the world around you? Don't lie to yourself and buy into the thought you are just one person in a great big world. Here is the fact: you are one person in a great big world that can be used by a GREAT BIG GOD in a GREAT BIG WAY.

Scripture: Matthew 9:35-38: "Then Jesus made a circuit of all the towns and villages. He taught in their meeting places, reported kingdom news, and healed their diseased bodies, healed their bruised and hurt lives. When he looked out over the crowds, his heart broke. So confused and aimless they were, like sheep with no shepherd. 'What a huge harvest!' he said to his disciples. 'How few workers! On your knees and pray for harvest hands!'" *The Message* by Eugene Peterson

Ephesians 2:10: "For we are God's workmanship, created in Christ Jesus to do good works, which God prepared in advance for us to do." NIV

Prayer: Dear Lord, give us sensitive hearts, ones that are not cold to the world around us. More importantly, Lord, help us to follow the feelings you drive into our hearts, the feelings that see hurt and desire to do something about it, the feelings that come from our first-hand experiences. Help us to follow your lead and calling in our lives. We ask these things in the name of the one who made us special, Jesus Christ, Amen.

A Day of Refreshing

There are some days I really look forward to besides the obvious holidays. These are days that are just nice days—you have yours, and I have mine. Here are some examples of mine.

I love the opening day of baseball. It is the beginning of a long season—and hope springs eternal. I love the night that the clock turns back and we get that extra hour of sleep. I love Fair Day—this is the day I go to the State Fair of Texas—a favorite for sure. And as a child, there was no better day than the last day of school—thus, sentimentally, I still love this day.

Today was a very special day in the lives of people who live in North Texas. It was the day the summer heat broke. I love this day. Let me explain. If you live in Texas you know with certainty it is going to be hot from June 1st until somewhere around Labor Day. "Oppressive" is the only word I can think of to describe the heat in Texas. You know the heat will not last forever, though it seems like it will. You just never know when the heat will break.

Today in Dallas the high was 87 degrees. Now for some of you, this might be hot, but for North Texans, it was pure heaven. When you walked outside in the middle of the day, the temperature was pleasant. When you played with the kids, you did not break out in a sweat and could play for more than ten minutes. Today was the day the heat broke, and we are thankful.

Here is my favorite part of this day; you can breathe again. It is like a breath of fresh air. This day signals to me that fall is just around the corner. Sure it is going to get hot again, but it is never the same. Days of refreshment are great. Some are offered by the weather, and others by God. Let me explain.

When you are living in the backwash of your sin and guilt, you feel as though you cannot escape. You can't breathe. Guilt stays with you like a hot summer day without a bit of shade to be found. "Oppressive" is the best description.

God never desires for us to live life that way. He desires us to live free from the guilt and shame of sin.

There is nothing like the "blue northern" that blows in when you know and feel the forgiveness of God. You can smile, you can breathe, you can feel good about yourself and the direction you are headed. There is a freedom that comes with being forgiven; oppressed no more.

Sure enough, someone is going to remind you of your sin and past, but once the sin is forgiven by God, it is never the same again. Let the cool breeze of forgiveness blow!

Having lived through the summer, I cannot imagine anyone who would choose the summer heat over a crisp fall day. Same with my sin—having lived in the pit of my sin, I cannot imagine giving up that refreshing that comes from knowing the God of the universe has forgiven me.

I feel a cool breeze blowing. Sit for a while, take it in. I think you will like the way it feels.

Scripture: Acts 3:19: "Repent, then, and turn to God, so that your sins may be wiped out, that times of refreshing may come from the Lord."

Prayer: Dear Lord, we thank you that you love us enough to forgive us of our sins. Help us to come clean with you, to seek to turn from our sins and to bring them to you that you might refresh our soul. We ask these things in the name of Christ, Amen.

Locked in a Cemetery

There are some positive things about funerals, and one of those is that often it turns into a bit of a family reunion. You see a lot of people you had not seen in a while, sometimes for years.

This past weekend I had such a reunion. One of my father's uncles died, and while at the visitation, it was nice to see a lot of seldom-seen relatives. As Kim and I left, we stopped in the parking lot and talked to one of my uncles, his wife, and my parents. As the day slipped away, we enjoyed reminiscing about some former days. Before too long, it was close to dark; my uncle and his wife needed to get to a hotel, Kim and I needed to get to church, and my parents decided to visit an aunt's grave in the cemetery.

My parents are still in okay shape, but perhaps they don't move as fast as they once did. This cemetery is one of the largest I have been around, and it is not easy to maneuver in. What my parents found is what many others have found; it is easier to get in a cemetery than to get out of one!

As the sun set, they made their visit, and then prepared to head home. Good idea. Too bad it was not that simple. Without knowing it, the time had passed for anyone to be in the cemetery and trust me, knowing this neighborhood, you do not want to be there after dark.

I had not heard of a cemetery being on lock down, but this one goes there. They lock the gates and shut it down tight. Sunday night, to my parent's unfortunate surprise, they found themselves on the wrong side of the cemetery gates after closing time. Never a good idea; on one side of the gates were the living, driving down a busy street; on my parents side were the dead, resting in peace.

Fortunately, there were three living people at that cemetery; my mother, my father, and a security guard in charge of the gates. They found the man with the key, he unlocked the gate, and away they went, narrowly avoiding a night with the dead. My parents were locked in a cemetery with the dead, and they knew it; unfortunately there are people locked in cemeteries of their own that seemingly do not know it or do not care.

Some are locked in the past of guilt, anger, resentment, shame, failure, and hurt. Others are locked inside the gates of present addictions, habitual sins, and personal disappointment. Either one or both are places of the spiritual dead.

Like my parents, they chose to drive in. Like my parents, they have found it easier to get into these places than to get out. Unlike my parents they fail to look for the one with the key. Christ holds the key; by his death burial and resurrection He overcame death and He can get you out of dead places as well. He is all about releasing the pain of the past and the heartache of the present.

Don't be like my parents and stay too long in dead places; stop living with the dead, let Christ unlock the gates, drive away, and never look back.

Scripture: Luke 4:17-19: "The scroll of the prophet Isaiah was handed to him. Unrolling it, he found the place where it is written: 'The Spirit of the Lord is on me, because he has anointed me to preach good news to the poor. He has sent me to proclaim freedom for the prisoners and recovery of sight for the blind, to release the oppressed, to proclaim the year of the Lord's favor.'" *This was Jesus' mission and still is!*

Romans 8:1-2: "Therefore, there is now no condemnation for those who are in Christ Jesus, because through Christ Jesus the law of the Spirit of life set me from the law of sin and death."

Prayer: Dear Lord, help us to not linger in our past where there is the reminder of past sin or to dwell in the present when we are living our lives apart from your Spirit's control. Guide us to know the freedom that comes from living for you and knowing your very real grace. We ask these things in the name of Christ, Amen.

Spiritual Karate

Say the word Karate and immediately my mind goes to people flying all over the place kicking, screaming, and knocking people everywhere. At times, something very close to that breaks out in my living room.

I grew up in the seventies. Thus, I have lots of references for this martial art, like Bruce Lee, the show *Kung Fu*, the movie *Karate Kid*, Chuck Norris, and even the classic song "Kung Fu Fighting" from 1974.

I can't tell you how many times as a kid I heard or said the phrase "don't mess with me, I know Karate." Of course, none of us did, but it made for a good threat, not to mention when we put our hands up in a Karate stance, it always made the other guy laugh.

Karate in its proper form is not an offensive tool, but a defensive one to be used only when pushed to defend yourself against the enemy. At least, that is what I learned watching *Kung Fu*, Chuck Norris, and *The Karate Kid*.

If we ask what "Karate" exactly means, this is what we find: Karate comes from two words, Kara, meaning empty, and Te, meaning hands. Thus, it means "empty hands."

So, what we have here is a means of defending ourselves without using guns, knives, or anything else to put in our hands. Being from Texas, my thought about Karate is that it is best used as a second option when you can't find those more conventional forms of defense—a last resort for lack of a better way of putting it.

In our spiritual life, there is a constant battle going on. In this battle, guns, knives, and anything in our hand will not do; we need something like Spiritual Karate. We come to the battle with empty hands, and quite honestly, we come against a force far greater than us.

So what do we do? Fortunately, God is aware of the battle and has made provisions for us ninety-pound spiritual weaklings. Below is a crash course in the art of Spiritual Karate.

A) **He is your refuge**—if you are looking for somewhere to retreat, go to God. "As for God, his way is perfect; the word of the LORD is flawless. He is a shield for all who take refuge in him." 2 Samuel 22:31

B) **Let your faith in God be your shield**—"In addition to all this, take up the shield of faith, with which you can extinguish all the flaming arrows of the evil one." Ephesians 6:16

C) **Gather spiritual wisdom; hang onto it**—"Do not forsake wisdom, and she will protect you; love her, and she will watch over you." Proverbs 4:6

D) **Ask God for help: start your day with prayer**—"But I cry to you for help, O LORD; in the morning, my prayer come before you." Psalm 88:12

The battle is real. Each day we approach it, we come with empty hands; lean on God to give you the tools to do battle against the evil of this world.

Scripture: Ephesians 6:12-13: "For our struggle is not against flesh and blood, but against the rulers, against the authorities, against the powers of this dark world and against the spiritual forces of evil in the heavenly realms. Therefore put on the full armor of God, so that when the day of evil comes, you may be able to stand your ground, and after you have done everything, to stand."

Psalm 46:1: "God is our refuge and strength, an ever-present help in trouble."

Prayer: Dear Lord, guide us to lean on you for our help and protection. Thank you for your love for us, and that in a world that is hard to trust, we can always trust you. We ask these things in the name of Christ, Amen.

The '74 Skeeters

In 1974, I was an average 12-year-old in my home town. I rode my bike all over the city, blasted firecrackers in my front yard on the 4th of July, and played every sport available. One of those sports was football, and though I loved the Dallas Cowboys, my hometown heroes were those Mesquite High School Skeeters.

Each and every Friday night, all of us would show up at the home stadium to cheer the Skeeters on. Win, lose, or draw (mostly lose), you could count on us to be there. In '74 though, something magical happened: the Skeeters got on a roll and ended up in the state championship game in Austin.

The memory of my first drive to Austin with my dad, grandfather, brother, and uncle is still strong. There was no way we were going to miss this game, and it turned into a family event. Unfortunately, the Skeeters took a loss that evening, but we were thankful for the season and the road trip to Austin.

At 12, you have heroes, and mine were many of those Skeeters. Thirty-six years later, I can give you many of their names off the top of my head. Names like Ford, Fincher, Crouch, and Singleton. To young football players, these guys were like rock stars with all of their great accomplishments.

I never thought of these guys as doing anything wrong. But as the years went by and I got to know both some of them and some of their siblings and found some rumors to be true, I came to find out that my heroes were a lot like everyone else.

Learning that my football heroes had flaws may have been my first lesson in grace. We see the people we look up to or those who have accomplished much through rose-colored glasses. We heap expectations on them we would never expect of ourselves. I had to learn to separate perception from reality. Only after doing so could I accept these people for who they really were: good football players with normal, every day flaws.

If there is one thing that can help all of us in our personal relationships, it is a serious dose of grace, especially within the home. Jesus was always good with grace. Let us learn from his ways:

1) **He treated everyone with equal respect,** no matter if it was a Pharisee coming to him at night like Nicodemus (see John 3) or the women at the well who had failed at several marriages. He heard them all out.

2) **He could put up with multiple failures** (see the life of Peter). Though Jesus kept teaching them about serving others right up to the last days of his life, they were arguing about who would be the greatest in the kingdom. These were his disciples, his closest associates—they should have known better after three years. How do you treat someone who just does not get it, especially in your home? A little extra grace might be just what they need.

3) **He was approachable.** Grace-giving people always are. Check the Bible out: people came to Jesus, all kinds of people. People who are able to work past their high expectations for others and dole out a heavy load of grace have more friends, laugh more, and live a more satisfied life. Graceless people are the direct opposite; few come to them. They live bitter lives and are never satisfied.

Those '74 Skeeters may not have been perfect, but they gave me memories that will last a lifetime. The least I can do is show them a little grace. What about your spouse, your child, your best friend, or the person sitting next to you at work? They may be flawed, but my guess is they have given you more good times than bad. How about learning from the master of grace and living out his example? They, like you, could probably use a little grace.

Scripture: 1 Peter 4:10-11: "Each one should use whatever gift he has received to serve others, faithfully administering God's grace in its various forms. If anyone speaks, he should do it as one speaking the very words of God. If anyone serves, he should do it with the strength God provides, so that in all things God may be praised through Jesus Christ. To him be the glory and the power forever and ever. Amen."

Prayer: Dear Lord, thank you for your grace that you offer to all of us. Help us in our lives to be full of your grace and love. We ask these things in Christ's name, Amen.

The Construction of Life

Just outside the community I live in, they are building a freeway. All around are the signs of change, and as I walk around the neighborhood, it struck me that the construction of a freeway is very much like what God does in the construction of who we are as individuals.

In the construction of the freeway, the first thing they did was take away something I loved about my area: the trees. They leveled them, and they did it quickly. Pile upon pile of bulldozed trees laid in the area until someone came and turned them into mulch. It broke my heart as I watched the change.

God does the same with us. When it is time for a change, many times he will take away something we love. He may take away a job you love that has given you security over the years. A friend may move away, leaving you to struggle with new friendships that fill the hole left behind. Maybe it is something more serious like the loss of your health that brings you to a new stage of life. Perhaps it is even the death of a spouse or loved one. These are serious: you love them, and would never in your own strength let go of them. But sometimes, many times, God has to bulldoze things you love in order to start a new period of your life.

After the freeway workers cleared the trees, they went to work on the ground and began to change the entire landscape. They started digging and moving dirt, creating hills where there were none and pushing deep into the ground in some areas. They also started creating the infrastructure, putting in pipes and laying wires that will be covered by concrete some day. This is the work that must take place underneath before the final stages can take place. It is a must, but it is not pretty.

God does the same in our construction. Right about the time we have started to recover from the loss of what we love, He starts to put in the infrastructure of our life. This is the most critical stage.

We learn to lean on him instead of our former life. We learn to take things one day at a time as opposed to making great plans for an unknown future. As the things we love change or go away completely, we start to take care of the "infrastructure" of our life. Things like dependence on God, praying with more power, loving and appreciating the little things we used to take for granted, like family. God starts to rebuild us from the bottom up, which is always the most effective. This perhaps is not the most fun, but certainly always the best.

They started the freeway several miles down the road from me at first, and so at times, I will drive a little out of my way to see what kind of progress they are making. Where used to be trees, where used to be dirt, where not long ago they were putting in the infrastructure is now concrete and bridge post. You can see progress being made, results of the process of hard work.

Results are the final stage of the construction of our life. After God has removed those things that stand in the way or our spiritual progress, after he has begun the building from the bottom up, results come.

We of course want results without all of that other stuff, but God's ways are best. He knows that without a good push, we would never put aside the things we love. We would never change our priorities, and we would be stuck in the same old mode. The bottom line is, we would never grow. Change must come. It is not always easy, but the results, when laid in the hands of God, are always best.

In three years, I will drive out of my neighborhood and jump on a freeway that will take me all over the city, saving me gas, wear on my car, and time. The trees will be a distant memory, the dirt and digging will be over. Progress will have taken place that at first I objected to, but in the end, it will be best for those I love and the city in which I live.

God is very likely doing the exact same thing in your life. He has stripped away things you love, or at the very least, changed their power in your life. Trust me when I say that in his time and in his way, before you know it, the new life will be the normal life. The old things will be found distant memories and the new life will be exciting and fresh. You will be stronger in your faith, closer to God, and more dependent on His touch. It will be best for you and for those you love.

Construction is painful at first, but progress in the long run. Don't take my word on it. Take God's.

Scripture: Ephesians 4:22-24: "You were taught, with regard to your former way of life, to put off your old self, which is being corrupted by its deceitful desire; to be made new in the attitude of your minds; and to put on the new self, created to be like God in true righteousness and holiness."

Jeremiah 29:11: "'For I know the plans I have for you,' declares the LORD, 'plans to prosper you and not to harm you, plans to give you hope and a future.'"

Prayer: Dear Lord, comfort our hearts at our losses and help us to see the bigger picture, your picture, your plans. Help us to stay faithful during the construction period of life and rejoice at the work you do in our lives. Help us in our faith and guide us through our doubts. We are thankful that you love and care for us; we ask these things in the name of Christ, Amen.

The Destructive Force

There are many forces that can affect our spiritual life in a negative fashion. Revenge is one of those at the top of the list. For a moment, think of revenge like a tidal wave. It builds up well out in the ocean and then unfolds in great destruction on its unsuspecting target.

Let's take a moment to build upon that analogy. A tidal wave almost always starts with an earthquake far out at sea. When the ground shifts, it starts a chain reaction. Revenge gets its roots with a life-shaking event. Someone is either hurt or certainly feels they have been. From that moment, the wave has now formed and started for the coast.

The wave does not hit immediately. It has hundreds of miles to build up steam. As a matter of fact, if it hit immediately, it would make much less impact. Same with the event—if it were dealt with immediately, it would have much less impact on the people involved. Instead, it builds; the longer they dwell on it, the more power it gains. With each new day, the desire for revenge builds until it consumes the offended.

The person involved can think of nothing but the wrong done them and how they are looking forward to the other person getting what they deserve. Always be careful with that thought. The wave builds; the target gets closer.

Finally, the wave hits the coast with a great destructive force. After just a moment, the area is overcome with water. When the wave recedes, the land has been swept clean, people are washed out to sea, and nothing looks the same.

Revenge is this way. It builds sometimes for years, then when it hits, it does so with a great destructive force. It destroys everything in its path. When the wave hits, it not only destroys the person who was the original offender, but also the person seeking the revenge. It rarely, if ever, leaves anything positive in its wake. There are no winners. Its force is great. Its destruction is final and can't be undone.

If the wave of revenge is starting to sweep you away, let me leave you with some thoughts to help you get your footing again.

Leave it to God, because he tells us to and because when it comes to justice, He is the only one capable and qualified. He alone gives true justice. Remember also that God is patient and may be patiently waiting for the offender to come to Him. Don't jump ahead of God and his mercy. There once was a time He waited on you, a time when you deserved justice but got mercy. Lastly, deal with the wave early while it is manageable. The longer it goes, the more powerful it is in your life.

Scripture: Romans 12:17-19: "Do not repay anyone evil for evil. Be careful to do what is right in the eyes of everybody. If it is possible, as far as it depends on you, live at peace with everyone. Do not take revenge, my friends, but leave room for God's wrath, for it is written: 'It is mine to avenge; I will repay, says the Lord.'"

Prayer: Dear Lord, help us to be people of grace, help us to follow the path you give us when wronged. Forgiveness is hard business for us. We thank you for the power you provide to be people who really forgive. We ask these things in the name of Christ, Amen.

The Trophy

When I was a boy, I played every sport imaginable except soccer, but I don't think it had been invented yet in America, so it doesn't count. When I played sports, you only received a trophy if you won or had a great individual achievement. Thus, a trophy was a much bigger deal than it is today.

I have two older brothers, the oldest named Randy. When I was young, he played for the beloved Galloway Hornets. The Hornets were not known for having great football teams, so team awards were not something they normally received. But in my bedroom sat what I thought was the biggest trophy ever awarded: my brother's most valuable player trophy for the Hornets.

Before I was old enough to play, I would look at that trophy and think "man, I want a trophy like that." I thought Randy had to be the greatest football player of all time. I can still remember looking at his team picture and trophy while admiring his accomplishments. As I awaited my day to play for the beloved Hornets, I knew I was going to have to work hard to get such a trophy.

Between the ages of 8 and 12, I did indeed get the privilege of playing for the Hornets. I worked hard and never missed a practice or a game that I can remember, and by the way why, would anyone want to miss practice or a game? I played hard, I worked hard, and I had a blast. Yet as was the norm, the Hornets didn't win much, so there was no team trophy to be had.

I never followed in Randy's footsteps and won the most valuable player award, but I was awarded a few smaller trophies and was quite satisfied with that. *What I learned in the process is that the fun is in the pursuit of the trophy, not in the trophy itself. Life is very similar, especially our spiritual life.*

Many today are simply satisfied in getting to heaven, and that will be good, no doubt. But there are rewards on the other side, and though I am a failed person like everyone else, I am looking for the trophy—not just to be on the team.

When we simply want to slip into heaven, then we settle for mediocrity in our spiritual life. We don't apply ourselves as we should and fall well short of our potential in Christ. We end up settling for second best.

The trophies of heaven are called crowns. I don't know about you, but just like with that big trophy Randy had, I want to look for the best crown possible. Also, as with the Hornets, I know that as I strive to be all Christ has for me, the pursuit will bring me satisfaction and blessings here on earth.

Are you shooting for the crown or just settling?

Scripture: There is a lot of scripture today; play close attention:
1 Corinthians 9:25: "Everyone who competes in the games goes into strict training. They do it to get a crown that will not last; but we do it to get a crown that will last forever." How is your training?

2 Timothy 2:5: "Similarly, if anyone competes as an athlete, he does not receive the victor's crown unless he competes according to the rules." Going by the rules?

2 Timothy 4:8: "Now there is in store for me the crown of righteousness, which the Lord, the righteous Judge, will award to me on that day—and not only to me, but also to all who have longed for his appearing." Are you eager for awards day?

1 Peter 5:4: "And when the Chief Shepherd appears, you will receive the crown of glory that will never fade away." Pay attention to the word "never".

Revelation 3:11: "I am coming soon. Hold on to what you have, so that no one will take your crown." Hang in there; keep your eye on the prize!

Prayer: Dear Lord, help us not to be satisfied with simply getting by. Put within us a desire to train, serve and love in such a way as to please you. We ask these things in the name of Christ, Amen.

Lighting up Church with Real Worship

If you are a pastor's child, there is one thing you can be assured of: you will spend too much time at church. Thus has been the case of all my children, and fortunately they have all handled it well. At times when Kim or I are busy at church, one of us will be left in charge of the children. The other night, it was my turn. I am not as good at it as Kim is, but I do try.

Basically, my strategy was to allow Gracie, our four-year-old, to walk the church. I simply followed. At one moment, she took me into a mostly dark sanctuary; while there, I experienced worship like I had not in a good while.

At our church, you start to attend worship at the age of four; this rule has not always made me the most popular guy, and I understand why. At small churches, you do what has to be done. Gracie has been battling it out with Kim for the last four months and has really been doing pretty well while keeping Kim and those around her busy.

There have been times when Kim has been a little frustrated about the progress she was making, feeling as though she was getting nothing out of church while wrestling with Gracie. Certainly there was the thought that Gracie wasn't getting much out of it, that is, until the other night.

Gracie took me to the dimly lit sanctuary, and as is her habit, began to boss me around. She had me sit down, and she proceeded to go to the stage. From there, she grabbed a microphone and commenced singing at the top of her lungs. Gracie has special needs and cannot speak like most four-year-olds, but this does not in any way stop her from communicating and was not stopping her at all from singing.

There she was, blonde hair flowing, smile on her face, singing to the Lord, raising her hands, and enjoying every second of it. I could understand her copying this from worship; she sees some of that every week, though I am still trying to figure out the hand-raising part, being Baptist.

343

After singing for a while, she stopped, looked at me, and then folded her hands into a prayer position. It was obvious she wanted to lead me in prayer. This caught me by surprise. It is not that we do not pray. It is that we do not fold our hands as we pray. Perhaps that happens at home, but not church. Somehow she knew the elements of worship and was leading me through it.

Though it may have appeared for the last four months she was getting nothing out of worship, obviously God has been speaking to her heart. Let me give you some reasons why I think that is so:

1) **Simple heart:** There is nothing complicated about Gracie or any child for that matter. They come to God and worship with no sense of needing to pray big, fancy prayers or sing songs with any kind of made up dramatics. She simply comes to God; we need to do the same.

2) **Joyful heart:** I have not seen anyone smile like that in years on the stage. She was almost laughing, she was so happy. We should come to worship with such a heart.

3) **Consistent Practice:** Gracie attends church more than most. There is no getting out of the practice of worship. It is a weekly event. It should be the same for all of us blessed with good health.

4) **Can't get enough:** I would get up to try and bring things to a close, and she would demand I sit back down. She never wanted it to end: the singing, the speaking, the praying—it could have gone on for hours. Many of us put a time limit of an hour or hour and a half once week on our worship. We need not limit our worship of God to a schedule or program.

I often laugh at the term special needs when it comes to Gracie. What she did for me in a dimly lit church was shed light on my real need to worship with a simple, open, and enthusiastic heart.

Scripture: Psalm 29:2: "Ascribe to the LORD the glory due his name; worship the LORD in the splendor of his holiness."

Prayer: Dear Lord, lead us to worship you with willing, joyful hearts that come thankful in your presence. We ask these things in the name of Christ, Amen.

The Forgotten Sign

When I took Driver's Education back in the '70s, we went over the importance of knowing what each street sign looked like and what it meant. For instance, a stop sign meant well, of course, to stop. This seemed boring and obvious at the time, but it is very important if you are going to be a safe driver.

It seems as though there is one sign that we in Dallas have a bit of a problem with. Even I must admit that my wife has accused me of having a little issue with this particular sign. It is the triangle yield sign. Perhaps we dozed off during this part of the lesson.

I believe that there are a few reasons why the yield sign is such a problem. First of all, it leaves a little room for interpretation. The whole thought is that you have to give way to oncoming traffic. For this sign to work correctly, a person has to decide what oncoming traffic is. For some, the question is not should you yield, but can you jump in front of the vehicle without getting hit. For some, yielding is not a command, it is a direct challenge of their manhood.

It seems as though the biggest challenge for drivers in Dallas is yielding to traffic coming off the highway. As cars zoom off the highway at 60 mph, most cars on the service road pay little attention and keep right on coming. Never mind that the driver coming off the freeway has the right of way. As a matter of fact, many times when you are exiting the freeway, you will find yourself yielding instead of the other way around just to avoid a wreck.

What I always like to keep in mind is that yield does not mean stop. So in my own personal driving, if I see no one coming, I keep right on going like I believe you are supposed to. What causes a problem is when the person directly in front of me sees yield and thinks stop when I can't see any reason for them to. On more than one occasion I have almost hit the guy in front of me because I thought they should have kept going.

The biggest problem with yield in the long run is not interpretation. It is in giving way to someone else. We have this problem on the roads and we certainly have the problem in our relationship with God.

We are proud people. We like to do things on our own. Yielding to anyone is a problem. For us, that proves that someone else is more capable or someone else has a better plan, and let's be honest here, that bugs most of us.

Mention the word "submit" (yield), especially in a spiritual sense, and we come unglued. Yet we submit every day. We submit to bosses, to teachers, and to all kinds of authority, no matter if we like to admit it or not.

So why fight it when it comes to God? Is He not our creator? Does He not have the overall plan and perspective for our lives? Does it not go better when we are submitting to His purpose and plan? If you call him Lord of your life, then here is a radical thought: let him be.

If you want one good reason to yield to oncoming traffic the next time you are driving around town, here it is: it avoids an unnecessary crash. The same thought applies to yielding to God in our life. It avoids an unnecessary wrecked life!

Read the signs, follow the rules, and I assure you, the journey will be much safer in life as well as in the car.

Scripture: Job 22:21-25: "Give in to God, come to terms with him and everything will turn out just fine. Let him tell you what to do; take his words to heart. Come back to God Almighty and he'll rebuild your life. Clean house of everything evil. Relax your grip on your money and abandon your gold-plated luxury. God Almighty will be your treasure, more wealth than you can imagine." *The Message* by Eugene Peterson

Prayer: Dear Lord, help us to seek your ways, to obey your commands, and to seek forgiveness when we sin against you. Remind us that your ways are best. Help us to acknowledge you in all ways, especially as the creator and lover of all things. We ask all these things in the name of Christ, Amen.

The Top Ten

I love lists and rankings, and I always enjoy it when a publication puts out its top ten on just about anything. I happened upon an old *Christianity Today* article that provided me with a very interesting list: the top ten most influential Christians of the 20th century.

As a public service to keep you from browsing though the internet, I am going to provide you with the list. Keep in mind, this is *Christianity Today's* list, not mine. Also keep in mind that one of my favorite things about lists is that they can cause people to get in such an uproar because they would have put someone else on the list. In no particular order, here is there top ten:

Karl Barth, Billy Graham, John XXIII, John Paul II, Martin Luther King, Jr., C.S. Lewis, John Mott, William Seymour, Alexander Solzhenitsyn, and Mother Teresa. My guess is there are some names here you have never seen, and some you are quite familiar with. My next guess is that many of you are shaking your heads and saying, "how did that person get on the list?" My next guess is that there may be a segment of you who really do not care about lists as much as I do. I am okay with that. Now I am going to stop guessing and get to the point.

Though some of these people might have had some effect on our lives through books, television, or maybe even at a personal revival, none were the most influential in our own personal life. For example, I have watched and admired Billy Graham for years and read some of his books, but he is not the most influential Christian in my life.

For another example, the first serious book I read as a Christian was *Mere Christianity* by C.S. Lewis. Though I have read it more than once and studied some of his other works, Lewis is still not even close to being on my own personal list of most influential Christians.

My personal list includes a saintly grandmother, a loving wife, parents who taught me to love all people, a steady father-in-law, a sister-in-law who is a prayer warrior, two sweet pastors of differing denominations and different demeanors who love God, love people, and love me. My list could include Godly deacons and loving neighbors, as well as my own children, who have taught me much about what it is to practice what I say I believe and whose innocence brings me back to reality. It could include older siblings who have showed me love and in many ways have been an example of perseverance through their personal difficult times. I could never pin down just ten, and you probably can't either.

On whose list might you be? The people on my list were not celebrities but normal everyday people who have passed through my life. The thought that they were influencing me one way or the other probably never crossed their minds.

Every day as we live out our lives, keep in mind that you may be more of an influence than you think and you never know whom you may be influencing. **The bottom line is that your actions and attitude matter!** My absolute final guess of the day is that you and I will never make the top ten list in *Christianity Today,* but we will make someone's. With that in mind, keep up the faith and stay the course.

- Assignment: Make out your list. Then, if it is in your power, tell some if not all of those folks how much you appreciate them and their Godly influence in their life. It will do them a great deal of good.
- Assignment: Ask yourself, "Is my example a Godly one, and would the way I am walking be a Godly influence to others? If so, great, keep it up; if not, write down things you need to change, then take the steps to get it right!

Scripture: Paul wrote both of these: 1 Corinthians 11:1: "Follow my example, as I follow the example of Christ."

Philippians 3:17: "Join with others in following my example, brothers, and take note of those who live according to the pattern we gave you."

Prayer: Dear Lord, we thank you for those you sent into our lives that showed us not only your love but how to practice it. Help us to live in such a way as to pass on their example. We ask these things in the name of Christ, Amen.

Tiz was 44

I was watching a music video the other night and noticed the image on television and the words to the song were directed at a very familiar person. In the mid '80s, this man owned Oklahoma, and all of us in neighboring states who loved basketball could only watch with admiration. True he was great at basketball but trust me this man was much deeper than sports.

He was born Wayman Tisdale on June 9, 1964, almost exactly two years after me. He was born to a well-known pastor in Tulsa, Oklahoma. He was given great gifts. Indeed, he could play basketball. I can still remember his sweet little left-handed jump shot. He was a 3-time All American at Oklahoma, won a Gold Medal with Michael Jordan in the 1984 Olympics, and went on to play professional basketball for 12 years. In 1997, he became the first player in any sport to have his jersey number retired at the University of Oklahoma.

Wayman always said though, that music was his first love. While in college, his coach Billy Tubbs altered Sunday practice so that Tisdale could play at his father's church on Sunday morning. After his basketball career was over, he went on to record several different jazz albums. He was an accomplished bass guitarist and had one album go to number one on Billboard's contemporary jazz charts. He would record 8 albums in all.

Indeed Tiz, as many of his friends called him, was gifted. But music and basketball were not his greatest gift.

Wayman Tisdale's greatest gift was his smile.

Almost 25 years later, I can still remember his great enthusiasm for what he was doing. Though I may not have been a fan of his university, you could not help but be a fan of Tisdale. His joy was contagious.

Billy Tubbs said, "He was obviously, a great, great player, but Wayman as a person overshadowed that. He just lit up a room and was so positive." Jeff Capel, the current coach at OU, noted Tisdale's "incredible gift of making the people who came in contact with him feel incredible special." Governor Brad Henry said, "...Even in the most challenging of times, he had a smile for people, and he had the rare ability to make everyone around him smile."

Wayman Tisdale died on May 15, 2009, at the age of 44. The first thing that came to my mind when I heard he had died was that we were very close in age. It put me in perspective with my immortality. Then, as I read more about his life, it was not the amount of years that he lived that impressed me but how he used his gifts in the years that he was given.

One thing I am certain of is this, "It is not the number of years you live, but how you live the number of years you are given that really matters."

Tisdale was a contagious, joyful Christian that used his gifts to make the world a better place. Shouldn't the same be said of us all?

Two closing thoughts for all of us this day. How are you using your gifts? And since we are all given a smile, how are you at sharing yours?

Scripture: Proverbs 15:30: "a cheerful look brings joy to the heart, and good news gives health to the bones." NIV
Proverbs 15:30, "A twinkle in the eye means joy in the heart and good news makes you feel fit as a fiddle." *The Message.* Got to love that paraphrase!

Prayer: Dear Lord, help us to be filled with your spirit in such a way as to share deep joy with those we come in contact with. Then, remind us each day that every day counts, that there are no guarantees, and that you love us and desire for us to use the great gifts you have given us. Guide us not to waste our time on earth. We ask these things in the name of Christ, Amen.

Out of Control

This is the time of the year that I love, cooler temperatures, football everywhere, and of course, the State Fair of Texas opens up here in Dallas. I grew up going to the fair and have hundreds of wonderful memories. I have one memory, though, that is not quite so nice.

We normally go to the fair in the middle of the week when the crowd is a little more tame than normal. One year we decided to go on dollar ride day. Since I have several kids, it normally costs me a small fortune for even one ride, so a dollar ride seemed like a very good idea.

As is our custom, we got out to the fair early and planned on staying late. We had a wonderful day, and as night arrived, we headed over to the rides to finish off our day. Just as we arrived, it seemed as though thousands of other people did as well.

The crowd went from small, to pretty large, to giant, to out of control in a matter of minutes. There was no room to move; Kim and I hung on to the kids with all we had. Finally the crowd became a mob. It was as close to a riot as I have ever been in.

We grabbed our kids and pushed through the crowd as fast as we could, Kim on one side and me on the other with some frightened kids in between. Dollar rides were the last thing on our mind. We were in survival mode. Finally, we weaved our way through the crowds and into open space, thankful to have made it without being crushed by the crowd or losing one of our kids.

During this whole event, I had two emotions: fear and lack of control. Both of these emotions were driven primarily by the crowd. Though you may not be at the fair, I believe people's emotions are very much driven by the crowd, with fear and lack of control being at the top of the list.

We are driven by fear when we allow the crowd to intimidate us into being someone we are not. The fear of not being liked, the fear of being alone, the fear of not being understood, or the fear of being a failure for the entire world to see can move us into making foolish and even sinful decisions. Fear drives us to be people we are not for people who ultimately are not important.

Control: we lose it when we allow the crowd to be the primary influence in our life. We say to ourselves the crowd is doing this, thus we should do it as well. We allow the crowd to push us in whatever direction the wind is blowing; trust me, the crowd is not always right.

Control: when we lose it, we lose sight of who we really are and who God wants us to be.

Two final words of advice: Spend the extra money on the rides at the fair, and stay away from a "crowd"-driven emotional life.

Scripture: Proverbs 25:28: "A person without self-control is like a house with its doors and windows knocked out." *The Message* by Eugene Peterson

1 John 4:18: "There is no fear in love. But perfect love drives out fear, because fear has to do with punishment. The one who fears is not made perfect in love."

Prayer: Dear Lord, help us to live our lives driven by your desires for us. Help us to have passions and emotions that match us as individuals created by you, not matched to the world around us. Help us have control and to know your love that drives our fear. We ask these things in the name of Christ, Amen.

Staying just a little longer than the rest: pays off!

I have three little ones that are still young enough to trick-or-treat on Halloween. On Saturday night they dressed up in what I consider very adorable clown suits, and off they went—John, Caleb, and Gracie, the cutest clown company of all time.

John, being 10, and Caleb, being 5, are the seasoned veterans of this trick-or-treating business. Gracie, on the other hand, is new to the business of going to the neighbor's doors and yelling at them until someone magically appears and gives out candy. "What a deal," she must think; she is probably wondering why her parents did not think of this sooner, and why we don't do it more often.

For the boys, it was all business. Their business plan went as follows: Go to door, yell trick-or-treat at the door, wait patiently for people with candy to arrive, hold the pumpkin out, say thanks, turn, and walk away. That plan has worked for decades, and the boys followed it to a tee. Gracie, well, let's say she was not interested in their plan.

Gracie had another plan. Being somewhat like her father, her plan was a little more personal than business-like. Here it is: go to the door, allow dad to hold the pumpkin (his personal privilege), yell something at the door, wait for the door to open, smile at the person handing out the candy, look inside the house for anything interesting, stick around well after the boys have left, blow kisses, and wave at each person in the house while they declare, "how cute you are," reluctantly walk away as dad prods her to do so, but only after she has signed thank you. Worked like a champ!

After about a block or so, we started to notice a trend with our company of clowns. Gracie seemed to be pulling in more of the loot. While the boys' pumpkins were getting full, hers was even fuller. So I watched, and just as we suspected, the longer she stayed, smiled, and visited, the more candy she received.

The boys were taking care of business. Gracie was taking care of business, but building relationships in the process. Conclusion: People want relationships from people more than they want someone to just take care of business.

God created us to be relational people. We need each other. We live in a world that has lost the art of sticking around and visiting, of taking time to give someone a smile and a hug. We are too busy finishing one task while thinking of the next.

To put it in the trick-or-treat perspective: we are busy getting to the next door, and in the process, we are missing out on really getting to know each other. It's a shame and has left our world lonely in the midst of millions.

We know hundreds, but know no one.

Perhaps this week, we can change our actions a bit. Maybe we can say hello to the check out person at the store, really listen, and give a serious response instead of the canned ones we all use. Forget for a moment that you have something else to do and pay attention to the people we are in front of right now.

We all want deep and rich relationships. Let's learn the lesson from the blonde in the hoop skirt clown outfit: be friendly, smile a lot, and take your time. It is, after all, how we were meant to act.

Scriptures: Romans 12:9-10: "Love from the center of who you are; don't fake it. Run for dear life from evil; hold on for dear life to good. Be good friends who love deeply; practice playing second fiddle." *The Message* by Eugene Peterson (I love Romans 12, by the way)

Prayer: Dear Lord, please be in complete control of our spirit and schedule. Help us to slow down long enough to build relationships. Help us to share a smile and the joy you have planted in us with those we come in contact with. We ask these things in the name of Christ, Amen.

25 Million Reasons to Live?

When you live in Dallas, whatever the Dallas Cowboys do is big news—even when it really isn't big news, if you know what I mean. This works out fine for me since I am a big Cowboys fan. This year has been extra interesting with the arrival of one Terrell Owens.

You do not have to be a big sports fan in Dallas to know at least a little something about T.O. Since his arrival, the cameras have been on him constantly, good or bad. Mr. Owens demands attention, and media of all kind are willing to give it to him.

I have found that most people do not like T.O., and though there are plenty of things not to like about him, I have found some things that show he is smarter than your average bear. No matter if you like him or not.

He is a very gifted athlete and from appearances works hard at it. Take one look at his body and you know that no one gets into that kind of shape by accident. It takes hard work. I also know he is gifted because wherever he has played, he has succeeded and has gained awards from his peers, who know best what it takes to be a great athlete.

T.O. loves attention, and I find him to be a great marketer of himself. He likes the spotlight and, my friends, he gets it, good and bad. What does this translate into? Money—and lots of it. For example, the last I heard, his No. 81 was the biggest-selling jersey of anyone in the National Football League. He has taken his gifts, work, and marketing savvy and turned it into a nice $25 million contract with the Cowboys. Not too bad, I'd say.

It is there at $25 million that I would like to land for a while. A couple of weeks ago T.O. took too many pain pills while recovering from a broken hand. According whom you choose to believe, he either took them by accident or tried to commit suicide. There is not time or space enough to debate this, and besides, only Mr. Owens really knows.

The day this news broke, the press was everywhere. You would have thought a president had been shot. After a day of speculation, the Cowboys called a news conference to explain the issue.

During that time, T.O.'s publicist, Kim Etheredge, started issuing denials, and then she made the statement that got my attention. Kim Etheredge said, "Terrell has 25 million reasons to be alive." Oh, really?

I guess for some reason Ms. Etheredge believes that if you make a lot of money, that gives you plenty of reasons to live. I beg to differ, but I am worried that many out there agree with her even though we never say it.

There are plenty of people with all kinds of money who are living lonely, desperate, and totally lost lives. There are also plenty of people out there who are making very little money that are also living lonely, desperate, and totally lost lives. There is no shortage of miserable people living in all kinds of economic situations. Money makes no difference whatsoever when it comes to reasons to live.

Ms. Etheredge has bought into one of the great lies of our society and I believe of the Evil one. That lie is this: how much you make, or what position you hold, is what gives your life worth. If that is what you believe, you will likely find nothing at the end of your rainbow except loneliness, emptiness, and a total lack of peace.

Why? You were not created simply to be rich or successful, at least rich and successful by the world's standards. You are worth something because you are a creation of God, and that is good enough.

Let's use a Biblical example of a great celebrity who had it all and was known the world over during his life. Solomon was a man who had everything honored by this world; he had great wealth, wisdom, and tremendous possessions. This is what he said in Ecclesiastes 5:10: "Whoever loves money never has money enough; whoever loves wealth is never satisfied with his income. This too is meaningless." Indeed, he was very wise.

In our wealthy, me-oriented society, we see each and every day the truth of what Solomon said in the scriptures lived out in broken and meaningless lives. You can never be successful enough; you can never have money enough. Enough is never ever enough. When you have 25 million reasons to live, you will want 25 million + one, I guarantee it.

Feeling empty? Looking for purpose? Looking for a reason to get up in the morning? I need only give you one reason: The God that created you loves you. Because He does, He has a purpose and plan for your life. In that plan, and with that God, you find real worth.

Scripture: Ephesians 1:11: "It's in Christ that we find out who we are and what we are living for. Long before we first heard of Christ and got our hopes up, he had his eye on us, had designs on us for glorious living, part of the overall purpose he is working out in everything and everyone." *The Message*

Prayer: Dear Lord, help us to avoid the traps of this world that lead us into depression and loneliness. Have us always to remember we are your children and that you love us even when it seems like the world does not. We thank you this day that you love us and sent your son to die for us and we ask these things in His precious and most holy name, the name of Jesus, Amen.

The Magnet Man

God has blessed me with the privilege of meeting some very unusual folks. Yesterday was just another good example. A friend and I were doing some work, and we noticed that the person supervising the work had stitches on the ends of his fingers. Not a big deal in most cases. Trust me, this was not the usual case.

As we asked him what happened to his finger, he said it was voluntary surgery. Now we thought that was interesting. He went on to tell us that over the weekend he had someone put magnets in the tips of two of his fingers. As my friend and I looked and smiled at each other, the question had to be asked: "why in the world would you do such a thing?"

This very sane-looking young man went on to tell us that since he works with electricity, this will help him feel electrical currents from the wires. Sure enough, as breaker boxes were opened, he could put his fingers close to the wires and know if that wire had any juice going to it and could even tell us which wires had more going to it than the other. He was a walking voltage meter.

This was very impressive to me, but the part I enjoyed the most was that he could pick up a paper clip without using his hand. They just stuck to his fingers like he had glue on them. Imagine all the bets this guy can win by telling people he can pick metal up without lifting a finger!

The bottom line is he had surgery to input a device within him that attracts certain metals. As always, the good Lord was way ahead of him. From the start, he put within us attributes that help attract people to Him and his love.

The Lord gave us eyes that can see not only the beauty of what he has created but also the people he sets in front of us. With our eyes, we can see the hurt that surrounds us: the lonely, the hungry, the cold, and the hurting. With our eyes, we can see the injustice of this world.

God gave us ears that we might hear what people say and the voices of those who have no voice in our society. He gave us ears that we can sit and listen to those who simply need a friend—not a counselor to give advice, but a friend to hear what is on their heart.

The Lord gave us knees to bow down and pray for His children. As we see a world in need of a friend, indeed of a Savior, and in need of help, God gives us the privilege of falling on our knees and bringing those needs before a loving and caring God.

He gives us hands and feet that move after we see the people of his world in need. With hands and feet, we feed the hungry, shelter the cold, and love the lonely. Our feet move us closer to people so our hands are able to hold those who need comforting and brush away the tears of the hurting.

Best of all, the Lord gave us a heart, a heart that breaks when our eyes show us the need and when our ears reveal to us the emotions and cries of those around us. He gives us a heart like His that cannot sit idly by as His creation struggles with daily needs or through great catastrophe. He gives us a heart filled with emotion that smiles at the birth of a new child or cries at the loss of a friend. Yes, the best thing He gave us was a heart.

One last thought is my friend spent a lot of money to have something attract to him. When we use the gifts God has given to attract people to us, we have wasted the gifts; they are rightly used when they attract people to God. This can be done—no stitches required!

Scripture: Psalm 36:7-9: "How priceless is your unfailing love! Both high and low among men find refuge in the shadow of your wings. They feast on the abundance of your house; you give them drink from your river of delights. For with you is the fountain of life; in your light we see light."

Prayer: Dear Lord, let use the gifts in a way that pleases you, gives honor to you, and most of all leads others to seeing and knowing the living God. We ask these things in the name of Christ, Amen.

Tooth Fairy Theology

At different times over the last 25 years, my house has been visited by a mysterious nighttime visitor. He comes in, slips money under a pillow, and away he goes with a tooth, always without ever being spotted. Yes, this visitor is the tooth fairy, and just the other night, he made his first visit to Caleb, my five-year-old.

Caleb is nothing but fun, and he's a great sleeper—we love that about him. Off to bed he went without any trouble with a tooth under his pillow in high hopes of reaping a great reward. A few moments later, the tooth fairy business completed, his mother and I headed off to bed ourselves.

About one in the morning, Kim felt a tapping on her shoulder and turned around to find Caleb there smiling, one tooth missing, but a dollar bill in his hand. Of all my kids, I do not believe anyone was ever as happy as Caleb to receive his gift for losing a tooth.

The next morning, while Caleb and I were enjoying a cup of coffee, I decided to quiz him a little about the tooth fairy. So I asked, "Did you see him?" His reply surprised me when he said "yes," so I went a little further. "Well, what does he look like?" That answer took a while.

He went off on a description that made me wonder about what this guy eats before he goes to bed. Come to find out, the tooth fairy is a she, not a he. She has all kinds of wings, dresses like a ballet person, and has glass slippers. She even carries a sword. I guess it is a little dangerous out there slipping in and out of people's bedrooms.

I want you to understand that I know the tooth fairy personally, and he does not look anything like this, and certainly does not own a sword. His wife would be afraid he would cut himself with it. What Caleb had in his mind was a combination of Disney movies, stories from his brothers, and his own vivid imagination. Though he had never seen the tooth fairy, he created her in his own imagination. Many today do the same thing with God.

We create the God we want instead of the God represented in the Bible. Here are just a few ways we create our own Tooth Fairy Theology:

- *Instead of coming to God in prayer for His will to be done in our life as we should,* we come to him with a wish list of things we believe we need. Instead of our Heavenly Father, we create a Heavenly Tooth Fairy to bow at our every need. We put our desires under our pillow and wait for Him to magically give us all we want.
- *Instead of calling on Him daily, which is the proper procedure*, we only call on him when we are in need or if something unusual happens. We have a theology that says "don't call us; we'll call you when we need/want you."
- We have taken God and combined Him with myths, other religions, and what we would like for Him to be. In so doing, we live in a confused state when He does not operate as we expect. Like Caleb with the tooth fairy, we have never seen God, but He is made clearer to us when we read His word, spend time with him in prayer, and walk according to His ways. *As we walk with Him daily, the real God appears.* Might I add, the real God is far better than any god we could create.

If you're five, Tooth Fairy Theology works just fine, as an adult, not so much. If we take our theology out from under our pillow and seek out God, we will find He is far better than any fairy tale could ever be. He created us, loves us, redeemed us, and has a plan and purpose for our life. What more could you ask for?

Scripture: 1 Timothy 4:7-8: "Have nothing to do with godless myths and old wives' tales; rather, train yourself to be godly. For physical training is of some value, but godliness has value for all things, holding promise for both the present life and the life to come."

Prayer: Dear Lord, guide us in our knowledge of you, help us to understand your ways and desires for our life is what is best for us. Give us power when we are weak and tempted to follow the world's ways instead of yours. We thank you for your love and ask all these things in the name of Christ, Amen.

Truly Rich, Among the Rich

She grew up in the depression and was an orphan by the age of twelve. She learned, like many people did during the depression, to be very frugal with her money. During her adult life, she bought her clothes from rummage sales, worked for the same company for 43 years, and invested wisely.

Lake Forest, the town she grew up and lived in, is one of America's richest. Grace Groner, college graduate and faithful employee, could have fit in well with the rich elite of that city, but chose not to. In a city filled with large homes and fancy cars, Groner chose to walk everywhere she went and owned a one-bedroom house hardly big enough for a dresser and twin bed.

During the Great Depression, she invested in three shares of 60-dollar stock that split several times over the years and turned into a fortune long before her death on January 19 of this year. It wasn't that she never spent money. She traveled often after her retirement, she often gave to people in need anonymously through her church, and she created a scholarship for her alma mater. She just spent it on the things that were important.

Let's say money was her companion, not her God. What can we learn from Ms. Groner who left somewhere close to 7 million dollars to the college she graduated from? Here are some points.

1) Her giving was not for show. In life as well as her death, she never attempted to be in the limelight. It was not about her ego but about the need. The other person's needs were more important than her need to be stroked for doing a good thing. *Matthew 6:1-4*
2) Though she lived among the rich, she felt no need to keep up with the Joneses. This temptation does many of us in as we attempt to have as much as the guy in the next cube, judging our success by our ability to have more. We lust after things instead of being satisfied with what we have. Things become our God when we allow this to happen. *Matthew 6:24*

3) Her pastor said she was very sensitive to other people's needs. She would see a need and make a gift. Two things here: though she did not have need, she could still be sensitive to the needs of others. Often, as we grow more comfortable, we forget what it was like to be in need. In a strange twist, many times it is the people who grew up poorest who are less benevolent after they have prospered. *1 John 3:17*

The second point is that when she saw the need, she did something about it. It is one thing to see the need; it is another thing to take action. *1 John 3:18*

4) Her lawyer made this statement, "She did not have the (material) needs that other people have...She enjoyed other people, and every friend she had was a friend for who she was. They weren't friends for what she had." When giving and living are done out of step, we attempt to buy our friends, no matter if we think so or not. Our status in America is often tied to what we have and we determine our friends to match our desire for higher status. Do you want to know who your real friends are? Find yourself in financial crisis or need. *Proverbs 17:17*

Ms. Groner gave much while she lived and even more after she died. That reminds me of a simple Jewish carpenter who did the same.

Scripture: Matthew 6:19-21: "Do not store up for yourselves treasure on earth, where moth and rust destroy, and where thieves break in and steal. But store up for yourselves treasure in heaven, where moth and rust do not destroy and where thieves do not break in and steal. For where your treasure is, there your heart will be also."

Prayer: Dear Lord, help us to use the resource of money you give with the right spirit. Guide us away from making money our God or using it to further our ambitions. Instead help us to use it in a way that gives glory to you and to your earthly purposes. We ask these things in the giver-of-all-things' name, Jesus Christ, Amen.

Turning on the Switch

I have been in my current home for a year and a half now, and it is every bit the blessing today as it was the first day we moved in. We enjoy all the rooms and what they have to offer. Evidently, we still have a little bit more to learn about the house.

We have a formal living room with a couch and a couple of nice chairs. This room is not our main living area, but a nice get away. It is a nice place to relax in every now and then, away from the rush of the rest of the house. I thought I knew all about it—guess not.

As some cleaning was going on, my daughter noticed a light switch in the room. She and my wife did not know what it went to. They played with it a little, even went outside and could not figure out what it gave power to. When I got home, I looked at it and for the life of me could never remember it even being there.

Of course, no one came in and put it there. It has been in the house all along, but for the life of me I do not know what it goes to. Of course, being the man of the house, I set out to figure this mystery out, but to no avail.

Here is the fact. We have a switch for power but never use it.

That sentence could match a lot of Christians' lives as well. We have the power of the living God at our disposal and fail to use it. Basically, many of us have not turned on the switch or have short-circuited the power. Let's look at how that happens:

- **We know God but do not trust Him.** We don't go to God because we have little faith. Remember, we are talking about the creator of the universe. We simply never flip the switch. *See all of Romans 4. Romans 4:20 & 21, "Yet he did not waver through unbelief regarding the promise of God, but was strengthened in his faith and gave glory to God, being fully persuaded that God had power to do what he had promised."*
- **We are living so far out of the will of God, His power is short-circuited.** We should not expect God to work in our life if we are living a life of disobedience. *Romans 8:5, "Those who live according to the sinful nature have their minds set on*

what that nature desires; but those who live in accordance with the Spirit have their minds set on what the Spirit desires."

• **We ask God for power for the wrong things**. We treat God like a Genie in a bottle that is there to grant our ever wish. We do not have because we ask with wrong motives. We are more concerned with pleasing ourselves than God. When we turn our hearts toward God and away from self, we will have more power than we ever imagined. *James 4:3. "When you ask, you do not receive, because you ask with wrong motives, that you may spend what you get on your pleasures."*

A light switch has a certain amount of power at its disposal. It does not matter if I know what it goes to or not. The power is always there, waiting to be used. Same with God. His power is always at our disposal, no matter if we choose to use it or not. He has more power than we could ever dream of. *Ephesians 3:20 and 21 says,* "God can do anything, you know—far more than you could ever imagine or guess or request in your wildest dreams! He does it not by pushing us around but by working within us, his Spirit deeply and gently within us." *The Message* by Eugene Peterson

Go ahead flip the switch; what do you have to lose?

Prayer: Dear Lord, guide us and teach us about your power. Help us to see it in the little things as well as the big. Help us to trust you in all we do. Guide us to respect your power; the one who has power to overcome death, to build the universe, and to heal our souls. We ask these things in the name of Christ, Amen.

Civil War

Abraham Lincoln presided over one of the most terrible times in the history of our country: the Civil War. During this time the country was separated mostly on the subject of slavery. What once was a unified nation became divided, and that division cost thousands of families everything they held dear.

As difficult a task as the war was, a very difficult task stood in front of the country's leadership just after the war. How to reconcile and bring a nation back together that had just finished shooting at one another for four years.

Lincoln was killed before the official end of the war in the spring of 1865, but before he died, he displayed the spirit that it would take to reconcile a country that had been fighting itself. In his second inaugural address on March 4, 1865, he stated these words that this day are on the side of the Lincoln Memorial, *"With malice toward none; with charity for all; with firmness in the right, as God gives us to see the right, let us strive on to finish the work we are in; to bind up the nation's wounds..."*

It is unfortunate that Lincoln never received the chance to put these words into practice. We will never know if or how he would have been able to "bind up the nation's wounds," but we at least know he had the desire to bring the family of states back together again.

Family battles bring out the worst in us. You do not have to be very old to remember some family battles. Maybe it was a divorce of your parents. They battled each other, they battled for custody, and they slung harsh words at each other through you.

Perhaps there was a death and a battle over money ensued. Once civil people make the battle personal with their words, their lawyers, and their hateful spirit, it is an ugly scene to say the least. Maybe a childhood rivalry turns ugly and words are spoken that shouldn't be. Then, brothers and sisters, sons and daughters do not speak to each other for years or perhaps ever again. It is sad, very sad.

Family battles are the civil wars of our times. I believe it grieves God greatly. It does not have to be this way. Let's look to Lincoln's speech for two points for the right way to reconcile relationships. I believe they are both good and Godly.

1) "With malice toward none": It is hard to overcome our anger when we feel we have been done wrong. Angry words last a lifetime. Be prayed up before attempting reconciliation or getting into a difficult situation with family members. Note: take the time you need to let your anger settle. Don't jump in too fast. That is a recipe for disaster.
2) "With charity toward all": Attempt, as hard as it may be, to see the other side of the story. They may have suffered some loss. They may have lifelong issues they are dealing with. It is very rare that anyone is 100 percent right and another person is 100 percent wrong.

As we close I want you to look at Lincoln's attitude, because attitude is everything when it comes to settling family civil wars. He realized that the battle was not the end, but reconciliation was. Binding wounds should be our spirit when dealing with difficult family situations, not compromising your position, but bringing a relationship back to where it needs to be. You may never agree totally (the battle). That is not the point. The point is to "bind the wounds" (reconciliation), and that is hard work, but work worth doing.

NOTES:

- Reconciliation is hard business; be sure and take the great reconciler with you: God.
- As perhaps the only believer in your family, your response will give you a chance to shine the light of Christ into the situation. Remember, God can use any circumstance to gain Glory and bring people to Him.

Scripture: Psalm 133:1: "How good and pleasant it is when brothers live together in unity."

I John 3:16-17: "This is how we know what love is: Jesus Christ laid down his life for us. And we ought to lay down our lives for our brothers. If anyone has material possessions and sees his brother in need but has no pity on him, how can the love of God be in him?"

Prayer: Dear Lord, help us to walk rightly with those we love the most, those within our families. Help us to reconcile broken relationships. May your spirit go with us and before us. Guide us in the use of our words and the actions we take; have them bring Glory to you. We ask these things because we know we are weak, and we need your help and guidance. We ask these things in the name of Christ, Amen.

The Uncommon, Common Man

He never wrote a book or saw his face on television. That I know of, he never saw his name in the local paper. If he was the boss at his job, I did not know it. He never held public office and would have been most uncomfortable with the thought. He lived in an average home and drove an average car. He was neither rich nor poor. He was your common man, an average Joe.

His name was Mr. Anderson to me, and thirty years later, his life still resonates in my memory. I played basketball with his son and took his daughter to the senior prom. We lived in the same common neighborhood, and his house was an open door.

Mr. Anderson was one of the first adult Christians I spent much time with. His impact was lasting. He never preached at me but always encouraged me. He was always, and I mean always, at our games and was leading on the cheers. We were not very good, but it did not seem to matter to him. When others might have criticized the coach, he was the coach's friend.

I did not hear him use swear words or make unkind jokes like some of the other adults. I rarely caught him in a bad mood, or at least that I could tell. In public, he was never caught cutting down his wife or having a big argument with her. He was strict, but not overbearing with his children. He had expectations of them, and they were to be met. If they were not, there was discipline, but it was in love.

He never preached a sermon, but loved and was faithful to his local church. Though I never went to his church, I thought well of it simply because he was a member. Of course, he was not a man without flaws, I just can't think of them at the moment because his good qualities stand out so much. To know Mr. Anderson was to love Mr. Anderson. It was an easy thing to do.

Some of you know a Mr. Anderson of your own. Some of you are a Mr. Anderson. I could have placed the name Mr. Thomas or Mrs. Smith just as easily, and you would have said, yes, I know that person. That is what makes them special: in the midst of a world that celebrates the famous, our world is built on the Mr. and Mrs.

Andersons. The average, everyday people who make an uncommon difference in the world because of their simple love of the Lord and the people the Lord placed around them.

When Mr. Anderson died of cancer somewhere around the age of 50, there was a hole left behind in the local community. Not because he was wealthy or served on the boards of the city, and not because he was a celebrity. No, a hole was left behind because an uncommonly common man was missing.

Why do we remember these people thirty years later? Because a great God took common people and made them and their love very uncommon, like only God can.

- **Assignment**: Take a moment and thank God for the everyday people he placed in your life that loved you in a very uncommon way. Thank them for their consistency, for their witness, and for their love for you.
- **Assignment #2**: Take a look at your life and make sure your witness is one that is being influenced by an uncommon God. You never know who is watching.

Scripture: Psalm 37:29-31: "The righteous will inherit the land and dwell in it forever. The mouth of the righteous man utters wisdom, and his tongue speaks what is just. The law of his God is in his heart; his feet do not slip."

Prayer: Dear Lord, we thank you for those who love you and have impacted our lives. May we live steady lives that give Glory to you and shine your light of love on those who surround us. We ask these things in the name of Christ, Amen.

Looks Good; Taste Great-Not Really

When it comes to new foods I am not exactly a thrill seeker. I like to stay with what I like. There are times though that I do attempt to grow up and try a new food. These are dinners my wife enjoys most of all.

She loves to watch my face as I chew into this new food, most of the time it is something green. She gives me the food then kicks back to watch my face. She does not want to hear my words; if I like it or not. No, all she needs to do is see my face and she will know for sure if I like it or not.

I know what is coming so in my wind I am working on my poker face. I am focused on eating the food and looking like I have enjoyed it. It really does not matter if I like it or not I just want to make sure that Kim does not get the joy of watching my face 'curl up' while I eat this new food.

Normally I fail. Kim with a smile on her face asks me if I like it. Thinking I can control my look I say of course. She just starts laughing and says you did not. She is correct and after a few more chews I admit defeat.

My voice says I love it, my face says I am eating Brussels sprouts. Same with our Christian walk at times; our voice says we love God but our actions look more like Brussels sprouts.

We must be careful to remember that our words mean little if our actions do not match those words. There is nothing worse in the world than all kinds of 'God talk' with little loving action behind it. We can give each other blessings, say God is this or that but if we do not back it up with Godly action the world will spot it a mile away and by the way stay at least that far from us.

We live in a world of talk and though we all hear it in the long run it means little. The world is looking for Godly action not great sermons. Here are 4 thoughts that need to be remembered:

- The world needs more loving action and less talk about those actions.

- We need to keep in mind that when we talk one thing and do another we fool no one especially God, who knows the motives of our heart.
- Attending church, always the right thing to do, can be one of the worst spots for God talk/wrong action. Simply attending church is no guarantee that your actions during the week are going to match your words. This takes some 'home work'.
- Sooner or later what is on your inside will show up on the outside and the world will know the truth of what you believe by your actions.

The question of the day: Does your actions say love or Brussels sprouts? Like Kim at the dinner table there is no fooling the world around us that watches us live out our faith day by day.

Scripture: Matthew 7:16-18, "By their fruit you will recognize them. Do people pick grapes from thorn bushes, or figs from thistles? Likewise every good tree bears good fruit, but a bad tree bears bad fruit. A good tree cannot bear bad fruit, and a bad tree cannot bear good fruit. Every tree that does not bear good fruit is cut down and thrown into the fire. **Thus by their fruit you will recognize them.**"

Prayer: Dear Lord, teach us your ways and give us the desire to follow them. Help us to think about our words before we say them and to ponder deeply the actions we take, making sure they match the message of love that comes from you. We ask these things in the name of Christ, Amen.

Stuck at a Shut Door

She was born June 27, 1880, in Alabama, born beautiful and full of life. Her first year-and-a-half was similar to any other toddler of that day until that fateful day at age 19 months when she was stricken with a serious fever that would shape the direction of her life forever.

The young baby was Helen Keller, who would become one of the most famous people of her day and the entire 20th century. Though seriously handicapped, she would grow to become a writer, speaker, and social activist. She would meet every President, from Grover Cleveland to Lyndon Johnson, until her death in 1968.

To say that Helen Keller lived a full life in spite of her disabilities is a gross understatement. To say she made an impact in the world around her would also be stating the obvious. That she surely met with some closed doors would also be an accurate thought.

Helen Keller was once quoted as saying these words, "When one door closes, another opens. But, often we look so long, so regretfully, upon the closed door, that we fail to see the one that has opened for us."

That is a wise statement that can speak to the heart of our relationship to God when we view it from a spiritual perspective. Let us do just that.

How are you currently dealing with closed doors?

Are you frozen in disappointment at that lost job, marriage, position, or other opportunity? Has the grief of your life overcome you to the point that to move forward is just too much? Have you allowed bitterness to become your constant companion as you stare broken at a door that will never open again?

When we choose to stand at the closed door, we get tunnel vision. We focus on the wrong done us by others, or our disappointment; or we beat ourselves up with our mistakes that cost us the opportunity. Often, this perspective of life leads us to deep depression, low self-esteem, or worst of all, into destructive behavior.

As we focus on what could have been, we miss what God has burst open for us. The best way to move past a closed door is to change focus and perspective.

We can learn from our past, but we are not to dwell on it. There is nothing most of us can ever do about the closed door once it is closed. That chapter in life is behind us. That is where it belongs. Look forward.

If we are to move forward, we are to focus on the one who loves us unconditionally and who always has our best interest at heart. As we turn our focus off the closed door and onto God, He will begin to sometimes slowly, and at times without us even knowing it, lead us to a new and even more exciting direction.

Keller dealt with physical handicaps, but today we are looking at spiritual ones. Life is filled with many different chapters: some doors that are slammed shut and others that swing open. Life is a journey in growing closer and more deeply in love with the one who gives life. Focus on Him, and before long, you will no longer see the shut door but the One in control of each and every chapter of life.

Scripture: Psalm 25:4-5: "Show me your ways, O LORD, teach me your paths; guide me in your truth and teach me, for you are God my Savior, and my hope is in you all day long."

Prayer: Dear Lord, help us to hold things loosely and to hold on to you tightly. Help us to lean on you for the "next steps" in life. We ask these things in the name of Christ, Amen.

Making the Garbage Man's day!

My creative mind works best on the move. Most Mondays can be difficult days because I am normally exhausted from my work on Sunday. Yet work must happen, and yesterday was a very busy day. But in the midst of the busyness, I had to get out, so Gracie and I took a walk around the neighborhood. It was great fun!

They are doing some roadwork around our house, so the neighborhood was busy and loud. There were lots of people for Gracie to say hello to, and she was having quite the time. All the construction workers thought it was nice to see Gracie as well, so it was working out for everyone.

Yesterday was trash day, thus the garbage man was in the area. Just by chance, as we were walking down a street, I looked up and there was the "garbage truck" and a big burly guy with a ball cap on his head, smiling in my direction and waving. Now I have had this occur to me enough to know he was not waving at me, but Gracie. Sure enough, I look down, and there she is waving with all her might to the garbage man.

For some reason, yesterday there were two men in the truck when normally there is just one. So as we keep walking, the other guy catches on, and he is waving at Gracie as well. So there I have it, two burly-looking guys with ball caps on, sitting in a garbage truck, waving like school kids at Gracie.

Now I know a good moment when I see it, so I look down at Gracie and ask her to blow them a kiss. Sometimes she will, and sometimes she won't; today she did. She looks up, blows them a kiss, and knocks both of them over with it. Their smiles turn to an all out laugh and all the while waving back at this girl on the sidewalk throwing them love. As they turn out away from us, you can tell they are still smiling, and she has just made their day. Classic Gracie—I was lucky to be there.

For some people, the garbage man is a low-class citizen, but not from my point of view and certainly not from Gracie's. Gracie would not know the garbage man from the CEO of Exxon/Mobil. She doesn't care if you are the clerk at Target or the construction worker banging out concrete on our street. She knows no partiality or prejudice. It is so refreshing. Here is the lesson we all need to learn: God sees things the same as Gracie.

We see status, education, financial condition, or star ability, but God sees His creation in us all. We have a tendency to judge people on where they are from and what their past consists of. God sees us (thankfully) for how we are and how He created us.

As Christians, we are called to see things God's way. The church should be the one place where we all come on common ground. When you walk through the door of a church, where you are from, what your history is, how much money you make, where you went to school, or even if you went to school should matter zero. In God's sight, we all come with a common need for grace, and He is all about giving it.

Gracie and God see things eye to eye when it comes to people. They are all special. Do you want to see your world smile more, follow their lead, and blow them a kiss of unconditional love? Trust me, the smile you will see in return is worth it.

Scripture: James 2:1, 5, 8 & 9:
1: "My brothers, as believers in our glorious Lord Jesus Christ, don't show favoritism."
5: "Listen, my dear brothers: Has not God chosen those who are poor in the eyes of the world to be rich in faith and to inherit the kingdom he promised those who love him?"
8 & 9: "If you really keep the royal law found in Scripture 'Love your neighbor as yourself,' you are doing right. But if you show favoritism, you sin and are convicted by the law as lawbreakers."

Prayer: Dear Lord, guide us to see people as you do, to look within first, and not pass judgment on others. Help us pass out unconditional love as you do. We ask these things in the name of Christ, Amen.

Pushing Buttons

Each child, at one time or another, enters a stage where they learn something you really wish they would not have learned. At times that comes from mental development, and at others it comes from physical development. Either way, it can cause a parent some trouble.

For instance, it is never a good thing when a toddler learns how to dig in the pantry. Instead of having peaceful control of calorie intake, you then have to battle it out with them as they learn the difference between Hostess Twinkies and Goldfish crackers.

My Gracie, over the last several months, has entered into such a stage. She has learned how to push buttons, especially those concerning the television. She can keep us hopping, trying to keep the video world in check.

Gracie can get us to screens we never knew existed, and our greatest fear is that on the next cable bill we are going to have purchased a show of let's say questionable viewing.

We will look up, and she will be recording a show, not that I am against that—I just did not know we could! The worse thing is that I have no idea of how to make it stop. Perhaps I should get her to give me a lesson on which buttons to push.

She is constantly moving us from video viewing back to the stations. This is only a problem because of the number of remotes we need for getting things right and the amount of time I have to spend looking for those remotes.

At times, if she does not like the video her brother has chosen, she simply pushes the button and turns it off, much to Caleb's displeasure. It may look like she does not know what she is doing, but don't let those sweet blue eyes and wavy blonde hair fool you: she knows exactly what she is doing.

When it comes to pushing someone's buttons, don't try to fool yourself or others. You, like Gracie, know exactly what you are doing. The difference is she is young and just getting started, while we have been pushing people's buttons for years.

Pushing buttons is an American art form. My definition of pushing buttons is choosing to do something that you know is going to irritate, anger, or frustrate another person. You're pushing their buttons if you know it will bother them before you do it.

Why do we push buttons? Here are just a few reasons:

- We push buttons to get back at people for things they did or said without it looking like we are trying to do it. Aren't we cleaver?
- At times, pushing buttons is a way of getting an argument started. Why we want to do that, I have no idea, but trust me, it happens. Some people just love conflict.
- We push buttons on people we do not like in order to get under their skin.
- We push buttons because we do not have the guts to come right out and say what we think in a loving spirit.

Whose buttons do we push the most? You guessed it: the people we live with and are supposed to love the most. We know their buttons the best and should know better but do it anyway. Siblings are the masters of pushing buttons!

What should we do about it? Simple, stop it. We are not four like Gracie. We are adults who claim the love of Christ. We should be looking out for the best interests of others, not for ways to drive them over the edge. Use the fruit of the spirit of self-control when you are tempted; *ask God for ways to lift up, not stir up.*

Scripture: 1 Peter 3:8-9: "Finally, all of you, live in harmony with one another; be sympathetic, love as brothers, be compassionate and humble. *Do not repay evil with evil or insult with insult, but with blessing,* because of this you were called so that you may inherit a blessing."

Prayer: Dear Lord, guide us in our relationships to care for the other person, to love them, to forgive them and to find ways to encourage them. We ask these things in the name of Christ, Amen.

Thank God for Role Players

If you watch sports from time to time, you will eventually see an All-Star game. This game is a collection of the best players in whatever sport they happen to play. It is nice to see all these superstars on the field at the same time, but it is rarely a good game.

You might ask, "Why is it a poor game with nothing but the best on the field?" Easy answer, someone is missing. Who is that someone? Another easy answer: the role-player.

For every superstar who gains the attention of the camera on television or the fans in the stand, there is someone who passed them the ball, blocked to make way for the run, or bunted the ball over to help get a guy in scoring position. Little guys who do not get much attention but are irreplaceable in helping the team win.

If you are having trouble grabbing the concept because you are not a sports fan, let me help you out. The role-player is the mom who makes sure the children do their homework or get to school with a coat when it is cold. They are the accountant who crunches the numbers while the salesman makes the presentation. You don't pay a lot of attention to the role-player but you know they are there. They are the unsung heroes of life: dependable, unassuming, and yet invaluable.

They are most needed in the big game, or as we are going to look at today, the crises of life. Four years ago to this very day, almost to the very minute I am typing this, I entered a crisis in my life. After six very healthy children, number seven entered the world with some unexpected trouble. With no warning from sonograms or doctors, she was born with Down syndrome. On top of that, she had health issues that would keep her in the hospital for a month and would later lead her to heart surgery. During this time, I found the true importance of the role players in my life.

Be sure you know this, long before you enter a crisis, God is setting up your role-players so they will be in place when you need them. For me, it was long-time friends who offered tears, prayers, babysitting, car rides, and financial support. People who I had probably taken for granted over the previous ten to twenty years were right there behind the scenes, lifting us up when we needed them.

Family members are often role-players; our family was no different. They were there from the very first moments, offering hugs, comforting words, telling us how much they loved us. They refused to allow us to stand alone and offered every help imaginable. They were so supportive that the written word cannot easily describe it. My heart skips a beat as I think of some of those moments. With role players like our brothers, sisters, nephews, nieces, and parents, we could not possibly have fallen.

I am certain God placed us in the church we attended with our specific need in mind. He does not do things by accident, and he had us right where we could be loved, where Gracie could be super-loved, and where prayers were being lifted up continually. Our church family played its role perfectly, supporting us with compassion, love, and respect.

God was busy arranging things at work well before the crisis began. He had moved me to the right position, in the right place, and had me working for and with the right people. He placed me with people who loved my family and me. He placed the proper loving supervisor in charge of my time. There was never a need to worry about the workplace. When it comes to role-players during crisis, with God there is no detail too small.

For the most part, the crisis has past. We entered our new normal long ago. Four years later, I can look back and see God's hand arranging and rearranging our role-players to help meet the urgent need, from the nurses who took care of us each day to the doctors who walked with us professionally and with a caring spirit. God never missed a beat.

The Most Valuable Player in any crisis is always God. He knows every need and loves us in an unconditional fashion. As I look back, I praise him for his care, and I give him glory that he loves us so. I know full well things could have turned out far different. His grace is truly amazing. Today though, more than anything, I thank him for the role-players he placed in our life to walk with us through a dark shadow of life: dependable, unassuming, yet invaluable. Praise be to God for his unsung heroes!

Assignment:

1) Take a moment and remember back to a time of crisis in your life. Think of the names of those who were there for you, for those who walked with you through those moments. As names come to your mind, pause and lift up a prayer of thanksgiving to God for sending these special people in your life. You may even want to send them a note or give them a call this day to thank them for their love and support. Don't put it off, or you might never do it. Role-players need encouragement, too!

2) Look around you. God may have you placed to play a role in someone's life. He may need to use your experience, your love, or your life skills to help someone in crisis mode. Be ready to jump in when needed.

Scripture: Psalm 23:1-4: "The Lord is my shepherd, I shall not be in want. He makes me lie down in green pastures, he leads me beside quiet waters, he restores my soul. He guides me in paths of righteousness for his names sake. Even though I walk through the valley of the shadow of death, I will fear no evil, for you are with me; your rod and your staff they comfort me."

Prayer: Dear Lord, we thank you for those you have placed in our lives to be with us in difficult moments. We pray that you will bless them greatly for the loving roles they played in our lives. We praise you because of your great love for us. We ask all these things in the name of Christ, Amen.

The Good Side of Crutches

Walking into work, well really almost running into work the other day, I ran into a fellow moving somewhat slower than I was because he was on crutches.

The gentleman in front of me and I slowed our pace and opened the door for him to allow him to take his time getting in. Where I work, you can only get in through revolving doors—there is no other way. So, if someone is moving slowly in front of you, you just have to take it easy and let them go. Of course, if someone is on crutches, you can have some sympathy for them, and their moving slowly does not bother you as much.

This man was very friendly, and you could tell he was new to crutches. He didn't operate them very well and was moving extra slow as he navigated the door. He smiled as we let him in, and he made a wonderful statement, "With crutches, you meet a lot of new and friendly people." That statement has stayed with me for more than a week.

Let's learn some lessons from our friend on crutches. One lesson is really a reminder that on the whole, people really do care about other folks. When they see someone in need, they will open the door, wait an extra minute, carry your briefcase, or even just simply give a smile and ask how you're doing. It's nice to know there is still a good side of people.

Really, it is not so much what I learn from knowing other people are nice to people, it is what the guy on the crutches must be learning that strikes me. When you are on crutches, you need other people. We go through life thinking we are very self-sufficient. It is only when we are hurt or hurting that we realize we can't do all of this on our own.

You need someone to carry your books, to open the door, to help with even the simplest of things. We try to be self-sufficient, but it just cannot happen. When on crutches, you are forced to look for help. I think that can be a good thing.

When you are hurt or hurting in life, it is good to be forced to look for help. God will use that time to lead you into a dependency on Him and on others that you would have never sought as long as things were going well. There are times that God puts you on "crutches" so that we can see the good in others and learn what it means to really depend on Him.

There are times in our lives that we all limp around on crutches. For example, a family member dies and you need some folks to hold you up spiritually and physically. It is good to have family and friends that are ready to stand in the gap for you with prayers and support. Another example is when someone accustomed to making a good living finds themselves out of work. It is hard for them to be able to swallow their pride and accept help from others. But in the long run, we are better for it.

Sometimes we twist our own ankle by making foolish decisions, and at other times, we step in a pothole we never see coming. No matter which way it happens, it always hurts, and there is always a time of recovery. One thing to keep in mind is that with short-term injury, crutches are there simply to help us through that period, not to be used forever. God has a lesson for us to learn, then leads us to throw off the crutches and get moving again. Accept those lessons, and then move on, possibly and probably in the direction of helping someone else with your newfound dependence on God.

God uses our pain, our moment on crutches, if you will, to teach us to draw closer to Him and others. In the long run, it is good for us. Even if we do not enjoy it at the moment, we can almost always look back and see how it helped us grow.

Right now, you might be limping alone. God has slowed you down, gotten your attention. Most growth is not found as you run through life, but as you limp. Somehow, like my friend walking in the door, we need to find the good in the crutches.

Scripture: Psalm 62:7: "My salvation and my honor depend on God; he is my might rock, my refuge."

Prayer: Dear Lord, help us to depend on you with all our hearts. Help us to learn the lessons you have in store for us to build us up, to draw us closer to you. Have us not to rebel against your messages. We ask these things in the name of Christ, Amen.

Trees, Trees; Everywhere Trees!

For over 30 years, with little exception, my family has been spending the weekend after Thanksgiving cutting down our Christmas tree at a Christmas tree farm. It is really a nice day. We get to go for a short road trip to the county and have a good time as a family choosing and cutting down our tree.

Here is how it works. The owner of the farm takes you on a hay ride, and leaves you with a handsaw in the midst of thousands (not exaggerating) of Christmas trees. From there, you find the one you like, cut it down, and wait for the tractor's return.

This year, I was particularly relaxed and really could enjoy the moment. As I did, I found some things at the tree farm that match in life. Here are just a few.

- Forty yards away, the trees always look perfect. Only when you get closer do you see their flaws. Exactly how we are with people. If you know them on the surface, people can look great, but when you investigate further, you see they are flawed just like you. Seeing people as people are is not a bad thing. We certainly need to keep that in mind as we put people on pedestals or consider looking the other way from our spouse. "The grass is always greener on the other side of the fence" is true on the farm and in life; in reality, it is a false read, don't be fooled.

- No tree is perfectly straight. Putting a crooked Christmas tree in a Christmas tree stand is a challenge. This challenge has not always brought out the best in me. So I look for a tree with a straight trunk. If you do the same, here are my words for you: good luck. It is just not out there. There are no perfectly straight trees, and there are no perfectly straight people, either. Here are two thoughts:

  a) If there are no perfect people, why do you keep expecting perfection from yourself? I am not saying don't try to be the best God has for you, but give yourself a little slack.

385

Stop beating yourself up. Accept you for who you are, an imperfect creation of the Father who the Lord loves, crooked trunk and all.

b) Stop expecting perfection from others. We are all flawed: that means the person who sleeps next to you is just as flawed as you. Or that child, or person at work, etc. Stop putting unattainable expectations on people, and you will find you can get along with others and accept them far easier.

- Tree sap is sticky. Do your best to keep your hands off. Same with people. The trees were extra sappy this year, and that stuff is like glue. It is annoying, and you can't shake loose of it. People with poor attitudes are like sap. They are annoying, and unfortunately their poor attitudes tend to stick with us. If you hang around saps, you can almost be certain you will be one soon. Word to the wise, stay clear of sappy people!

It is amazing what you can learn amongst the trees. Remember, keep your hands off the sap, look for a straight trunk, and keep in mind that they all look good when you put lights on them. It's the same with people. We may not all look pretty, but in the light of Christ, we can all shine brightly.

Scripture: 2 Corinthians 13:11: "Finally, brothers, goodbye. Aim for perfection, listen to my appeal, be of one mind, live in peace. And the God of love and peace will be with you."

Prayer: Dear Lord, help us to see things clearly in our relationship with you and other people. Help us to forgive ourselves and move on to the life you have for us, then help us to forgive the flaws of others as you have forgiven us. Guide us to your light of love. We ask these things in the name of Christ, Amen.

Stay Away from the Edge

A phobia is an irrational, intense, persistent fear of certain situation, activities, things, or people. With that in mind, ask yourself this question, "Do I have any?" I am thinking most of us have at least one. After looking at a list of phobias on the internet, I am thinking I have a phobia about phobia names! Goodness, there are many of them. Let's take a look at a few.

- Do you have Ablutophobia? That is the fear of bathing, washing, or cleaning. I know several five-year-olds with this phobia!
- How about Claustrophobia? This is the fear of confined spaces. Here we find one of mine. Never ask me to go to a cave, never.
- What about Decidophobia? The fear of making decisions. We suffer from this one each time we try to decide where to go eat.
- Many people I know have Glossophobia. The fear of speaking in public, or of trying to speak.
- Phonophobia? Fear of loud sounds. Anyone with this problem should stay a minimum of two miles from my house!

Acrophobia is the fear of heights, and again this is one that I can certainly relate to if not confirm 100 percent that I have. I will go up to tall buildings or rides, but do not ask me to get too close to the edge for any amount of time. Honestly it really freaks me out.

While I was in community college, the subject of phobias came up once, and I started to discuss my fear of heights with my professor and the fact that I became afraid near the edge. I asked him what I should do about it, and his answer is as clear today as it was almost 25 years ago. Here are his words: "Stay away from the edge." Now, why didn't I think of that!

These words are simple but good advice when dealing with heights and when trying to stay away from sin. Too many times we attempt to see how close we can get to sin without actually committing sin. Godly people and the Bible warn us to stay away from certain situations, but for some reason, we think we will be the first person to be able to stand on the edge and not fall. You know the results of such thinking as well as I do: disaster.

People choose to stand on the edge at the local bar, the no-tell motel, the gossip's phone call, and in our personal business dealings to name just a few. Friends, take it from someone who has fallen over the edge: do not stand on the edge. Get as far away from sin as you possibly can. Do not even entertain the thought. The fall is too great, too painful, and too hard to recover from.

I guess I have Edgeofsinphobia. That is the fear of standing on the edge of sin and falling into it. The only way to avoid this problem is to take the advice of my wise professor and the Lord himself: stay away from the edge!

Scripture: Romans 8:12-14: "So don't you see that we don't owe this old do-it-yourself life one red cent. There's nothing in it for us, nothing at all. The best thing to do is give it a decent burial and get on with your new life. God's Spirit beckons. There are things to do and places to go!" *The Message* by Eugene Peterson

P.S. —There is good news for those of who have fallen over the edge, which includes most of us. God is there to pick us up, forgive us, and put us back on the mountain. If you have fallen, don't stay down. Get up. God always offers redemption.

Scripture: Psalm 32:1: "Blessed is he whose transgressions are forgiven, whose sins are covered." Blessed indeed!

Prayer: Dear Lord, we ask for your Spirit to convict in such a way as to move us away from sin when we get close to the edge. Help us to discern evil from good and to be obedient to your Holy Spirit's calling. We ask these things in the name of Christ, Amen.

The Right Response to the Wrong Action

One of the most important things you can do when you are pulled over by a policeman for a moving violation is respond in the right way. A wrong response could be very dangerous. With this in mind, I searched the Department of Motor Vehicle web site, and they tell us exactly how to respond. See below:

1) Slow down immediately, put on your blinker, and pull over as soon as it is safe.
2) Breathe deeply and calm down from the initial adrenalin surge of realizing you're being pulled over.
3) Stay in your car unless instructed otherwise.
4) Follow all instructions exactly.
5) Move slowly and keep your hands visible. Quick moves can be misinterpreted as a threat.
6) Be absurdly polite.
7) Sign the ticket. If you do not, the officer has to arrest you. It is not an admission of guilt.

There you go. That is exactly how the DMV says you should respond when the lights come on, and you have committed a moving violation. That is nice to know, because from time to time, everyone gets a ticket.

It is good to know how you should respond after you have sinned while driving your car; it is also good to know how to respond when we have sinned in our life. Just as the DMV has a place for such information, we have the Bible as our guide. See Below:

1) When you realize your sin, pull over long enough to get the proper perspective. Sudden moves here are often fatal, spiritually speaking.
2) Don't try to fix your sin yourself. You are not capable. This normally only causes the issue to get worse and take longer to resolve. Remove yourself from the situation or temptation and then lean heavy on God.

3) Follow His instruction completely:

   a) Admit Sin—(Romans 3:23)
   b) Turn from your sin—(Acts 3:19). This is repentance—don't just say you are sorry. The proper response to your sorrow is to remove yourself from the situation. Being sorry is remorse; turning from it is repentance. Big, big difference.
   c) Claim God's love for you in spite of your sin. (Romans 5:8)
   d) Know that He forgives you and stop living under the cloud of guilt you have pressed upon yourself. Once he forgives you, he forgives you. Stop going back to that sin and letting the enemy dominate your thoughts. This is very important. Many people are defeated by not taking this step. (Psalm 103:11-13)

Speeding in life is dangerous; you could hurt someone or yourself. If you do it long enough, I guarantee you that you will be stopped by the law eventually. Sinning in life is more dangerous, I assure you if you keep at it long enough, it will take its toll, and eventually, we will all meet the judge.

The worst thing about getting pulled over is paying the ticket. No doubt there is a price to pay. The best thing about taking the right steps spiritually when you have sinned is that someone else has already paid the price. It was paid 2000 years ago on an old, rugged cross.

Scripture: Psalm 51:1-3: "Have mercy on me, O God, according to your unfailing love; according to your great compassion blot out my transgressions. Wash away all my iniquity and cleanse me from my sin. For I know my transgressions, and my sin is always before me." *This was written by a sinner, King David. The entire chapter is worth the read.*

Prayer: Dear Lord, we thank you that you forgive us of our sins. Convict us where we are wrong and lead us down straight paths. You are a good and merciful God, and we ask these things in the name of Christ, Amen.

Need a Purpose?

Normally when I write about Gracie, I write about a nice event; her smile melts a heart, her attitude wakes me up concerning my own, or she reminds me of what is really important. All of those are on the money, but it does not tell the complete story.

There are challenges in raising someone with special needs that we experience every day. Language barriers, developmental delays, and it looks like she has a triple dose of stubbornness: she has two very stubborn parents and apparently, the Down syndrome must add to the mix a bit. Oh yes, and two more things; she must be watched 24/7/365, and she likes things her way.

If left alone, she can dismantle a house in a matter of moments; when she gets busy, look out. She is on the move from one thing to the next, and there is no stopping her.

She likes her routines, and normally I go along. For example, when we get home and park in the garage, Kim normally undoes her safety belt. Now most would just get out of the car on Kim's side and go to the house—not so with Gracie. She wants to get out on my side.

So, she starts to walk across the seats to ever-waiting dad. When she gets about halfway, she will take a detour. She will go to the back or visit the front and generally just check the place out. I patiently wait, and then finally, knowing that without a change this game could go on for hours, I do something about it.

What I have found works best for her is I give her a purpose. For example, I will give her a grocery bag to carry in. She picks it up, jumps out the car, and away she goes. Sometimes, I will let her push the button to bring down the garage door. She takes the command, heads for the door, and once again, mission accomplished.

What we have found about Gracie in the garage is what also works in the house; give her a purpose, and things run smoothly; cut her loose with no direction, and you will find that trouble is just around the corner. Guess what? The same goes for you, and God knows it.

Everyone needs a purpose in life, period. Everyone needs a reason to get up in the morning. People without a clear definition of their purpose in life will do what Gracie does; they will go from one thing to the next until they find themselves in trouble.

It does not have to be spectacular; just be you. Take what you enjoy, and do it as unto God. Work with kids, mentor a teenager, start a company, sing in a choir, run for office, run an office, help a struggling family, counsel a young married couple in trouble, and the list goes on and on. I don't know your purpose, but God does take the question to him. Then get busy.

Side note: I have found that most people know their purpose and are not involved in it. Experience teaches me these people are the most miserable in life.

Side note two: When I say "get busy," I mean get busy with your purpose. Most people are busy with stuff that will amount to nothing in life. Get busy with the right thing, God's purpose. As a matter of fact, if you narrow your business to your gifted area, you might find yourself happier and less busy!

Scripture: Jeremiah 29:11: "'For I know the plans I have for you,' declares the Lord, 'plans to prosper you and not to harm you, plans to give you hope and a future.'"

Ephesians 2:10: "For we are God's workmanship, created in Christ Jesus to do good works which God prepared in advance for us to do." (Love this verse!)

Prayer: Dear Lord, help us first to seek your way, second to find our way, and third to get on the way of doing what you have called us to do. We ask these things in the name of Christ, Amen.

The Best of Intentions

No niece or nephew could have a better aunt to watch their every move than four-year-old-Gracie. As you might expect from any aunt, but especially one that is a "young" aunt, at only four years old, she loves to get right in their face, give them big hugs, remove and then replace their pacifiers, follow them, and pat them on the back. They may not love it so much, but she sure does.

The other night her big brother and I were working in the nursery during an event at church—what a team! Anyway, Gracie was in there with her nephew and niece. She was very busy getting in her niece's face, and we were having to work hard to keep said niece from getting too upset about all the "in your face" attention.

At that moment I said to my son, "Gracie means well; she just does not do well."

It is here that many of us find ourselves spiritually, is it not? We mean well, we want to do what God wants us to do, but our actions don't always match that desire.

We, like Gracie, go about our business and are trying to do the right thing but never take the quiet moments to learn from the Lord. Or we never learn from others' reactions to us, and instead of doing good, we end up finding ourselves in trouble.

It is not that we don't try to correct Gracie, it is just that at this stage in her life, she is so focused that she does not hear what we are trying to say, and so she just keeps on going. Once again this action is exactly how many of us are spiritually; we are so focused on what we want to do, what we think is right (without asking God) that we never listen to God trying to cool our jets or get us to move our attention elsewhere. God's still, small voice gets louder and louder, but still we do not stop, we do not hear. With this attitude, we simply run in place spiritually.

Another part, the reason we try to move Gracie away from the little ones, is we are afraid that, without intending to, she might hurt one of them. Trust me, if you know Gracie, that is the last thing she wants to do. The look on her face when that happens will tear even the most insensitive person up emotionally.

Once again, here we find ourselves; the last thing we would ever want to do is hurt someone else. The thought breaks our heart, but when we refuse to listen to instruction, refuse to respond to the warning signs and stay the course, inevitably that is exactly what we end up doing. This results in one of the worst emotions: regret. We regret the damage we have done not only to ourselves, but also to others.

Gracie is young and just wants to help. She does not know better, though we are working with her on it. She does what she does out of love. You might be the same. You might be young, and surely you could easily be doing things out of love. It simply could be that God is working with you to improve your life and the relationships in it.

Take some simple steps. Slow down and take a look at those around you. How are they responding to your actions? Stop long enough in your daily routine to hear God's voice. Often he can't get through all the busyness in your life. Then, even if it does not seem like something you want to do, if you determine that God needs for you to make a change, do it.

When you do this, you will move your life from "wanting to do well and just not doing it" to "wanting to do well and completing the task!"

Scripture: Romans 7:17-20 "But I need something more! For if I know the law but still can't keep it, and if the power of sin within me keeps sabotaging my best intentions, I obviously need help! I realize that I don't have what it takes. I can will it, but I can't do it. I decide to do good, but I don't really do it; I decide not to do bad, but then I do it anyway. My decisions, such as they are, don't result in actions. Something has gone wrong deep within me and gets the better of me every time." *The Message* by Eugene Peterson. *Seems as though Paul had the same problem as us!*

Prayer: Dear Lord, simply help our actions to match our heart's desire to please you. We ask these things in the name of He who gives us the power to overcome, Christ. Amen.

Who Are These People?

Over the last five years, something suspicious has been happening at my house. I strongly believe that someone, while I was not looking, reached in and replaced my three older kids. What is so good about their undercover work is the fact that they have replaced these children with ones that look just like my own. Very interesting, and very sneaky.

They think they have me fooled, but I am on to them now. I am a little slow to catch onto things, but I do get it after a while. These supposed children of mine are now 21, 19, and 17 just for reference. Here is what has tipped me off to this replacement program. They do things I would never dream of doing. Let me explain.

For my son's 21st birthday, as well as for Christmas, he requested, received, and enjoyed getting power tools! The only power tool I can think of in the Harris household for the last 23 years is the electric toothbrush used by my 9- and 6-year-olds. I have absolutely no interest in tools of any kind, much less ones that have the ability to cut my finger off. There is no way a son of mine would want a power tool or even know what to do with it. Even more suspicious is that I have watched him, and indeed, he does know what he is doing. Hey, they can't fool me. This son is an imposter.

Then there is my 19-year-old daughter. Her heart's desire is to be a nurse. From what I can tell, nurses hang out with sick people, taking their temperature, giving shots, and taking blood. And that is the stuff I can only write about in a family devotional. My stomach gets queasy just thinking about people getting sick, much less cleaning up after them. I know this cannot be my daughter because I remember holding her down when she was 6 or so when the doctor tried to give her a shot. I thought I was wrestling an alligator. Yes, indeed, these imposters are fooling me no longer.

What about my 17-year-old? Well, I caught onto to this guy real fast. Last week he goes to (are you ready for this?) *guitar lessons*. The words "Harris" and "music" are rarely heard in the same breath. None of us can play a lick, especially the father, unless of course you include that harmonica Matt got for Christmas. Now I am watching some guy walk around my house strumming on a guitar. It just ain't right; no rightful kid of mine is going to be playing an instrument. Yes, indeed, I am on to them. My real kids are missing.

Or are they? God created us in His image. Each of us is special in His sight, and we have gifts that were created only for us. There is only one you, nobody else.

Yes, unfortunately for my kids, they do have some traits of mine, but they are not me. We do well when we remember that each child is different. They are individuals created in the image of God to do works He has set aside for them. When we remember this, it is easier to release them into the world. Keeping this in mind also helps us to have patience with that child that does not conform to our way of thinking. God just may have set them up different than you.

As we keep in mind that each of us is different, yet special, it should allow us to let our children explore different interests. I love sports, but not every one of my children will love sports as I do. Maybe they want to play the harmonica or guitar; maybe they want to write or volunteer with the handicapped. Let 'em try; give 'em a chance. How else will they discover who it is God created them to be?

Power tools, guitars, and nursing. What's next? Only God knows, and I am glad. It's fun watching His image grow.

Scripture: Genesis 1:27: "So God created man in his own image, in the image of God he created him, male and female he created them."

Prayer: Dear Lord, we rejoice that you chose to make us special. We are thankful you have a place for us to be and a gift for us to use. Help us to listen to your voice and follow your directions so we will be where you want us to be. Be with us as parents and grandparents to allow our children the freedom to be who you have created them to be. We ask these things in the name of Christ, Amen.

'Tis the Season for a Smile

When I think of a parade, I think of it as the buffet of life rolling down the street. During a parade, you see it all, and there is something for everyone, just like a good buffet. For children, there are clowns, funny looking cars, balloons, people on stilts, candy thrown from cars (my kids' favorite), and different animals, like horses, that city kids don't normally see, especially walking down the street. For adults, there are cool-looking old cars, bands (my favorite), floats, and then, of course, you can add all the things kids like, 'cause adults like 'em too.

I go to four parades every year almost without fail. They are all different, and all have their good points. One is in the spring, one is at the end of the summer, and then there are two Christmas parades. The Christmas parade has something to offer none of the others do.

The Christmas parade in my hometown is short. That comes in very handy when you are wrestling with an 18-month old, but that is another devotional altogether. My favorite aspect of this parade, other than it being short, is that it is at night. So what is a normal parade turns special because of all the Christmas lights on the trucks, cars, and floats in the parade. It really makes it nice. You're going to figure out real fast I like Christmas, and I like Christmas lights.

There is one other thing I noticed last night about my hometown parade that I like. It's the smiles. As I stood there in the cool night with my three youngest children by my side, I noticed the smiles. My children were doing their normal parade thing—collecting candy and all kinds of literature to be read by adults later. But as I watched, I noticed that during this parade, unlike all the others, people were looking right at me. They were saying Merry Christmas, singing happy songs about the birth of Christ, and in general, they smiled more than at other parades.

Now, there are a great many churches that participate in this parade. They represent a wide spectrum of the religious community. Like a good buffet, there are plenty of different denominations to choose from. They all have something different to offer. Each had their good points, all were theologically okay, but the ones that I enjoyed the most were the ones who gave me a smile and presented a message of hope.

Christmas is about a smile. We as Christians can get so hung up on sharing Christ with the world that we forget that folks have plenty of choices to follow, but they all have the same need. They, and we, all need hope, and it can start with a simple smile.

We think this Christianity is serious business, and it is. But if we can't put a smile on our face, then really, what do we have to offer? I am not talking about some fake smile that covers up the pain inside. I am talking about a smile that says, "I am just like you, struggling, but I have hope." Hope is the greatest gift of Christmas. Maybe it has been a bad year for you; you can look to Christmas, the miracle of the virgin birth of our Savior, and have hope. Maybe you have suffered loss, or maybe the situation seems hopeless. You can look to the scriptures and find an angel that says, "All things are possible with God."

In the parade of life, there are people out there that are waiting for the normal. There are the people rushing by trying to give you the gospel in two minutes, the lights that brighten up your life for just a moment and then are out of sight, or the superhero Christian covering up an inside that is not so superhero.

I say let's give them something on the buffet they really need: the hope of Christ. It can all get started with eye contact and a smile.

Scriptures: Luke 2: 10: "But the angel said to them, 'Do not be afraid. I bring you good news of great joy that will be for all the people.'" People who bring good news normally have a smile on their face; we are in the good-news-bringing business.

Luke 1:37: "For nothing is impossible with God."

Prayer: Dear Lord, help us to present the good news to a world that is in desperate need of good news. Help us to reach out with a good spirit and hope. Thank you for the hope you give us in our Savior, Jesus Christ. Most of all, thank you for this special time of year that we can celebrate His miraculous birth. In Christ's name, Amen.

Drawing Names

My family has fifteen children in it, and so for many years we have drawn names at Christmastime to keep each family from going broke buying gifts for so many people.

In case you have never done this, let me tell you how we work it. Somewhere around Labor Day, we take everyone's name and put it in a hat. We draw out names for the number of people in our families. Then we keep the names a secret and go out and buy a gift for each person within the agreed upon price range. Let's say that the limit is $25.00.

This is a fine system, and it works out well for us. For me to have a really nice Christmas, the names we draw are very important. Let me give you my thoughts. There are two types of people here—the names you want to draw and the people you want to draw your name.

First of all, you do not want to draw the name of anyone who already has everything. You know, the people who have enough money during the year to get whatever they want and have absolutely everything. What in the world can you get someone who has everything for less than $25.00!? You just feel very inadequate bringing your small gift to the table.

Then there are the people who you want to draw your name. These are the people who have plenty of money this time of year and totally ignore the $25.00 limit. You know you're going to get something nice and have a great time on Christmas Eve because the gift is going to be really nice. These people, of course, are my favorite relatives.

As I thought about this, one thing is very obvious about both names I mentioned. The person whose name you do NOT want to have and the person who you DO want to draw your name is the same person.

I find this situation to be very similar to God. When it comes to God, what can we give Him that He, the Creator of the universe, does not already have? There is no way we can match His great gift of eternal life or even the simplest of blessings that He daily gives.

Then, on the other hand, we love the fact that God is in the business of blessing our lives. He has all the resources of the entire universe at His disposal, and He never seems to hesitate to use them as He richly blesses each of our lives. I am so glad that God does not set a previously arranged limit to how He wishes to bless us. Or, if He does have a limit, He seems to go over the limit constantly.

What I know for absolute certain is this—I am glad that God drew my name.

Scriptures: Ezekiel 34:26: "I will bless them and the places surrounding my hill. I will send down showers in season; there will be showers of blessing."

James 1:17: "Every good and perfect gift is from above, coming down from the Father of the heavenly lights, who does not change like shifting shadows."

Prayer: Dear Heavenly Father, may we during this season give praise to You and give thanks for your beautiful gift of Your Son. Lead us to be people who acknowledge your blessings, not only at Christmas, but also all year long. In Christ's name we pray. Amen.

Blowing Fuses

I am a huge fan of the outside Christmas lights; always have been, always will be. We put ours out the week before Thanksgiving while the weather was good. Officially though, the lights can't come on until 6 o'clock on Thanksgiving Day, and not a minute earlier; those are Harris rules.

After we put ours up, we waited until the evening to turn them on, and when we did, they looked great—for five seconds. Then the fuse blew, and out they went. This was a little frustrating, but I knew how to resolve the issue. So I rounded up an extra fuse and replaced the old one. Problem solved.

For a few days the lights worked well, but then, without warning, a section of the lights went out again, the result of another blown fuse. I like for my lights to work, and I do not enjoy replacing the fuse all the time.

The temptation was to blow my fuse about my fuse-blowing lights. Fuse-blowing, whether it is with lights or your temper, is never a good idea. Let's examine some reasons why.

A. Fuses blow for a reason. There is something overloading the system. That is exactly what happens to us. We blow our fuse because of an overload somewhere in the system. I find myself losing my patience much more often when I have over- committed my schedule. Something has to give— change your schedule before you blow and have to apologize or ask for forgiveness for some sin.
B. Even if you don't see things from a biblical perspective, let me assure you blowing your fuse too often is bad for your physical well-being. Heart attacks, ulcers, and strokes are a good place to start. Something is churning inside; God did not create the body for unresolved stress. God gives a peace that passes all understanding; take hold of it before the body breaks down!
C. If you lose your temper for a certain reason and that event keeps occurring, then you are acting like me with my lights.

Something was causing the fuse to blow, but all I was doing was replacing the fuse. I had a good idea concerning the real issues, but instead of fixing the cause, I just took care of the symptom. Bad idea. I went for the short-term answer instead of the long-term. We do this all the time concerning anger, and for some reason, we are surprised that we keep losing our temper. To truly resolve the issue we must take the long-term stance to change what is happening in our life.

An out-of-control temper is an outward expression of an inside condition. If you are struggling with this area of life, take a step back and get a good look at your spiritual life. Anger and temper are a destructive force; they destroy families, marriages, careers, and churches. Take control of this force before the lights go out; you won't regret it!

Scripture:

Matthew 5:9: "Blessed are the peacemakers, for they will be called sons of God.

Ephesians 4:26: "'In your anger do not sin': Do not let the sun go down while you are still angry."

Ephesians 4:31: "Get rid of all bitterness, rage and anger, brawling and slander, along with every form of malice."

Philippians 4:7: "And the peace of God, which transcends all understanding, will guard your hearts and your minds in Christ Jesus."

Galatians 5:22-23: "But the fruit of the Spirit is love, joy, peace, patience, kindness, goodness, faithfulness, gentleness and self-control."

Prayer: Dear Lord, lead us to be people who are in control of our emotions and tempers. Help us be people of love and not anger, we ask these things in the name of Christ, Amen.

Getting off the Island of Misfit Toys

It has been colder than normal around here for the past week, and that means that any outdoor activity has been put on hold for better days, and it also means that I have been watching a little more television than normal.

Thankfully, this is the Christmas season, and there is some decent stuff out there to watch. For example, I have always been a fan of the animated version of *Rudolph the Red Nose Reindeer*. We have little evidence that Rudolph existed, but his story has many lessons for all of us to learn.

Actually, there are so many lessons that I had a little trouble deciding which one to go with. After much consideration, I have decided to speak about those toys that landed on Misfit Island. We shall call them, from now on, misfit toys.

Now, if you have not watched the show, Rudolph runs away, and after traveling some distance with some interesting characters, he ends up on Misfit Island. What, you might say, is Misfit Island? Well, of course, it is where all the misfit toys go. Here is their place of refuge.

What, you might ask, is a misfit toy? Goodness, haven't you watched television in the last 40 years? It is a toy that is not quite normal. For example, there is a Jack-in-the-Box named Charlie. Thus, he is a Charlie-in-the-Box, and that makes him a misfit. As I think of it, I can see all kinds of little mistakes on these toys; for example, there is an elephant that keeps walking around with spots. She, too, is a misfit toy.

Somehow they have all landed on Misfit Island and are there waiting for Santa Claus to come and pick them up. Each year goes by and each year they are disappointed because Santa never comes. These toys have high hopes, but they know who they are — misfits.

These toys are very unhappy because they believe they will never be used. They believe they will never be played with by any children, even though that was their intended purpose. Someone somewhere made a mistake in their construction thus creating misfit toys that are useless to the normal world. At least that is what they think.

In reality, we live in a world of misfit people, do we not? Broken bodies, broken lives, misplaced priorities that lead us to regret, foolish decisions, shame, disappointment, sin, and all these things lead us to declare ourselves to be misfits. From there, we spend our lives in isolation away from all of those normal people we see who have it all together. We are useless to the world; at least that is what we think.

I have good news for all of you folks worried about these misfit toys. Rudolph goes back to the North Pole and tells Santa about them, and sure enough, on Christmas Eve, here comes Santa to pick them up and take them to little boys and girls. I am telling you, these misfit toys are very excited when Santa shows up. What a happy ending to the story.

I have equally good news for us misfit people. Believe me when I say this—get off that island. There are no normal folks out there—we are all misfits. We are all important to Him. Please do not isolate yourself thinking that because you are not like the rest of the world you are of no use to God. I do not understand all of God's ways, but I know this—He is a great lover of the misfit. Here are some examples:

Misfit Moses—stuttered and couldn't speak in public.
Misfit Paul—had some thorn in the flesh, not to mention a history for persecuting the church.
Misfit Jacob—was a trickster.

And what about all of those misfits Jesus used to show the power and glory of God? The blind, the sick, the lame, the deaf, sinners, lepers, and even the dead were misfits to the world, but to God, of great use.

Let me give you the final bit of good news. Just like those misfits toys who were rescued on Christmas Eve, you received a welcomed visitor on Christmas day. In the town of Bethlehem, a Savior was born for you. His name is Jesus. Instead of coming on a sleigh with reindeer, He was born in a stable with sheep and cattle.

Because He came, we are no longer misfits. His desire is not only to save us from our sins, but to use us for His intended purpose.

When a misfit comes to Jesus, there is some celebrating going on that only fellow misfits can appreciate. This season, get off the island, come to Christ, and allow Him to use your "misfitness" the way he had planned all along.

Scriptures: 1 Corinthians 1:26-29: "Brothers, think of what you were when you were called. Not many of you were wise by human standards; not many were influential; not many were of noble birth. But God chose the foolish things of the world to shame the wise; God chose the weak things of the world to shame the strong. He chose the lowly things of this world and the despised things—and the things that are not—to nullify the things that are, so that no one may boast before him."

Prayer: Dear Lord, help us to know that in our flesh we are weak but in the power of your Holy Spirit we are strong. We praise you name. Because of your love for us you sent your Son to rescue us from our sins. We ask all these things in the Savior we love's precious name, Jesus Christ. Amen

Jesus is Missing

Cheviot, Ohio, has a real problem on its hands. In this Cincinnati suburb, there is a thief on the loose. The stolen item—baby Jesus! Apparently someone slipped into their nativity scene while no one was looking and stole a life-size figure of baby Jesus lying in the manger.

This is not the first time they have lost baby Jesus. Some years back, it was taken but was returned when the police were given a tip. In that case, it was missing only a day. According to the authorities, they have no leads this time.

I am not sure what value a life-size figure of baby Jesus has out on the open market, but city official Steve Neal said, "If something happens to one of the figures, I don't know where I would go to get a new one." That makes the figure pretty valuable to the City of Cheviot.

You may not be too concerned about what the value is, but you might be asking what good a baby Jesus would be outside the manger. For that question, I have one answer. Priceless.

Yes, indeed, there is a Jesus missing. He is missing in our workplace, He is missing in our homes, He is missing where we play, and He is even missing in some churches.

Much of the world in which we live never takes Jesus out of the stable in Bethlehem long enough to apply Him to their daily lives. A baby in a manger is nice and safe. But take Him out, let Him challenge you not to hate your enemy, or lust after your next-door neighbor, and that is a whole other story.

The world has seen enough of observing baby Jesus in the manger, yet nowhere evident in our daily lives. Though the City of Cheviot may be concerned about a missing figure in a manger scene, we should be much more concerned about a missing Christ in the world in which we live.

Might I add, this missing Christ is not the responsibility of the world that does not know Jesus, but instead of the Christian world that does. They need to see that He is real to us. A baby in a manger might be safe but is totally useless unless we take Him with us all year long.

Though this all may sound very negative, let me spin it back around and say that it is very exciting to take the baby Jesus out of the manger and apply Christ in your everyday life. Though He challenges you to live right, He also gives you great opportunity to experience things you would have never dreamed of if you will simply listen to His leading. Being a Christian is not, and was never meant to be, a boring, never-take-a-chance life. Faith, as a matter of fact, is the direct opposite. It is anything but boring.

Soon Cheviot will pack away all the characters in their manger scene. I hope, when they do, they have found their baby Jesus. Soon we will pack away our Christmas season, and when we do, I hope that we will leave Jesus out to be adored all season long.

Missing in the manger, but found living in our lives—all year long.

Scripture: Matthew 10: 5-8: "Jesus sent his twelve harvest hands out with this charge: Go to the lost, confused people right here in the neighborhood. Tell them that the kingdom is here. Bring health to the sick. Raise the dead. Touch the untouchables. Kick out the demons. You have been treated generously, so live generously." *The Message*

Prayer: Dear Father, remind us each and every day of the New Year that you are important, that you matter not only to us but to the world around us. Guide us to follow you all year long, not just at Christmas. As we celebrate the babe in the manger, help us to be reminded of the victory of the cross. In Christ's name, Amen.

One String of Lights

We live in a world that is changing at lightning speed. Though preachers and politicians preach about change as a positive thing, most of us struggle with it at least a little. In reality, we all like to have consistency in our lives.

In February 1985, my wife and I, along with our newborn son moved into a small, two-bedroom house on 5th street. That first Christmas, we did what we had always dreamed of doing, we put up Christmas lights on our very first house.

Proudly we worked together, moving the ladder into place and putting in some very small nails to help hold our lights on the house. One thing Kim and I have always agreed on was the type of lights we would have: the big, multi colored lights. Old school lights, if you will, of orange, white, red, green, and blue.

So right across the front of our house went one simple string of "old school" lights. Nothing fancy, nothing in the bushes or any-where else on the house. Just straight across, hanging from those small nails.

In '86, we added a daughter, but the string of lights stayed the same. In '88, still another son, same house, same string of lights. From '88 to '96, we didn't add children, but we did add some twist to our lights. We put some in the bushes, then some around the win-dows, and after a while, we even placed some near the sidewalk. Though we had some additions, you could always count on the same string of multi-colored lights going across the face of the house.

In '96, children started to arrive again, and for the next 10 years, God would bless us with four more. For 23 years, we lived our lives out on 5th street. We grew as a family together. We laughed, loved, cried, and played together. We fought through some tough times together, built and rebuilt relationships with each other. We suffered loss during those years, and we celebrated great joys.

Though many things changed, and the house began to shrink, one thing stayed the same. At Christmas time, there may have been other lights at other places, but there was always one string of old school lights across the front.

Christmas means so much to so many people, and for me it means a lot as well. But one thing that is not lost on me is the consistency of the season. For one moment in our busy lives during the year, we can count on Christmas. The manger is always there, calling us home, giving us hope in our circumstances and peace to our unsettled hearts.

It is a time of traditions, of remembering the good old days, even if they were not so good. It's about friendships, old and new, about families and friends. It is a time of forgiveness and putting the grudges of the past behind, if only for a little while. It's about giving gladly and receiving joyfully.

In a world gone mad with change, Christmas and the celebration of our Lord's birth with the hope that it brings is a constant we can all be thankful for.

At some point this season, I will drive down 5th street, and I will look to a small house with old, rusted nails stationed across the front waiting for one string of big, multi-colored lights. At that moment, I will be thankful for the time God gave me there, for his many blessings within those walls, and most of all, for the "light of the world" that I celebrated with those lights each year.

Thank God this year for the constancy of his love.

Scripture: Luke 2:10-11: "But the angel said to them, 'Do not be afraid, I bring you good news of great joy that will be for all the people. Today in the town of David a Savior has been born to you; he is Christ the Lord.'"

Prayer: Dear Lord, we are thankful that in a fickle world whose love is conditional, your love never changes. We celebrate this season the greatness of your love, and we ask these things in the name of Christ, Amen.

Real Heroes of Love

When Paul Ferguson passed away last week, the news made the papers. He happened to be a survivor of Pearl Harbor, and as it happened, he and another survivor of that same event died in our area within a week of each other. Men with that experience are a dying breed.

He, of course, was a war hero serving his country, as all veterans do, no matter if they happened to be at Pearl Harbor or in another conflict. For 60 years, he never spoke of his experience on December 7, 1941. But when he felt people were forgetting about the lessons from World War II and patriotism, he began to speak. Those who heard him speak said he was like a grandfather, and he was well loved by everyone who heard him.

Today I see him as another kind of hero, another dying breed that I find more important in these times. I find him as a hero of love. Packed away in the article about him was the fact that he had been married for 60 years.

Imagine all the experiences that a couple could go through in 60 years. The good times of family, friends, graduations, celebrations, vacations, and time together. Then, of course, there are the dark days that a couple would go through — the deaths, disappointments, dreams unfulfilled. Think, too, of all the times someone could have walked out, could have found greener pastures on some other hill.

Listen to a quote from a friend about his last days. "At the last minute he was trying to stay alive, not in a frantic sort of way, but because he wanted to take care of his wife." In his final moments, his final thoughts were of his wife and caring for her. A hero of love always is thinking of the other person.

His wife, well, she is a heroine of love herself. Listen to her words about her final moments with the man she had loved and walked through life with for 60 years. "I knew he was dying…but I just wanted to love him and take care of him and hold him. And that's what I did." To hold him one more time, to take care of him for his last moments, that was her only desire. How great it would be if we could all die in the arms of someone who loved us so much.

I stand humbled in the presence of such love and am privileged to have read about it. Heroes of love, both of them. Hear the words once spoken in every wedding, "For better, for worse, for richer and for poorer, in sickness and in health." It is rare to say these words in a wedding any longer, but to a hero of love, those words of commitment must ring true. For the Fergusons, they did, and their reward was great because of it.

"Love is a fruit in season at all times, and within the reach of every hand." — Mother Teresa

It is within the grasp of everyone to become a hero of love. Let us ignore the world's outlook on life that emphasizes short-term gain, lust, and getting what you want at all cost.

Perhaps you have failed at love in the past and fallen for the world's traps. Today is another day. It is never too late. Today commit to be a hero of love. See love from a Biblical view and not a worldly one, and you too will receive a rich reward.

Let us close by reading the scripture to form our guideline for love.

1 Corinthians 13:4-8a, 13: "Love is patient, love is kind. It does not envy, it does not boast, it is not proud. It is not rude, it is not self-seeking, it is not easily angered, it keeps no record of wrongs. Love does not delight in evil but rejoices with the truth. It always protects, always trusts, always hopes, always perseveres. Love never fails… And now these three remain: faith, hope and love. But the greatest of these is love."

Prayer: Dear Lord, help us to keep our commitments, to love as you would have us to, to be quick to care, to put others first, and to be quick to forgive. Help us to lean upon your Holy Spirit when the flesh tempts us. We thank you for your great love, that though others will let us down and at times we may not feel loved or even love-able, we can always know we are loved by you. We ask these things in the name of Christ. Amen.

When the Easy Days End

When we first had a child with Down syndrome, we heard all the naysayers and listened to all the doctors' endless negative predictions. Kim and I both are blessed with very stubborn spirits, so we listened, but we refused to succumb to all the bad and bold predictions.

In the early days after Gracie's heart surgery, we went through a time where life really was pretty easy. Support was great (still is), stares were at a minimum, and Gracie herself looked much younger than she was, so if there was a developmental delay, no one really took notice. We often turned to each other and said these words, "These are the easy days." We are finding out the truth of those words in very real ways lately.

We just knew that if the doctors or therapist gave us a date for Gracie to have something mastered, we would beat it. That date would be for other children, not our own. We come to you today admitting we were not as good as we thought we were.

The last several months, things have been a bit tougher than normal. Gracie has her father's need for speed and cannot be left alone for even a minute without something interesting going down. We are now facing the challenges of having someone older with special needs, and at times it can get the best of you, no matter what your support system is. Each car drive, dinner out, or visit can be a new adventure in patience.

If that sounds like whining, let me assure you, it is more about being honest than complaining. Simply because I sit behind a keyboard or stand behind a pulpit does not remove me from the full range of emotions all people experience.

We love Gracie, we know she is special, and we would not trade her for all the "normal kids" (I hate that phrase) in the world. Every day we assure ourselves of how much worse we could have it compared to others, and we tip our hat to those who travel much more difficult roads.

At times I might be tempted to have a pity party. At those times, God is right on time with some intervention. Thus has been the case recently.

Just recently at a soccer game I attended, a lady and her cousin had an accident, and I was tending to them. As I did, I found that the cousin, a young adult, had special needs. He had trouble speaking but could be understood. As we talked, he took me on a wild, long ride of imaginative speech. The lady tried to stop him, but I stopped her so he could talk, and I could listen. I was super busy, but God needed to interrupt me for a moment so I could appreciate the blessings He does give and remind me of how good I have it.

The lady had raised this man up from the time he was a month old. She had three youngsters of her own and had been out of work for quite some time. She knew struggles far beyond what I will ever know; message received.

God was not through with me yet. Today, as I sat in a meeting with other pastors, I sat by someone I knew only on a surface level. As he spoke, he said something about a new TV show on, and he mentioned something about a nine-year-old with cancer. He went on to say that every time he saw the show, it was like watching his own nine-year-old grandson die all over again. I was humbled as I listened, and my heart broke for this man of God and his family.

God is good to me. Each time I am tempted to grow bitter or frustrated or to have a little pity party, God takes time out of my day to provide for me a reality check. I am grateful He does that for me.

The best thing I learn from these moments with God is that I am blessed not because I have it better than anyone else. We all have our issues. It is never about who has it best or who has it worse, that is not the point and never is with God. The point with God is to use each experience to mold us more each day into His image.

We may not be able to relate on all levels; we all have different needs. But we can all relate to needing a God that cares for us in the midst of whatever circumstance we find ourselves in. The good news is we have one.

He is not a distant God or one made of stone; He is an ever-present God, standing with us in all circumstances. Let Him stand with you today.

Scripture: Philippians 4:6-7: "Do not be anxious about anything, but in everything, by prayer and petition, with thanksgiving, present your requests to God. And the peace of God, which transcends all understanding, will guard your hearts and your minds in Christ Jesus."

Prayer: Dear Lord, you are a dear Lord, and we thank you that you walk with us through difficult and different days. Help us to learn the value of walking and learning your lessons daily. Guide us to apply what we learn from you to our lives. We ask these things in the name of Christ, Amen.

Holding Little Hands

Gracie's brothers had just returned from the pool. The pool is too cold for her at the moment, and I felt like she needed a little special attention, so we took a walk. It was a good walk for all concerned.

Gracie is often on the move, and it is hard to slow her down, yet this night there was a simple calmness to her as she reached up to hold my hand as we walked hand-in-hand in our circle. It felt good to be able to wrap my hand around hers, and better that she allowed me to do it without attempting to pull away.

As we walked, I felt close to her as she allowed me to touch her hand and walk alongside her. For some moments, instead of her following her plan to her next destination, she allowed me to lead without fighting back.

I thought: this is how God must feel when I finally reach up and allow Him to hold my hand without any resistance. How He must long for those few moments when I stop from my busy schedule long enough to allow Him to guide. I thought of how He must enjoy the quiet moments when I finally allow it to be just the two of us.

As Gracie's oldest brother and his own family drove away, she took her hand I wasn't holding and blew kisses and waved to them at the stop sign before they got away. The fact they could not see her didn't bother her. She simply smiled at me as I commended her for her sweet good-byes.

I thought to myself of how God must love to hold our hands and watch us as we take time to love one another with the simple love that a child has. Not a polluted, worldly type of love, but an unconditional one that could only come from Him. Surely God must smile at our innocence.

At the end of the circle, I tried to move her back toward the house, but she would have none of it. In her silent way of communicating with her father, she started to point me a little further. She saw the street light ahead and headed for it. A part of me wanted to take charge and head for the house, but the wiser part kept walking in the direction she wished to go. She squeezed my hand, smiled, and walked that walk that only Gracie can. I was holding her hand, but she felt she was in control.

Surely God loves to hold our hand as we seek out new adventures. I thought of the times I believed that I was in control, only to realize in looking back that it was the Father who allowed me to go a little further for the experience of it all while all the time holding my hand tightly. I thought how He must love it when we walk toward the light, holding His hand for security as we face the unknown, together.

A few houses from the end of the street where the light awaited us, Gracie decided she was finished walking. She turned, stood right in front of me, and reached both arms up toward her father. The choice was to run over her or pick her up—easy choice. I finished the journey to the light with a smiling, safe, and satisfied girl in my arms. I felt unusually good as I carried my girl home.

For just a few moments, I knew how it must feel for God when we, His children, grow tired and weary, and instead of attempting to take matters into our own hands, we simply reach our hands toward the Lord. How He must yearn for the moments that we give up and reach up.

Gracie got to the light, but not on her own strength. She reached her destination on the strength of her father.

How assuring it is to know that as we walk toward the light with all of this world's distractions, heartaches, and failures, that when the day comes, we can reach our arms up to our Father, and He will carry us safely home.

What a good God—one that holds our little hands.

Scripture: Isaiah 49:16: "See, I have engraved you on the palms of my hands; your walls are ever before me."

Prayer: Dear Lord, we thank you that you love us enough to walk with us each day. In Christ's name, Amen.

The Temptation of Christmas (Cookies)

Over the last several months, I have been in a battle. I have recognized that my weight is starting to get out of hand. So, I decided it was time to take some steps to get it under control.

You know, the typical stuff—start exercising more, getting more rest, trying not to eat Jack in the Box tacos at 10 o'clock at night on the way home from church.

Although the taco deal is a problem, a bigger problem was just watching what I eat and how much. The place of my greatest struggle with watching what I eat is at work. I decided to take control there, and I brought oatmeal, grapefruits, oranges, and enough Campbell's tomato soup to stock a good-sized grocery store.

Now, I have been doing pretty well, but this Christmas thing has overtaken me. Everywhere I walk, there are sweets. At almost every turn is some kind of cake or cookie. Today, I counted five desks that had donuts, peanuts, Christmas cookies, and some candy for the season. This fails to mention the huge spreads at two different Christmas parties. There is only so much temptation a guy like me can handle.

I must admit I have stumbled. I have eaten my share of cookies, and I sure enjoyed those donuts. I have even begun to rationalize it by saying, "I will enjoy the food now during the season, but right after the first of the year, it is back to the Campbell's soup and oatmeal." I ask myself, "How bad can it be?" I also tell myself, "It would be rude to turn down all these nice offers for food, and of course I wouldn't want to be rude. What kind of witness would that be? It is just a few weeks anyway. What will it hurt?"

I have named my challenge the Temptation of Christmas (Cookies).

I find in my struggle to stay away from cookies some issues we all come face to face with in our daily walk. Let's take a look at them; it will keep my mind off the sugar cookies in the next cube for a few moments anyway.

A first thought is that no matter how hard you try to avoid temptation, it is always out there. As a matter of fact, the more you try to remove yourself from a certain challenge, it seems the more it finds its way back in your mind. You must be willing to surrender to the Lord whatever it is that is tempting you and allow him to protect your thoughts. (Philippians 4:7)

Many times, it is your friends who unknowingly put you in difficult situations. They may not know your struggles, or worse, may not care. For example, they simply put the plate out as they always have and expect you to eat like you always have, not realizing that you no longer want to take part in what is going on. It takes a culture change sometimes to avoid temptation. Sometimes you have to avoid the cube. That means you may have to change friends or avoid them for a while as you allow God to help you gather strength. That is why good Christian friends are so important, and, might I add, that is why it is so important to be a good Christian friend. Paul says in 1 Corinthians 15:33, "Do not be misled: bad company corrupts good character."

Rationalization is one of the great dangers of our society. You can convince yourself with any number of reasons that whatever is tempting you is fine to do, even morally right. Satan loves to help your rationalize. Once you have convinced yourself you're right, you are doomed to failure and heartache. If it goes against God's word, then don't do it. It's not right. It's as simple as that.

Lastly, you will need to look for ways out. I have had to change my route to avoid places where I know cookies are out. When people invite me to breakfast, I have to have a ready answer like, "I am eating oatmeal." My example is trivial to someone who is fighting the demons of drugs, alcohol, or pornography, but the point is solid and biblical. God allows for ways out. We must work to take them (1 Corinthians 10:13). Soon Christmas will be over, the cookies will be gone, but temptation never will be. Lean on the Lord, hang onto His word, and He will deliver you.

Scripture: Matthew 6:13: "And lead us not into temptation, but deliver us from the evil one."

Prayer: Deal Lord, in our daily walk, help us to avoid the temptations that will lead us into sin. Reveal our weaknesses to us. Give us a strong sense of evil when it lurks around the corner. Help us to find the way out. We ask these things in the name of the one who loves us, Jesus Christ our Lord. Amen.

Just Lights

Picking out and decorating our Christmas tree is one of the big events of the holidays for us. It is filled with tradition, and we work it around our schedule now so everyone can be a part of the events.

We travel to one of the many Christmas tree farms about an hour out of town. We take a hayride out to where the trees are and walk among hundreds and hundreds of trees. We take our time and check out as many trees as we can. Finding the kind of tree we want and making sure everyone agrees is starting to get a little more difficult as my children get older. Standing among all of those trees, everyone has to keep one thing in mind—no tree is perfect.

After we have found the tree for us, we take it home and get to spend a night decorating it. There is a moment in decorating the tree that I like the best. It is after the lights have been placed around the tree, and we turn on the lights for the first time. There the tree stands by itself, nothing but lights shining on it. It is perfect to me just like that. I keep telling my family that one of these years I am going to just have a tree with nothing but lights on it. No tinsel, no balls, no candy canes, just lights. No little lights or flashing lights either, just the big, old-fashioned ones I like the best.

No matter what a tree looks like out in the woods, when you cut it down, it always looks good when the lights are shining off of it. There, we can find ourselves as well. Among a crowd of people, are we not just like all of those hundreds of trees in the woods? Some are big, some are skinny, some are fat, and some are tall. Few really stand out as anything special. In the woods of life, few really stand out. There are no perfect trees.

Yet when you take a person, any old average person, and let the light of Christ shine off of him, then it changes everything. What once was a normal, average person among thousands becomes something very special. I believe you can take the ugliest tree in the forest, put lights on it, and it will look good. I believe Christ works the same way. He can take the most messed up life, the ugliest heart, and when His Spirit penetrates it, it can be the most beautiful heart, pleasing to look at, lighting up a dark world.

Really, there is no need for all the ornaments we try to add to our life. We try to prove we are so "Christian" by how we talk or by what we know. Really, we just need to shine. God can do His own decorating in our life, adding what he wants, when he wants. Our life is His to decorate.

My favorite part is that moment when we turn on the tree lights, turn off the rest of the lights in the house, and look at the tree in the dark. There, a simple tree, with all of its flaws, gives light to the house. You cannot see its imperfections; all you see is the light. Your life well-lived, with the Spirit working in it, will not show the world your imperfections. They simply see the light.

Let it shine. It's a beautiful sight.

Scripture: 2 Corinthians 4: 5-6: "For we do not preach ourselves, but Jesus Christ as Lord, and ourselves as your servants for Jesus sake. For God, who said, "Let light shine out of darkness," made his light shine in our hearts to give us the light of the knowledge of the glory of God in the face of Christ."

Prayer: Dear Father, help us not to dress ourselves up, but to be obedient and follow your lead, to be who you have created us to be. Help us just to shine for you in a way that points away from us and points directly at you. In Christ's name, Amen.

Something for Nothing

My glasses live in a constant state of peril. If I take them off, they are open season for any small hands that love to pick them up and give them back to me. They have been bent more ways than an Olympic gymnast. I have to rescue them often. Unfortunately, they are not always rescued in time.

This time I have no one to blame but myself. I laid down on the couch, put the glasses in their usual spot, then rolled over, and rolled over onto the glasses. They were bent, and I needed some professional help on getting them back in shape.

My friends at the optometry department at our local store know me well. Whenever my glasses meet with some major event, they are always there to bail me out. They have given my glasses at least nine extra lives.

This time I took them to my friends and said, "I am going to go shopping; take your time, and I will come back and get them when I am through." The lady said, "no problem," and away I went, my glasses in the trusty hands of my local eye care professional.

After taking our time and doing some shopping in the store, my wife and I went by to pick up the glasses. Our friend said she had put in some new screws and put them in for a super cleaning. When I put them on, I was amazed at how clean they were and how good I could see. That was all I could focus on. They felt great, and I could see even better than before. We thanked her and walked away.

As we walked away, Kim kept staring at me. Now, of course, with my good looks, that should not have surprised me, but this was not that kind of look, it was kind of a perplexed look. Finally, she looked at me and said, "those are not your glasses."

I took them off and looked at them, and sure enough, she was right. They were the same name brand, but not the same color; same design, but not the same earpiece. They were my same lenses, but they were not in my frames.

We turned around, took the glasses back to the clerk, and told her what the deal was. I did not want her to get in trouble for putting my lenses in someone else's frames, and I did not want to receive something without being charged for it. She said absolutely that those were my lenses; she never committed fully to the frames. She said if they were new, we would have to pay for them, and they weren't new. We laughed about it with her and tried to work it out, but finally we gave up and walked out of the store with new frames.

Something for nothing; new look without the cost—not a bad deal. That is exactly the deal God gives us: new look, no cost; eternal life free of charge. Not a bad deal if you can get it, and we all can! God has seen our bent lives and loves us anyway.

Why fight it; accept the gift and get on with the new life and your new look!

Scripture: Romans 5:8: "But God demonstrates His own love toward us, in that while we were still sinners, Christ died for us."

Ephesians 2:8: "For by grace you have been saved through faith and that not of yourselves; it is the gift of God."

2 Corinthians 5:17: "Therefore, if anyone is in Christ, he is a new creation; the old has gone, the new has come!"

Prayer: Dear Lord, we thank you that you take our old, broken lives and make new ones of them. Have us to live our lives out in thanks for your free gift! We ask these things in the name of Christ, Amen.

Where Are They?

I hope you are prepared for the simple/truths animal test this morning. A good night's sleep would have been good and a little study wouldn't have hurt. I guess since I did not give you any warning, you will just have to work off of your already-great knowledge. Below is a list of animals. Tell me where each of them live at this time. Good luck, and you will not be graded on the curve.

- Badlands Bighorn Sheep
- Giant Deer Mouse
- Louisiana Vole
- Arizona Jaguar

Now, if you have seen any of these animals, please report to your nearest mental health professional for further evaluation. All of these animals at one time lived in North America, but they are now extinct and have been for some time.

Okay, for the second part of the quiz, tell me what these animals have in common:

- Monoplacophora
- Coelacanth
- Laotian Rock Rat
- Gracilidris

Give up? All of these animals are called Lazarus species because at one time they were thought to be extinct but reappeared at a later date. The name Lazarus comes from the friend of Jesus that He raised from the dead in John 11.

Anytime we see animals that are in danger of becoming extinct, we put them on an endangered species list. If they are on this list, we do everything possible to help them survive and eventually thrive. Below is a different kind of endangered species list I am aware of. See what you think.

- The man who leads his family in a spiritual fashion. The one who talks about spiritual leadership, then actually follows through.
- The Christian who knows God's grace and actually tells others about it.
- The believer who knows gossip is wrong and actually does not spread any juicy tidbits when they hear them.
- The Christian who spends as much time loving, caring, and meeting people's needs as they do sitting in service, Bible studies, listening to sermons on television, or reading Christian books.

These, and others just like them, are aspects of the Christian life that are passing into the distant past.

Why do animals become extinct? In the days we live in, there can be several reasons: poaching, loss of habitat, and pollution to name just a few. Why is the last list going into extinction? Lack of concern, preoccupation with the things of this world, and total lack of discipline are just a few of the reasons.

Let's look within today and make sure the ways of Christ are not falling into extinction in our own life. Make an endangered species list, and then treat it as such. We may need to change our environment (the people you hang out with). We certainly may need to spend more time in prayer and study, asking God to guide and protect our mind and give us the power to live our life as He would have us to. Trust me, if all the ways of Jesus were extinct, the world would miss it. And on the other hand, if we lived out his ways completely, the world would be a far better place.

Let's not let the world find the ways of Jesus extinct.

Scripture: Matthew 5:14-15: "You are the light of the world. A city on a hill cannot be hidden. Neither do people light a lamp and put it under a bowl. Instead they put it on its stand, and it gives light to everyone in the house."

Prayer: Dear Lord, give us the desire, discipline and dedication to be the light of this world. We ask these things in the name of Christ, Amen.

Up in Smoke

In 1914, a great fire ripped through a factory owned by Thomas Edison in West Orange, New Jersey. Over ten buildings were lost, and the total loss financially was seven million dollars. Edison was insured for two million. Edison was 67 years old as he watched much of his life's work go up in smoke. The fire means little to our thoughts today. I want to point you toward his attitude.

The day following the fire, as he was walking through the rubble, Edison made what I think is one of the great quotes of all time: "There is great value of disaster. All our mistakes are burnt up. Thank God we can start anew."

True in the business of invention; more true in our relationship with God. Maybe you have made a few mistakes in your life. Others may remember. The mistakes continually haunt you, but perhaps it is time to just let them burn!

Our God is the God of second chances, and for that, we can be most thankful. Focus on that middle sentence, "All our mistakes are burnt up." He had no more reminders of past failures. They were all burned in the fire.

The world may want to remind you of your past failures; they love to label. The devil may bring your failures to mind almost daily in an attempt to beat you down emotionally. Don't listen to them. Look to God.

God loves us and does not wish for us to live in the backwash of our past failures or disasters. God wishes to forgive us and set us free. He gives us a chance to start new. Listen and learn from Edison again: "Although I am over 67 years old, I'll start all over again tomorrow. I am pretty well burned out tonight, but tomorrow there will be a mobilization here, and the debris will be cleared away, if it is cooled sufficiently, and we will go right to work to reconstruct the plant." He said this as he watched the flames destroy his building. Here is what I take from that:

- Look at his age, 67. It is never too late to start over!
- Look how fast he was going to get started: the next day. Don't wait, or you will be waiting forever. Start new today!
- Clear out the debris; get rid of the trash of your disaster. Don't let the past hang around. You may need to change friends, change jobs, or change neighborhoods; do what it takes clear the debris.
- He used the word "we" when speaking of reconstructing the plant. It takes help. Get it. Find a Godly person to confide in, someone you trust. Build your support system. You will be shocked to find so many others who have been through the fire.

Oh yes, Edison: how did he do after the fire? Three weeks later, he presented the world the phonograph. As with Edison, I am certain the same is true of you. God has great plans for your life. Let the past burn in the smoke of a forgiving God. Start new today.

Scripture: 2 Corinthians 5:17: "Therefore, if anyone is in Christ, he is a new creation; the old one has gone, the new has come!"

Romans 8:1: "Therefore, there is now no condemnation for those who are in Christ Jesus."

Prayer: Oh Lord, how we thank you for second chances and for redemption. Guide us to live not in the past but under the umbrella of your loving grace. We ask these things in the name of he who loves us so, Christ. Amen.

Baby Jesus is late!

When you have a Children's Christmas pageant at a small church you never know what might happen. The only thing you know for sure is that it is going to bring a lot of smiles to people's faces. Normally though, this follows several tense moments for the adults. This year did not disappoint.

After months of practice, the big night arrived and the parents and grandparents were filing in right on time. Normal start time is 6:30. If you know me well enough, you know there is nothing normal about the way we start service. Only know this—I have never started a children's musical on time.

This year we had a last-minute baby Jesus. Mary, Joseph, and baby Jesus gladly stepped in, but there was one snag. They already had a family reunion planned some distance off from the church. The leader of this threesome promised me he would do all he could to get the volunteer savior and his parents back in time for the play.

At about 6:25, I am standing out in the parking lot, greeting a few visitors as they come in, but also keeping a good eye out for Jesus. At 6:30, with curtain time arriving, I watched as cars came into the parking lot—but none of them represented the one I was really looking for: Jesus.

The children had rehearsed several times. The people were in their seats. The cameras were charged up, as were the leaders of the production. The church musicians were beginning to run out of songs to play before the event started. Everything was ready, but no savior had arrived.

It is never good to start late, but trust me—it is never good to start late when preschool children are involved. Their attention span has a short shelf life, and you have to fire when they are ready.

Finally I walked out of the parking lot and into the church where I found Jesus' chauffer seating in the proper place. Jesus, Mary, and Joseph had arrived minutes earlier. While I was looking for him in one direction, he came in another.

Actually Jesus had been there on time—it was me who was looking in the wrong place. There we find ourselves often. Standing in the cold, looking for Jesus, but doing it in the wrong place!

We look for a savior in our possessions or our position. We look for him in our checkbook or in our successes. We look for him in religious activity or self help books. We look for him with the clothes we wear or by the words we can say.

Why do we never find him? Because many of us spend our time looking for Him in the empty things of this world when Jesus has been right there with you the entire time.

He is as close as a prayer. Call His name, and know His presence is real. There is no guessing in what direction he will come. He will come straight to your heart.

Oh yes, and He always comes right on time!

Scripture: Matthew 1:23: "The virgin will be with child and will give birth to a son, and they will call him Immanuel"—which means "God with us."

Prayer: Dear Heavenly Father, we thank you that you are not a distant God. Help us to seek you in the proper way, have our eyes and ears to be open to your presence. Be with those who are seeking you, with those who are hurting and lonely, help them to find and know your love. We ask these things in the name of Christ, Amen.

The Gift of the Harmonica

My wife and my sister-in-law are two of the most reasonable people I know. But when it comes to their "babies," reason is thrown right out the window. These normally sane people will do some pretty unreasonable things. Add Christmas in the mix, and it really gets interesting.

Before I go on, you need to know that my house is loud—very loud. There are a lot of people in a very small amount of space. I don't mind the space, and I don't mind the noise. As a matter of fact, I enjoy the closeness that all this brings. There is no hiding in my house. I am sure when the kids grow up and are on their own that I will miss the noise and the cramped space.

The last thing a loud house needs is a kid with a harmonica. Yet my wife and sister-in-law, both college-educated, God-fearing, levelheaded people, both bought my kids a harmonica. For the sake of space, I will not even mention the kazoo that was found in my six-year-old's stocking. What were these people thinking? All around my house, even in my car, my nine-year-old plays and plays his harmonica. He loves it, and he loves to play it—never mind he has no idea about how to play a song on it.

Of all the gifts we gave my son, his favorite gift is a $2.35 harmonica. All the saving, all the cutting corners, and all the doing without throughout the year so that we can buy nice things for our kids at Christmas, and the most popular gift cost under $3.00. There is a lesson to be learned there.

When friends ask him what he got for Christmas, he always leads off with "a harmonica." Some of those same friends laugh when in the background during phone conversations they can hear little Matt playing his harmonica. When I asked the children at church what they got for Christmas, each child named some great gifts, their favorites I am sure. Guess what mine said—you got it: "the harmonica."

A small gift given in love, stuffed in a stocking, almost an afterthought, turns out to be a young child's favorite. In our spend-as-much as-you-can, got-to-have-the-best-and-biggest society, there is much to be learned from the gift of the harmonica.

First is the simple fact that the gift does not have to be expensive to be special. Matt never asks how much anything costs, and he surely doesn't at Christmas. It's not the cost he cares about—it is the gift. They are all special to him, and he is glad to receive them. When will we learn that the greatest gifts that we give people are the simple ones? Things like love, attention, compassion, and friendship. They all cost us very little, but they are gifts from above to the world around us.

My second thought is that it is who gives you the gift that makes it special. My children have very little money of their own, and when the little ones buy things, they use my money. That does not matter to me. What matters to me is that they care enough about others to want to give a gift. What also matters is who they are to me all year long; they are my children. We are God's children, created in his image; we please him when we give gifts of love to others. It does not matter to Him that you use the resources He supplies.

Another thought is this—nothing makes a person happier than seeing the gift they give to someone being used and appreciated. Though I am not thrilled with a harmonica blaring in my ear, especially in my van, I am given joy by watching the happy look on my son's face while he plays. God gives us gifts to use for His service; His greatest joy is when he sees us using those gifts. My friend, play that harmonica. No matter what it is, it pleases God.

Keep this in mind; no gift you give or receive can match the greatest gift of all that God gave us in his son, Jesus Christ. We need to keep in mind any gift we give to God or anyone else is not much more than a $2.00 harmonica compared to the incomparable gift that God gave to us. It was costly no doubt. Who could imagine sacrificing their own son? But what makes it so special is the person who gave it, the living God.

A little boy with a harmonica—he loves the gift and he shows love to the giver. It is sweet music to my ears. A creation of God, using His gifts for God's glory, makes a sweet aroma of worship to the living God.

431

I guess my wife and sister-in-law are still as smart as I thought they were.

Scripture: 1 Peter 4:10: "Based on the gift they have received, everyone should use it to serve others, as good managers of the varied grace of God."

Prayer: Dear Lord, we thank you for the gifts you give. We praise you that you allow us to use your gifts to serve others. Have us to love in the simple ways each day; help us to be good managers of your grace. In Christ's name, Amen.

CPSIA information can be obtained at www.ICGtesting.com

229573LV00001B/45/P

9 781612 151212